A world of difference?

Comparing learners across Europe

Marilyn Osborn, Patricia Broadfoot, Elizabeth McNess, Claire Planel, Birte Ravn and Pat Triggs

with Olivier Cousin and Thyge Winther-Jensen

Open University Press

Open University Press
McGraw-Hill Education
McGraw-Hill House
Shoppenhangers Road
Maidenhead
Berkshire
England
SL6 2QL

email: enquiries@openup.co.uk
world wide web: www.openup.co.uk

First published 2003
Reprinted 2009

A catalogue record of this book is available from the British Library

ISBN-10 0 335 21101 1 (pb) 0 335 21102 X (hb)
ISBN-13 978 0 335 21101 2 (pb) 978 0 335 21102 9 (hb)

Library of Congress Cataloging-in-Publication Data
CIP data has been applied for

Typeset by RefineCatch Limited, Bungay, Suffolk
Printed in the UK by Bell & Bain Ltd, Glasgow

For Theo and all the other children who will be the young European learners of the twenty-first century

Contents

List of figures and tables

Figures

Tables

Acknowledgements

This book reflects the efforts of many people in the three countries in the study, Denmark, England and France. Above all we would like to mention Stephanie Burke, the project secretary, who coped so well with the complexities of working in several different languages and Imogen Newman who took the manuscript to completion. The late Oz Osborn provided early statistical guidance, particularly with the design of the questionnaire for analysis. Ahmed Sharif provided all the subsequent data analysis and statistical advice. Many other academic colleagues in the Universities of Bristol, Copenhagen and Bordeaux II helped us at various stages in discussing ideas, problems and strategies. We would like to thank them for their support. We are also grateful to the various administrative staff of the three universities who helped us in many ways during the project.

In France, Maroussia Raveaud provided invaluable help with fieldwork, and a number of research students working with Olivier Cousin gave us much needed support in the fieldwork stage. François Dubet and his team of researchers at the University of Bordeaux II were involved in early discussions of the project proposal.

In Denmark, Birte Kjaer Jensen at the Ministry of Education and Research gave us valuable support and help. We would also like to express our thanks to the Danish Research Council for the Humanities who funded the Danish contribution to the ENCOMPASS study and to Trine Holst Mortensen, Susanne Wiberg and Thomas Bille, students at the University of Copenhagen who helped with collecting and discussing the Danish data.

We would like to take this opportunity of acknowledging the debt we owe to the many individuals working in the education systems of the three countries. Without their help this comparative study would not have been possible. In particular we wish to thank the pupils, teachers, headteachers and other staff of the study schools in England, France and Denmark who allowed us access into their schools, staffrooms and classrooms and who so actively cooperated with us in the process of data collection. We hope that they, above all, will find this an important and valuable study.

Finally, we extend our grateful thanks to the UK's Economic and Social Research Council (ESRC) who funded the ENCOMPASS study.

Note: The study was designed above all to give a voice to young learners in the three countries. For this reason, in the case of France, where pupils are quoted we have provided the original quotes as well as English translations. In the interest of space this has not been done in the case of the adult interviewees, nor has the Danish original been provided, since so many Danes, including the young people, are polyglots, and since relatively few other readers will be able to read Danish. Throughout the study pseudonyms are used for schools, pupils and teachers in order to protect their anonymity.

PART 1
Introduction and Methodology

1 Education for a changing world

Introduction

Are schools in crisis? As the twenty-first century dawns, there is mounting evidence that the institution that has served industrial society so well in training, socializing and selecting successive generations of young people to take their place in society may be less well placed to serve the rapidly developing world of the twenty-first century. This is because we live in a world of change. A world in which, in developed countries at least, there are unprecedented opportunities for individuals to make choices about values and about lifestyles. The dawn of the third millennium offers the citizens of such countries access to a level of material comfort and a breadth of experience unparalleled in any previous era. It also offers unprecedented challenges for the organization and conduct of education. The information revolution, coupled with major changes in the labour market, requires traditional institutional structures to become more flexible in order to provide for the development of the skills and attitudes that will be needed if learning is to become sufficiently responsive to these changes. At the same time, the erosion of value-consensus and the growing cultural diversity within industrialized societies is focusing attention on the role of educational institutions as a mechanism of social integration and control. In particular there are expectations that schools will play a major part in the inculcation of moral values and notions of citizenship.

Indeed the evidence both from scholarly research and from popular press articles points to a situation in which schools are increasingly being charged with the responsibility of containing the fall-out of societies in which diversity, normlessness and even violence are becoming the defining characteristics. Yet schools in their turn appear to be less and less equipped to undertake this responsibility. Many of the children now growing into adolescence and young adulthood around the world are challenging the ethos of an institution which appears to have little relevance to their daily lives and fails to recognize their individual identity and needs.[1] For every young person who is successful at school and finds it motivating and rewarding, there are two others for whom, to a greater or lesser extent, the experience of their daily life at school is at best only neutral, made tolerable by the opportunity it offers for contact with friends and 'having a laugh'. For a significant minority, school offers a daily reality of failure and the erosion of self-esteem as they struggle to achieve what many perceive to be the arbitrary and unobtainable goals that the system imposes upon them.

As Andersson (1995) suggests, in the twenty-first century many young people will spend a quarter of a century, or a third of a lifetime, in educational settings, a reality that is bound deeply to affect the individual, both intellectually and emotionally. And yet, his research in Sweden reveals that only 30 percent of the 1200 students he studied were happy at school, finding it stimulating and meaningful and contributing to their positive self-esteem. For the more ambivalent majority the reality was a lack of meaning and responsibility with many feeling alienated and unsuccessful. Similar findings are reported by Csikszentmihalyi *et al.* (1993) following their international survey of the roots of success and failure among teenagers. For the vast majority of young people, they suggest, life at school alternates between boredom and apprehension. Likewise Barber's (1996) survey of 30,000 English adolescents revealed widespread student alienation, apathy and disaffection (cited in Elliott *et al.* 1999). Providing as they do, a more or less traditional diet of academic subjects, teacher-dominated lessons and an authoritarian regime in which the balance of power between teachers and pupils is profoundly unequal, it is not surprising that schools do not provide a positive and motivating opportunity to learn for many of today's young people. As Jenkins suggests:

> A British School is well attuned to those who are well attuned to school. It plays to their strengths and thus validates its own assumptions. Any professional ivory tower can do that. But the test of a school should be its ability to stimulate those who see no point in it, yet who most need the 'drawing out' that is the definition of education.
>
> (Jenkins 2000: 20)

Rudduck and Flutter (2000) suggest that 'Teachers are very aware of the difficulties of engaging all pupils in learning and know that schools have changed less in their deep structures in the last 20 or 30 years than young people have changed.' Yet students, it seems, are less and less content to be the passive recipients of authority. Like workers who are more productive when they are active participants and understand their part in the overall enterprise, so students at school arguably need to be actively involved and consulted if their interest is to be actively engaged.

If the above findings from research are indeed representative of a widespread educational malaise, of a situation in which young people around the world are forced to spend longer and longer in institutions that they find unfulfilling, they represent a challenge to all those engaged in the educational project to consider at the most fundamental level, the long established assumptions about what education is for and how it is best delivered. Indeed there are several reasons why such an exercise is becoming daily more pressing.

First, as already suggested, the 'stakes' for individual countries in terms of overall national levels of educational achievement are becoming higher year by year as the intensity of international competition grows in direct proportion to that of the global knowledge economy. Policy-makers around the world are becoming increasingly obsessed with national standards as reported in international comparisons of student achievement (Winther-Jensen 2000). Thus, for example, when the results of the Third International Maths & Science Study (TIMSS) study were published in Denmark it produced a national shock which changed the focus of national educational policy significantly. Rightly or wrongly, there is now a widespread international assumption that those countries with the most 'successful' education systems will be those that forge ahead in the global economy of the post-manufacturing age. Thus, ways must be found of encouraging students to learn more.

Second, the social impact of globalization has been one of the key factors in the erosion of traditional community values. The cultural diversity and social fluidity that have replaced these values in many cases represent a challenge to accepted relationships and practices such as those between teacher and student or families and schools. Moreover the advent of marketization, which casts parents in the role of educational consumers rather than relatively powerless associates, has weakened the traditional authority of educational institutions and of the teachers who work in them. Thus studies of teachers in England (Rudduck and Flutter 2000; Osborn *et al.* 2000), France (Cousin and Felouzis 1998), Germany (Graudenz and Randoll 1997) and many other countries report a general concern about rising levels of bad behaviour in schools, a widening gulf between the cultural world of teachers and that of their students leading to difficulties in communication between teachers and students and increasing tensions between home and school.

'How schools develop a positive learning culture – where pupils (and teachers) feel it is "cool to learn" often against a background of scarce resources and competing priorities' (Maden and Ruddock 1999: 13) becomes then a pressing question. In particular it is necessary, as Randoll (1995) suggests, to identify the deep-seated cultural factors that either support or inhibit educational engagement, for it is clear that it is changes in the wider society – in its culture – that are prompting many of the contemporary tensions within education.

The comparative perspective: past, present and future

But if many of the tensions now manifest in education are the result of relatively recent social, economic and political developments, the fundamental purposes of education remain what they have always been. The aspiration is not new that mass school systems should equip future generations with the skills and knowledge required for employment while at the same time, moulding the young into responsible and law abiding citizens. In Europe at least it can be traced back to the origin of modern mass education systems in the nineteenth century where the landmark legislation that in each case ushered in such a system typically articulated these defining principles. For the last century and more, these two purposes have continued to serve – more or less explicitly – as the defining goals of education in the industrialized world. During the twentieth century a growing concern with individual rights, and more recently with the ability of individuals to take full advantage of the new educational opportunities becoming available, has led to a third theme being woven into the other two. This is the role of education in supporting personal development.

But if the industrialized world was broadly as one historically, in defining the need for universal access to an institution which would be charged with the fundamental social responsibility of shaping and training future generations, the realization of such provision on the part of particular nation states was in practice very varied. If the conceptual skeleton of schools and classes, teachers and curricula was and remains, well nigh universal, the institutional flesh with which these bones were subsequently clothed exhibited significant variations. The choice of educational priorities, the structure of educational provision, the degree of central control, the scale of public resources invested, the training and status of teachers, the system of examinations are but a few of the many dimensions in terms of which, education systems have come to diverge. The design of each education system is a reflection of the gradual accretion of policy decisions. These policy decisions are in turn a reflection of the informing ideological and cultural traditions of a particular society.

Thus the contemporary policy debates of many different national education systems display a dual tension. On the one hand there is evident in all such systems a chronological tension between the past and the present; between the models of mass educational provision that emerged to serve the novel challenges of the nineteenth century and the challenge that the increasingly different needs of the twenty-first century presents. On the other hand there are the more specific tensions arising from these broader social developments and the particular curriculum content, pedagogy and assessment practices that have evolved as a result of specific national traditions.

Understanding the source and significance of such differences is the central project of comparative education. Since the very beginning of modern forms of education, comparative educationists such as Comenius, Jullien and Matthew Arnold, as well as Sociologists such as Max Weber and Emile Durkheim, have sought to compare and contrast the specific institutional arrangements for educational provision of a particular time and place. In each case their initial goal was to understand the way in which prevailing economic and social imperatives were mediated by the ideological and cultural traditions of any particular society to produce the idiosyncratic characteristics of any one national education system. More importantly, however, their goal was also to understand the significance of such differences; to use them to illuminate those features of education and of industrial society which are pervasive and shared and hence, constant, and those which are idiosyncratic and hence, context specific. Are there universal truths about the nature of the educational enterprise that can be discovered regardless of contextual variations? Are there lessons that can be learned about educational provision from the systematic juxtaposition of common problems and different responses? How can one educational system best learn from another?

These questions lie at the heart of comparative education and are its defining rationale. They highlight the many forms that comparative studies can take – not just contemporary comparisons of one national system with another but historical comparisons of the same country over time; or of different regions of the same country in which variations in culture or in external conditions may lead to significant differences in practice. Even the comparison of different social groups – boys and girls, for example, or high and low achievers – can shed significant light on the factors at work in any given social setting. Thus comparative educational studies can usefully be conducted between individuals in a particular classroom; between individual classes and schools; between geographic regions within and beyond national states; of phenomena which transcend national boundaries, and of those which are defined by them. At one extreme they are uniquely well placed to study the impact of international phenomena such as multiculturalism, globalization and postcolonialism; at the other, they are equally well placed to study individual expectations and attitudes and the impact of peer group cultures and family life, all of which are likely to have an impact on educational experience. Comparative studies arguably have a unique power to reveal what that influence is and how it is realized in practice.

Historically, however, comparative educational studies have tended to focus overwhelmingly on the macro agendas of policy formation and educational inputs. They have tended to be more concerned with variations in structural provision, with the inputs and outputs of educational systems rather than with the beliefs and values, perspectives and aspirations of the individuals participating in that system. Hence the topics chosen for comparative educational study have tended to be ones in which the meta-narratives of national settings and policy decisions have tended to eclipse a focus on individual agency and its significance.

Recently, however, this historical imbalance has begun to be rectified as the pressures for educational change become apparent not just at the level of policy decisions but at the level of schools, teachers and students as well. Scholars have recognized that as organizations, schools too face conflicting priorities and must reconcile new demands with existing institutional practices, which are rooted in a particular socio-cultural tradition and sanctioned by the prevailing power structure (Gewirtz *et al.* 1995). Equally they have recognized that just as schools mediate prevailing social, economic and cultural realities through their own traditions and practices, so too do the actors within them. Teachers and pupils thus interact with the institutional ethos created and through their actions; both reflect and help to shape educational priorities. But as comparative studies become increasingly fashionable among policymakers searching for novel educational solutions, the need for them to embrace both perspectives becomes correspondingly more pressing.

It is not surprising that in an increasingly international world which is characterized by a 'knowledge economy', the relative success of national educational systems in terms of their production of 'human capital' has become an explicit concern of policymakers. There has been, as a consequence, a growing tendency to 'borrow' policies and practices that appear to be effective in achieving high educational standards. And yet the research evidence suggests that the powerful influence of the particular national setting and the potential significance of the cultural context into which such policies will be imported ought to receive as much, if not more, attention. However, tempting as it is to borrow apparently successful practices from elsewhere, it is important to recognize that the success or otherwise of any given educational strategy depends on the context as much as it does on the specific intervention; not only on what teachers do but also, crucially, on what the students themselves bring to the learning encounter.

Moreover the educational context is itself a complex of variables that need to be carefully teased out. The network of factors at work includes those associated with the individual student's 'learning biography'; teachers' understandings and professional priorities; and the ethos and arrangements of the particular classroom and of the institution as a whole in which the encounter takes place. They also include the culture and policy priorities that characterize any given country at national level. Here again the dangers of one sided comparisons are evident. The power of international league tables of achievement, for example, is dangerously seductive when divorced from a consideration of the attitudes and experiences of the students themselves.

The importance of starting with learners themselves rather than with teachers or policymakers as the focus for comparative studies, is now increasingly being recognized. A series of recent studies has demonstrated the relationship between national context, institutional ethos and particular classroom practices in mediating the development of a learner's identity. Such studies throw new light on the significant variations in national levels of achievement recently revealed by a series of international studies (see for example Elliott *et al.* 1999; Broadfoot *et al.* 2000).

Perhaps part of the reason for the relative neglect of the learner perspective in comparative studies up to now is that the history of formal educational provision as we know it today has itself been dominated by concerns about delivery. Initially these debates were about who should provide what education to whom, for how long and at what cost. Subsequently they have also come to embrace concerns about quality – the best way to design textbooks, the most efficacious teaching methods, and the most effective way of managing a school and developing the professionals who work in them. Amid the clamour of competing claims, and the ebb and flow of educational fashions, learners themselves have remained in shadow, the daily reality of their experience as it accumulates into a more settled personal identity, subject only to the most cursory categorizations of effort and ability.

Learning and culture

As this book will reveal, comparative studies have the capacity to redress this imbalance. With their unique capacity to compare one context with another in a systematic way, comparative studies have a potentially very significant role to play in exposing the extent to which an individual's capacity to learn, their motivation and their eventual success, is closely linked to the particular combination of cultural experiences that constitutes their 'education'. They can demonstrate the importance of recognizing learning as a social, as much as a psychological, phenomenon and the implications such recognition has for the way in which learning experiences are organized and conducted. It is significant that, despite the existence of an enormous volume of psychological research on various aspects of learning, there is as yet relatively little that can guide the development of a learning environment that is more in tune with the needs of young people in the twenty-first century.

One reason for this is because relatively little of that research is explicitly comparative in seeking to understand how a particular cultural context may affect the learning process. The way in which individual pupil's needs, interests and abilities interrelate with and are affected by the various socio-cultural settings they experience at home, at school and in their peer group is still relatively poorly understood, although its significance is increasingly being recognized. After more than a century in which educational theory has tended to assume that it is an individual's cognitive ability – often called their intelligence – that determines their potential to learn, it is now finally being recognized that learning dispositions combining both cognitive and affective dimensions are of crucial importance in this respect, just as they are in the successful execution of workplace roles (Goleman 1996). Confidence, motivation, perseverance – even creativity – are all beginning to claim a place as key components in successful learning and, hence, in the creation of a positive learning culture.

The recent rapid growth of interest in lifelong learning has served further to underline the need to understand what it is that motivates and empowers an individual to take advantage of the learning opportunities available to them; to shift the focus of research concern away from the *provision* of educational opportunities, from the factors that influence the *ability* to learn and towards those that impact upon the *desire* to learn. Inevitably such a shift highlights the impact of social factors, as these shape an individual's continually developing identity and sense of self. It argues the need to develop a 'social theory of learning' (Coffield 1999) that constructs the potential success or otherwise of learning in terms of aspects of the social setting rather than in terms of the quality of the tools in an individual's head.

Efforts to develop such a social theory of learning inevitably centre on the notion of culture since culture is central to social life. Wertsch argues that:

> The basic goal of a socio-cultural approach to mind is to create an account of human mental processes that recognises the essential relationship between these processes and their cultural, historical and institutional settings.
>
> (Wertsch 1991: 6)

Stenhouse expands upon this individualist and subjective notion of culture in describing it as:

> a dynamic field within and through which individuals make contact with one another . . . a medium bridging the gap between the lonely, subjective experiences of minds which communicate with one another . . . culture consists of a complex of shared understandings which serve as a medium through which individual human minds interact in communication with one another. It enables us to recognise as familiar the way other people think and feel and thus to share their feelings. It also enables us to predict and thus to anticipate the actions of others so that we can cooperate with them . . . This learning and sharing takes place as we cooperate and communicate in groups, and it depends heavily on language, with which culture is intimately related . . . The central fact is that both creative thinking and critical thinking grow from the culture, and that between the two there is a

> continuous dialectic. Individuals develop because their creative thought is disciplined by critical standards; and in education both the creative impulse and the critical reflex are important, for education is but the drama of culture set upon a small stage.
>
> (Stenhouse 1967: 13,16,37)

Stenhouse's analysis of the curriculum in these terms arguably goes to the heart of the current crisis of schooling. It provides a powerful rationale with which to critique the contemporary educational emphasis on the inculcation of predefined bodies of knowledge. This latter view of the educational project is rooted in an externalized view of culture. The transmission model of education reflects the view of culture referred to above as the defined and objectified morals, beliefs, values, skills and knowledge of a whole society. Parsons (1952), for example, argued that culture is transmitted, that it constitutes a heritage or a social tradition, that it is learned and that it is shared. Such a perspective of culture is closely linked with a transmission model of education in which it is the teacher's job to pass on to their pupils predefined elements of the knowledge that have been collectively generated within a particular epistemological culture.

By contrast the more dynamic, constructivist, socio-cultural approach to culture outlined above implies that the capacity to motivate individuals to acquire the necessary cultural tools and to interact with others on the basis of shared understandings and values is central to the conceptualization of good teaching and learning. It emphasizes the essential relativism of the educational project, which is shaped by culturally specific values and understandings and is designed to provide for an individual's progressive mastery of the relevant cultural tools.

It is possible to develop a theoretical model with which to structure the diverse dimensions of culture. Such a model would need to recognize the existence of a range of dynamic cultural settings which are, to a greater or lesser extent, concentric, ranging from pupil sub-cultures through to national and international policy discourses. Four linked themes can be mapped onto these different settings. The first of these concerns the issue of identity and its creation. There is arguably a need to establish the relationship between context and individual action in terms of three planes of analysis – the community/institution, the interpersonal and the personal (Rogoff 1995: 141).

The second theme is more explicitly educational. Building on these core notions of individual identity it recognizes the need to construct a rationale for 'meaningful' education in terms of a socio-cultural theory of learning.

The third theme concerns the role of different pedagogic structures and practices – what these represent and how the different ideological and institutional traditions from which they are derived both represent and reinforce the culturally specific character of particular institutional and systemic arrangements.

The fourth theme is conceived at the most macro level and provides an analytic structure for the cross-cutting discourses of, for example, marketization, social inequality and globalization, as framed within the central question of the perceived purpose of education.

These four analytic themes provide the core structure of this book. The chapters which follow will show how, linking them, both empirically and theoretically, within a comparative perspective can throw light on the complex interplay of factors – personal, social and structural – that influence a young person's engagement with learning. As we show in this book, comparative studies provide a particularly powerful way of illuminating the significance of national culture in education, of the impact of the specific configuration of educational values and understandings that in any one society are the result of historically embedded institutional traditions. Such institutional traditions are in turn a reflection of that society's more generic educational ideologies. The use of an explicitly comparative focus to study the socio-cultural reality of school experience for young people is thus a potentially key source of insight for understanding the variety of factors that impact upon an individual's learning. By the same token, it also offers some much needed guidance on the challenges that schools face if they are to engage the interest and commitment of young people in the twenty-first century.

The ENCOMPASS study

This book is an attempt to provide such a demonstration. The ENCOMPASS study on which this book is based, builds on earlier comparative work by the project team which clearly demonstrated the significance of national cultural influences on both teachers' and students' perspectives. In a series of studies (Teachers' Conceptions of their Professional Responsibility in England and France (BRISTAIX 1988; Broadfoot and Osborn 1988); Primary Assessment, Curriculum and Experience (PACE) (Osborn *et al.* 2000); and Systems, Teachers and Policy Change (STEP) (Broadfoot *et al.* 1996) we have shown how the construction of primary teachers' professional identity and hence their priorities and what they define as their responsibilities are heavily influenced by the national culture and national educational traditions in which they work. These studies indicated that teachers' classroom practice is a reflection of both these nationally distinctive professional values and associated understandings about the choice of pedagogic approaches to pursue these. Using a comparison of two national contexts with very different educational traditions – England and France – we were able to document the way in which teachers in both countries mediate the external requirements placed upon them, in terms of nationally specific professional values and understandings, to produce interpretations of both their priorities and desirable classroom practices, which are often very different from those intended by government directives (Broadfoot *et al.* 1996; Osborn *et al.* 1996).

A parallel comparative study of pupils in primary schools (Quality in Experiences of Schooling Trans-nationally (QUEST) explored the way in which the national cultures and educational traditions of England and France lead to significant differences in the way in which pupils define their relationship to school. We found that the resultant variations in children's attitude to school, in the sources of their motivation to learn and, in consequence, how they defined the role of the teacher, combined to create very different classroom environments in primary schools in the two countries (Broadfoot *et al.* 2000). The study reported in this book builds on this earlier work in trying to understand the significance of these various national differences for the development of a young adolescent's developing identity as a learner.

Thus although there are already a number of influential studies of children's learning in different cultures, for example, Richards and Light (1986), Whiting and Edwards (1988) and Alexander (2000), much previous work in this field has been small scale and anthropological in nature; one of the distinctive contributions of the present study was its larger scale as well as the opportunity to use existing longitudinal data sets.

We also included a third national context with a distinctive and very different educational system and educational priorities – Denmark. The Danish focus on collaboration, democratic decision making and the importance of the affective dimension in education, provides a striking contrast with education in England and France. It therefore provided a significant source of additional insights in the quest to illuminate the relationship between the national context, the institutional context and the nature of pupils' school experience.

The study was conducted between January 1998 and March 2000. Its aim was to elucidate the relationship between national culture, individual biographies and classroom practices in creating the context for learning, and the significance of national educational cultures and the encroaching pressures of globalization for pupils' different patterns of engagement with school and with learning. In the ENCOMPASS project we chose to compare these three contrasting national education systems in order to illustrate three fundamentally different approaches to the provision of compulsory education and schooling, and to investigate the effect of different policymaking on pupil experience.

In particular the research project was designed to explore the significance of the cultural context in which learning occurs, by examining the perspectives of pupils in these three European countries on the purposes of schooling and on themselves as learners. Our previous studies led us to hypothesize that although students in the three countries would be likely to share many common concerns associated with their age and the global youth culture, they would also have very different attitudes to, and expectations of, themselves as learners, their teachers and their school. Thus the broad aim of the project was to explore the social reality of schooling for students and the relative significance of the factors that influence the development of learner identity in the three national settings.

We recognized the necessity of addressing all levels of national educational activity from policymaking by ministers and civil servants at one extreme through to the myriad of individual interactions between teacher and pupil, and pupil and pupil, at the other. Thus our data collection, details of which are discussed in Chapter 2, was designed to enable us to respond to a series of research questions couched at these different levels as follows:

1 At the level of national policy discourse in the three countries, what are seen as the main aims of secondary schooling?
2 How are these national policy discourses mediated by institutional structures at the school level, such as school organization and ethos, pastoral care systems, rules and norms of behaviour?
3 How do teachers mediate these agendas to pupils?
4 In the light of all the above, how do children construct an identity as a learner and as a pupil, and what are the main sources of influence on their perspectives on learning, schooling and academic achievement?
5 What is the relative significance of intra-national differences in social class, gender and ethnicity as compared with international differences?
6 To what extent is children's experience of secondary schooling becoming more similar or moving towards convergence in the context of Europeanization, globalization and the internationalization of adolescent/peer culture?

Thus at the most general level our goal was to compare the educational experiences, attitudes to schooling and approaches to learning of secondary school age students in England, France and Denmark. We wanted to situate contemporary policy debates about raising educational standards, which are so much a feature of today's comparison obsessed world, in a more explicit understanding of the way in which the different cultural traditions of these three countries shape the reality of school experience for the young people growing up in them. More specifically however, we were concerned to understand the significance of such national differences as a series of case studies that could throw light on the nature of the relationship between system and action, individual biography and social context and, hence, on the social nature of learning itself. Our aim was to engage in a comparative study of learning, to pursue what we have referred to elsewhere as a 'comparative learnology' (Broadfoot 2000), in which the focus of comparison is not policies or organizations, differences in teachers' practice or other educational ingredients, which are the more traditional fare of comparative educational studies, but on learning itself and the light that a comparison of cultures can throw on it.

The theoretical orientation of the study is socio-cultural, drawing upon the work of Bruner (1990) and Wertsch and Smolka (1993). They in turn have drawn on the work of Vygotsky (1978) to highlight the important influence of social interaction in the development of higher mental processes through the mediating effect of the tools, signs and patterns of action which are embedded in different cultures. Forms of meaning and intellectual capacity have to be understood and located within the social context from which they derive. What is significant is not necessarily the 'objective' feature of a learning situation, but the ways in which these are construed and interpreted by subjects within that culture and setting (Bronfenbrenner 1979).

Thus the social and educational project for individual pupils within a particular culture involves the gradual appropriation of the mediational means (Bakhtin 1986) in order to negotiate their developing academic, social and personal identity. The construction of the individual 'pupil' which is largely the responsibility of the formal curriculum may be regarded as taking place within the broader context of the construction of the more general identity of 'child' or 'youth', involving peer group and family influences. It is important to ask, however, how far such processes are now being influenced by increasing European integration, the internationalization of adolescent peer culture, and the effects of globalization (Eide 1992; Masini 1994). Thus, in this book, we explore whether there are trends towards greater cultural homogeneity in the light of increasingly convergent economic and social structures. Are students' experiences of schooling becoming more similar? Are their efforts to construct their identity as learners and as adolescents pursuing increasingly similar trajectories? How far are young people's efforts to negotiate pathways that lead to success in terms of academic achievement, peer status and social conformity comparable from country to country? (Keys and Fernandes 1993; Rudduck *et al.* 1995).

We felt it was likely that differences in the three countries in terms of school structure and organization, school ethos and environment, and in the learning culture of classrooms would continue to impinge significantly on the creation of students' identities and on their views of themselves as learners. Other research evidence suggested, for example, that it may be difficult for students in England to negotiate strategies which achieve a balance between academic success as a pupil; social and peer group success as an adolescent; and success in conforming to school norms for social behaviour (Hargreaves 1967; Lacey 1970; Woods 1990; Abrahams 1995; Raphael Reed 1996). In France and

Denmark other research suggested that the process of negotiation and the strategies required were still very different, mediated as they are by idiosyncratic national traditions, school ethos and structures (Charlot *et al.* 1992; Jensen *et al.* 1992; Frønes 1995; Dubet *et al.* 1996).

After outlining the research design and method of data collection in Chapter 2, we explore the continuing differences that the ENCOMPASS project identified in the above respect in Chapter 3. In exploring the interwoven fabric of culture, context and policy in each of the three countries we show how the prevailing ideological traditions in each country remain very different, with an emphasis on differentiation and individualization in England; on republicanism and universalism in France; and on collaboration and consensus in Denmark.

Chapter 4 builds on this discussion of the historical origins and cultural characteristics of the three systems in examining the differences that can be identified between the schools themselves in the three countries. It explores the relative roles of government, parents, students and teachers in the running of the school. Particular attention is given to the balance between the affective and cognitive purposes of schooling since this was identified from the outset as a potentially key dimension of variation between the three countries. Significantly, the chapter shows that even such ubiquitous words as 'school', 'class' and 'headteacher' can represent very different realities in practice.

Chapter 5 provides an investigation into the differences that characterize teachers in the three countries. It identifies significant variations in emphasis in terms of teachers' views of subjects, teaching methods and their educational priorities. As such the chapter goes to the heart of the issues that divide the three systems in terms of their overall goals and the means chosen for achieving these goals. Equally though, the chapter emphasizes the importance of recognizing both structure and agency in these distinctions, of the influence of national culture on the one hand but also of the teacher's own individual biography and values on the other.

Chapter 6 completes the part of the book that is concerned with portraying the different elements that inform the provision of schooling in each of the three countries. It describes some of the typical features of day to day classroom encounters and the very different experiences of the pupils in them. From the analysis presented we identify the underlying values that appear to inform the different systems – individualism and empiricism in England; egalitarianism, collectivism and intellectualism in France; and a mixture of all of these in Denmark.

The central question of the ENCOMPASS study concerns the way in which culture influences the development of a young person's identity as a learner and what this can tell us about the forces that support or inhibit learning. Chapters 7 and 8 attempt to provide some answers to this question. They report on the views that students themselves offered concerning aspects of their home and school, and of their social life with their friends. Again, as expected, significant differences between the three countries are reported. However, there are also some things on which the young people in all three of the countries appeared to agree, notably concerning the characteristics of 'good' teaching and the importance of education for future life. The paired case studies of individual students that we present in Chapter 8 provide a graphic picture of what it is like to be a particular type of pupil in each of the countries. They emphasize the importance of understanding that it is the complex interaction of a whole range of factors covering school, classroom, friends and family that combine to shape any individual's learning career and emerging identity.

The ENCOMPASS study would be justifiably open to criticism if it had not made the effort to compare the relative significance of *different* cultural settings on students' experiences and perspectives. Are the undoubtedly important differences that exist between individuals within the same country as a result of their socio-economic background or their ethnic identity, ultimately more important than the type of between-country differences referred to above? How far are the much heralded differences between boys' and girls' performance a determining factor in the development of learning identity? Chapter 9 makes it clear that such intra-national variations have considerable significance but these appear, perhaps surprisingly, to be less significant overall than the international sources of variation.

This book thus paints a picture of three education systems that share a broadly similar European heritage but which are marked, nevertheless, by the very distinctive patterns of organization and practice that have emerged over a century or more in response to prevailing national cultural priorities. The book paints a second picture as well: of young people growing up in a changing world, a world of great opportunities but of considerable pressures and uncertainty as well. The book describes their aspirations and their doubts; their friendships and their frustrations; their day to day experiences in school; and the lived reality of an increasingly global peer culture. It attempts to capture a vision of what influences the success and failure of young learners in the secondary schools of three different countries; of the influences and views that they have in common; and of what divides them. Ultimately the book seeks to paint a picture of learning; of how it can best be encouraged; and of the new challenges that appear to be confronting teachers and students in all three of the countries in our study. Thus the last chapter in the book attempts to answer the question with which this chapter began. Are schools in crisis? What are the challenges they face for the twenty-first century? How far are these the same in England, France and Denmark, and to what extent is it possible to conceive of common solutions? Our conclusions are both radical and challenging. But they are not unrealizable.

Note

1 Recent reports suggest that this disaffection is marked even in Japan where pupil conformity and commitment have, until recently, been the envy of many other countries.

2 New methodologies for comparative research? the research design of the ENCOMPASS study

Introduction

In recent years there has been a growing tendency to 'borrow' educational policies and practices from one national setting where they appear to be effective and to attempt to transplant these into another, with little regard for the potential significance of the cultural context into which they will be imported. Thus international comparisons have been used to legitimate claims about the condition of national systems of education and to justify radical changes in educational policy (Alexander 1999). Many of the studies which have been used in this way have employed large scale survey methods and international studies of educational achievement. By their very nature such studies have been unable fully to take culture into account. Yet such an understanding of educational perspectives and practices within their cultural context is fundamental to understanding how learning takes place. This chapter argues for the importance of seeking to understand, through cross-cultural comparison, the relationship between national context, institutional ethos and classroom practices in mediating the development of a learner's identity. It describes the multi-layered comparative methodology employed by the ENCOMPASS project and emphasizes the strengths of linking both macro and micro levels of comparative research.

In the first part of this chapter we draw upon examples from the ENCOMPASS study and from the programme of comparative research which preceded it (see Chapter 1) to discuss particular issues which arise in comparative studies, and the way in which the research team attempted to resolve them. The second part of the chapter describes the methods employed in the research. Throughout the chapter we highlight the potential value and power of a multi-layered approach which combines quantitative and qualitative methods, particularly when designed and implemented in a cross-national collaborative research team.

Particular issues in comparative research

In many ways comparative studies provide an ideal 'educational laboratory' since they allow ethnocentric assumptions to be identified and challenged by the existence of alternative practices, which are at least as deeply rooted in their own cultural context. As we hope will be apparent from the account of the outcomes of the project which follows, such in depth international comparisons can provide a unique set of insights and can yield contrasts that are the basis for developing new theoretical perspectives.

The fact that comparative studies of this kind are relatively rare, however, despite their undoubted strengths, is indicative of the methodological difficulties involved. It is far less challenging to carry out a national case study or studies of particular aspects of educational provision which take little account of the critical influence of the mediating national contexts. In spite of its rapid growth in recent years, much comparative educational research still lacks both theoretical and methodological rigour, either because educational systems are chosen for comparison on the basis of convenience rather than logic, or because no attempt is made to build on the comparisons made to formulate more general insights into the relationship between education and society.

In recent papers both Broadfoot (2000) and Alexander (2000) have attempted to delineate a range of activities which might be called comparative research. Alexander draws a distinction between the 'old' and the 'new' comparative education and between 'comparative education' and 'policy directed educational comparison'. Broadfoot distinguishes between the major international quantitative studies which have been used to heighten awareness of differential achievement and more qualitative studies which have contributed to a collective understanding of the interrelatedness of the various cultural factors concerned and of the dangers of crude policy borrowing. She argues for a kind of 'third way' in comparative research which uses 'more post-modernist conceptual tools' and which focuses on individuals and their access to learning rather than on systems and problems of provision (Broadfoot 2000: 363). It is in this latter spirit that the ENCOMPASS project was designed, with a focus on individual learners and how they are situated within a larger cultural context. It was designed to be explicitly comparative, studying three countries with a coherent rationale for their selection in order to illuminate 'constants' (those factors which might be seen as universal to a particular situation such as being a secondary school pupil) and 'contexts' (factors which are likely to be more culturally specific).

In an early paper on our programme of comparative projects (Broadfoot and Osborn 1992) we described some of the issues that have to be resolved drawing upon Warwick and Osherson (1973) who identified certain basic problems that occur in comparative analysis whether the method of research is the sample survey, participant observation, historical analysis or some other approach.

These are issues of:

1 conceptual equivalence;
2 equivalence of measurement;
3 linguistic equivalence;
4 sampling.

Although these problems may arise with any research method, they are brought into sharpest form by the use of combinations of methods as used in the ENCOMPASS programme of study and in particular by the questionnaire/ survey method.

Conceptual equivalence

One of the most basic theoretical questions in comparative analysis is whether the concepts under study have any equivalent meaning in the cultures under study. Concepts may be more or less culturally specific – even, as emerged from this study, such an apparently unambiguous one as 'teaching style'. Particular terms may not have exact counterparts in all cultures. A major challenge for comparative research then is to 'provide conceptual definitions that have equivalent, though not necessarily identical, meaning in various cultures'. These problems are lessened to some extent, but not eliminated, when comparing two western industrialized societies. There may be more shared concepts but there are still problems of conceptual equivalence. For example, in our study of primary teachers in England and France we found that 'accountability' had no equivalent meaning in French and therefore the expression 'professional responsibility' was chosen, since it appeared to have validity in both countries. Later examples included very different meanings for assessment in Denmark and the other two countries.

Equivalence of measurement

In addition to choosing variables that can be given comparable conceptual definitions in the societies under study, there is the further challenge of developing equivalent indicators for the concepts. Concepts may differ in their *salience* for the culture as a whole, or respondents in some countries may be unwilling to discuss sensitive topics such as politics, sexual behaviour, income or religion. For example, in an early study of adolescents in Denmark where teachers were asked to consider analytically the characteristics of their adolescent students, Lerner (1956) commented that 'Despite their willingness to co-operate, the Danish teachers claimed that they were unaccustomed to considering analytically, matters of adolescent interactions and could express no judgements or opinions'. Eventually this component of the investigation was abandoned. A similar problem occurred in the ENCOMPASS programme where French teachers found the concept of 'teaching style' problematic and were unaccustomed to reflecting upon their 'teaching style' in an analytical way.

In another early paper Dujykes and Rokkan (1954) suggested that one effective approach to equivalence lies in a study design involving collaboration between knowledgeable members of the participating societies. They indicated a number of ways in which this may be achieved, but conclude that by far the most direct approach to equivalence is the 'joint-development-concurrent' model where the research design is arrived at jointly by collaborators from the different cultures involved, and the study is carried out more or less simultaneously in these cultures. However, they were able to cite the existence of few such studies. This is the approach adopted in the ENCOMPASS programme of study, which allowed at least some of these important methodological difficulties to be overcome.

Linguistic equivalence

There still remains the difficulty of obtaining linguistic equivalence through translation. 'Back-translation' was seen for a time as the answer to these difficulties, in which the questionnaire is translated from language A to language B by a native speaker of B, then from B to A by a native speaker of A, then from A to B by a third party, and so on until discrepancies in meaning are clarified or removed. This approach later came under heavy fire, however, since it was clear that such methods, although designed to produce equivalent words in the two languages, could not ensure that these literally equivalent words or phrases conveyed equivalent meanings in the two languages. Warwick and Osherson (1973) offer suggestions as a guide to setting the problem of linguistic equivalence within the broader framework of conceptualization and research design. These include ensuring that the research problem is salient to all the cultures involved; that the primary emphasis in translation is on the conceptual equivalence – comparability of ideas – rather than of words per se; and that there is extensive pre-testing of the research instruments in the local culture.

The ENCOMPASS study attempted to confront these problems by employing a method emphasizing joint production of research instruments by the researchers from the three countries in the process of which concepts and their meanings could be extensively discussed. Thus, final drafts of instruments were produced more or less simultaneously in three languages. This is detailed in a later section of this chapter.

Sampling problems

The comparability of cross-societal studies may be greatly reduced by, for example, the use of noncomparable or low quality sampling frames; differing procedures for selecting the sample; the oversampling of some groups and undersampling of others; and the high, or varying, nonresponse rates. The ENCOMPASS study adopted a more qualitative approach which involved the matching of secondary schools in each of the three countries with schools which were as comparable as possible in terms of their pupil intakes, with relatively similar socio-economic and ethnic backgrounds. Questionnaires were administered in their classrooms to the entire year group in each of the study schools with a researcher present to explain the purpose of the study, help with any difficulties and to collect the completed questionnaires. This ensured a high response rate, although pupils were told that they had the right to refuse to take part in the study and some did so.

Some solutions to the problems of cross-national comparison?

Arguably many of the problems previously discussed stem from an exclusive reliance in much comparative research on single methodologies. Significantly, Warwick and Osherson (1973) make a plea for more 'innovative combinations of methods in comparative research'. Many of the limitations of survey methods in comparative study, for example, would be much less serious, 'if the study also contained extensive qualitative information on the societies covered'. The combination of survey and qualitative methods in comparative research is a fruitful one and provides the analyst with additional sources of information for interpreting the findings, as well as immediate evidence on the validity of the data.

Another strong case for including a more qualitative research design was made by Crossley and Vulliamy (1984), who have suggested that case study or ethnographic methods can play a vital role in comparative education in examining the hiatus that may exist between the policies and the practice of schooling. Their later book (Crossley and Vulliamy 1997) demonstrates by example how detailed qualitative case studies can provide significant comparative insights. Case studies of schooling can expose the gap between rhetoric and reality and lead to theories about the processes of schooling. They can also, in combination with questionnaire surveys, act as a method of 'triangulation', helping to atone for some of the problems inherent in the questionnaire/ survey method. For example, it is well known that questionnaire surveys are prone to 'the reproduction of rhetoric'; that respondents are often unwilling to admit 'failures' or doubts about what they are doing, and that there is a tendency for respondents to present what they think researchers want to hear. In addition surveys tend to make assumptions about the meaning of both concepts and actions for the respondents and, in the positivist tradition, necessarily tend to impose the researcher's meaning on the respondents. As cited previously, these problems can be intensified in cross-cultural research.

Pepin (1999) and Tobin (1999) also put forward compelling arguments for qualitative comparative work. Tobin, for example, makes the case for a comparative classroom ethnography, drawing upon his own studies of preschool in three cultures in order to illustrate how such comparative analysis can be a powerful tool to 'make the familiar strange and the strange familiar' in order to highlight what we take for granted in our own educational institutions. The work of Elliott *et al.*. (1999) also makes this point powerfully in comparing and seeking to explain the very different educational experiences of pupils in the UK, Russia and the US. Most recently, in a masterly study of pedagogy in five cultures, Alexander has used qualitative research to 'unravel further the complex interplay of policies, structures, culture, values and pedagogy' (Alexander 2000: 4).

This steady growth of more qualitative comparative approaches has developed alongside the 'rapid and powerful rise' of major international quantitative studies such as the international comparisons of educational achievements (Broadfoot 2000: 362). Relatively few of these, however, have attempted to combine both quantitative and qualitative approaches using a cross-national comparative team. This chapter argues for the unique insights which such a powerful combination can provide. Thus, as Miles and Huberman (1994) argue, although not referring to comparative studies, in a combination of quantitative and qualitative methods each method can be strengthened by using the intrinsic qualities of the other so that when 'good quantitative studies are combined with the 'up-close, real world contexts that characterise good qualitative studies, a very powerful mix can result'.

Such an argument applies with yet more force in comparative studies where this 'powerful mix' can illuminate our understanding of how individual, group and national identities are mediated by cultural tools that may both facilitate and constrain how individuals engage with a situation (Wertsch 1991). Thus, such a mix may illuminate the relationship between the national cultural context, educational institutions and the way in which these are mediated to teachers and through them to learners. Such in-depth comparisons of French, English and more recently Danish education have been conducted over a number of years by the ENCOMPASS team. In a series of comparative studies we have used a combination of quantitative and qualitative approaches to illuminate our understanding of the significance of culture in shaping the organization and processes of education within an educational system. Thus our studies of teachers and pupils have revealed 'deeply rooted differences in national educational priorities, in epistemologies, in institutional traditions and in professional values' (Broadfoot 2000: 362). They highlight the significance of cultural context in shaping teacher strategies and pupil responses to teaching, learning and schooling at both primary and secondary level. The methods adopted by the ENCOMPASS research are described in the remaining sections of this chapter after a short discussion of the issues involved in working collaboratively in a cross-national team.

Building a cross-national research team

Most researchers who are involved in comparative work would agree that such cross-national collaborative research, by its very nature, can involve more compromises in methods than a single study approach. This may be why many researchers either adopt the 'safari' approach (where a single researcher or single-nation team of researchers formulate the problem, design the research instruments and carry out the same study in more than one country) or the 'lone-ranger' approach where data is gathered by individuals and teams in each national context and then presented side by side without being systematically compared, after which the researchers go their separate ways.

As Hantrais (1996) argues the problems of building and maintaining a cross-national research team may only be resolved after much negotiation. There is no doubt that the process of building and managing such a team can be time consuming and sometimes the quality and level of the contributions to multinational projects may be very uneven. There may be inequalities of funding or other issues of inequalities of power between the researchers from the different countries involved. As Lauder (2000) points out, this may be particularly the case when some of the researchers are drawn from an oppressed group which may be being researched, as is the case when postcolonial peoples are researched by former colonizers. Although good project management cannot in itself be sufficient to overcome these problems it is certainly the case that the managerial skills and experience of the co-coordinators are critical in holding the team together and negotiating agreement without such compromise that the end product becomes bland.

However, the advantages of building a cross-national team where every stage of the research from initial conceptualization and research design to analysis and writing up is carried out by a genuinely multinational group can pay dividends, as we shall see in the description of the projects which follow. In particular, such a cross-national collaborative method of working can contribute to in-depth debate and understanding of the research issues and can, in a sense, become part of the data. Thus, in initial planning meetings in the ENCOMPASS project, which took place both face to face and via email, conceptual and linguistic issues were discussed and very different perspectives emerged from the researchers in the three countries on what were the central issues. These became a subject of debate and contributed to the way in which the team were able to reach a greater understanding of meanings and 'taken for granted' realities in the three countries. One small example of this was the greater centrality of parental involvement in the Danish system and the different understandings which existed about the importance of assessment. This process of discussion and re-conceptualizing continued during the coding, analysis and interpretation of the data.

The ENCOMPASS programme of research

As Chapter 1 outlines, the ENCOMPASS research adopted an explicitly socio-cultural theoretical approach. The study was designed to explore the different inputs, processes and outputs which shaped secondary students' educational experience of the three European countries – England, France and Denmark. The broad aim of the project was to explore the social reality of schooling for students and the relative significance of the factors that influence the development of learner identity in the three national settings.

In the light of the discussion of methods which follows it is worth re-stating the key research questions of the study. These were:

1. At the level of national policy discourse in the three countries, what are seen as the main aims of secondary schooling?
2. How are these national policy discourses mediated by institutional structures at the school level such as school organization and ethos, pastoral care systems, rules and norms of behaviour?
3. How do teachers mediate these agendas to pupils?
4. In the light of all the above, how do children construct an identity as a learner and as a pupil, and what are the main sources of influence on their perspectives on learning, schooling and academic achievement?
5. What is the relative significance of *intra*-national differences in social class, gender, and ethnicity as compared with *inter*national differences?
6. To what extent is children's experience of secondary schooling becoming more similar or moving towards convergence in the context of Europeanization, globalization, and the internationalization of adolescent/peer culture?

Research design and methods of data collection

As will be apparent, the questions required us to collect data at a variety of levels: at the level of national policy, at the level of the school and classroom, and at the level of the individual teacher and learner. In addition to working at these different levels, the research design needed to include both quantitative and qualitative approaches to data collection in order to maximize both the breadth and depth of the insights generated. This approach built upon the strengths of the previous programme of work by the team of researchers in which the clear patterns of response evident in a large questionnaire survey supported the validity of generalizations about national differences, while in-depth individual and group interviews and classroom observation allowed the processes which underlay these differences to be explored in greater depth. However, the design of the current study contained some unique and innovative features in cross-cultural study, including the method of reflecting back in group interviews selected quotes about schooling, teaching and learning from pupils in the three countries, and the inclusion of an 'insider' and an 'outsider' perspective, as detailed below.

The research design included three levels and three phases of data collection. At *national policy level,* government policy documentation from each country was collected and national policy discourse analysed in order to establish what were seen as the key goals of the secondary education system, the main means of achieving these goals and the major areas of tension.

At *school level,* documentation such as prospectuses, policy documents and school development plans were collected and analysed. Interviews were carried out with headteachers, year heads and form tutors, or the equivalent, in each country. These focused on educational priorities for the children, and on the structures and organization in place in each school to provide for personal development and support (for example, pastoral care systems and personal and social education) and the understandings which the staff held about the purposes of these.

The *sample of secondary schools* in each country was matched and selected to be as representative as possible of a socio-economic mix. In England three comprehensives, one in an area of relatively high socio-economic status in the Midlands, one in a 'mixed' area in the southwest and one in a highly disadvantaged area in London were selected. These were matched as far as possible with schools in Denmark, two of which were in Copenhagen and one in the west of Denmark, and with three schools in France, one in an area of relatively high socio-economic status in the southwest, one in a 'mixed' suburb of Paris and a third in a highly disadvantaged suburb of Paris. In these schools all the qualitative data collection, teacher and pupil interviews and classroom observations were carried out. However, for the questionnaire phase of the study which required a sizeable sample, since English comprehensives are considerably larger than comparable schools in France and Denmark, in order to collect comparable numbers of pupil responses we included twenty additional schools in Denmark, where the schools were very small, and one in France. In both cases these were drawn from areas of 'mixed' socio-economic status.

Data collection at *pupil level* combined quantitative and qualitative approaches and took place in three phases over the two years of the study. In *phase one* approximately 1800 12- and 13-year-old pupils in their second year of secondary schooling, all of whom were drawn from the sample of schools outlined above, completed questionnaires containing both fixed response and open-ended questions.

The questionnaire (see Appendix 1) focused on young learners' perspectives on schooling, teaching and learning in general and, more particularly, on their own schools, their teachers and their views of themselves as learners. In devising any research instrument for cross-cultural comparison, particularly questionnaires, a number of important issues arise as discussed in the earlier sections of this chapter. Careful consideration was given to linguistic and conceptual cross-cultural differences in the construction of the questionnaires and in their translation. As a result, these were extensively piloted and revised a number of times. Production of both French, English and Danish questionnaires took place simultaneously with team members from all three countries present, and discussion over meanings and conceptual equivalence formed an important part of the understanding of the researchers before they went into schools. For example, it quickly became apparent that issues such as parental involvement, selection and assessment had very different meanings in Denmark than in either England or France.

In *phase two* a sub-sample of 18 'target' children was then selected for further detailed study over the course of the two years of the project, which included individual and group interviews and classroom observation. The target group included equal numbers of boys and girls who were chosen to represent a mix of high, medium and low achievers, from a range of socio-economic and ethnic backgrounds.

The 18 pupils in each country were first individually interviewed in depth (see Appendix 2) about their views of teaching, learning and schooling and then later in groups (see Appendix 3). Each group interview included one target pupil and four friends chosen by the individual target child. Approximately six group interviews took place in each school and 18 in each country. These were designed to elicit insights into peer group culture and the relationship of this to children's identity as learners, and to school culture (Dubet *et al.* 1996). The aim was also to follow up insights gained from the analysis of the questionnaires and individual interviews. To extend and validate the findings of the first phase the researchers fed back to the groups some of the findings concerning: what children in their school, their country and in the other countries had said about their experience of schooling. Selected quotations (see Table 2.1) from children in all three countries were used to stimulate group discussion and were followed up with a series of probes designed to explore meaning and to examine some of the influences on children's perspectives.

In *phase three* individual follow-up interviews were carried out with target pupils in order to investigate their options and choices in relation to the next

Table 2.1 Examples of pupil quotations used to stimulate group discussion

Good pupils and peer groups
Themes: gender, ethnicity, friendship, social background, success, 'coolness', conformity.

Good pupil

'A good pupil is a little cute blonde girl with a brain which falls out of her mouth when she speaks'

Prompt Does it make a difference if the pupil is a girl or boy?
Prompt Does what colour you are make a difference?

'A good pupil is a keener – a really clever person – posh – and they do everything proper'

Prompt What does it mean to be a 'keener'?
Prompt Does what kind of home you come from make a difference?

'A good pupil is someone who always does good work'

Peer groups

'A good pupil doesn't get into the wrong crowd'

Prompt What does 'getting into the wrong crowd' mean?
Prompt What does being 'cool' mean?

'You can only be different if you're popular'

Teachers and assessment
Themes: motivation, self esteem, identity as a learner, concept of 'interesting' lessons.

'Teachers judge pupils too much by their marks'

Prompt What effect does getting a bad mark/doing poor work have on you?
Prompt What effect does getting a good mark/doing good work have on you?
Prompt What does 'good work' mean?

'Teachers shouldn't make you feel like a loser'

'I learn best when the teacher makes the lesson interesting and enjoyable'

phase of secondary education or employment. In addition, during all three phases of data collection, evidence such as school reports and any available assessment results were collected for all the target pupils. These were analysed in order to be able to investigate pupil perspectives in relation to attainment.

Techniques that the research team had used successfully in previous projects, including the extensive piloting of all the research instruments and the presence of the researchers during completion of the questionnaires in the classroom, helped to minimize some of the many problems associated with cross-cultural research of this kind. In any method of researching with young adolescents there are potential problems of authenticity of response and researchers must accept that their presence in the setting and their relationship with the children may have influenced the outcome to some extent (Connelly 1997). However, through triangulation of the findings using multiple methods we hope that these problems have been minimized. For example, the researchers were able to explore in more depth many of the issues which arose from the questionnaires through a combination of individual interviews with a sub-sample of pupils, teacher interviews and classroom observation.

Throughout the research the team made use of both 'insider' and 'outsider' perspectives (Schratz 1992) in order, where possible, to gain three way cultural insights and to minimize the risks of ethnocentricity. Thus, following the method adopted by Judge *et al.* (1994), each researcher wrote up data from a country that is not their own. Cross-checking and validation of these accounts by the host country then took place.

Part of the value of cross-cultural research is the extent to which it is able to identify both constants and contexts in educational experience (Broadfoot and Osborn 1988). Cross-cultural comparisons of pupil experience identify pupil responses to learning which are more universal to the situation of 'being a secondary school pupil' from those which may be more culturally specific. As we have attempted to show in this research, pupils in England, Denmark and France have to engage with school contexts and teacher mediations which relate to cultural, philosophical, political and historical differences between the three countries. These in turn are mediated by pupil concerns and perceptions of schooling and learning and will ultimately affect behaviour and learning outcomes.

Conclusion

This chapter has discussed some of the particular issues and problems that can arise in comparative research and has outlined the ways in which the ENCOMPASS study has attempted to resolve these. The specific contribution of the research has been the attempt to shed light on the complex interplay of factors – personal, social and structural – that influence young people's engagement with school. Thus the study has used a comparative multi-layered perspective which combines both quantitative and qualitative methods to underline the importance of problematizing what it is to *learn* as well as what it is to teach, in different countries. For this purpose the methods used were designed to try to establish the 'constants' and 'contexts' in learners' experience and perspectives. In Part 2 of the book, which follows, we describe the findings from the documentary analysis and interviews with teachers, headteachers and year heads in the three countries. Here we outline the national educational policy context for the research and the distinctive features of school organization, teaching and classrooms experienced by young learners in the three systems.

PART 2

National Cultural Contexts: Schools, Teachers and Classrooms

3 Culture, context and policy

Introduction

The second section of this book uses data from documentary evidence, semi-structured interviews, observation and fieldnotes to describe and analyse the national school settings within which the target pupils experienced learning and created their multiple identities. It moves progressively from the historical and ideological origins of the three national systems to the present day national, school and classroom arenas in which policy is successively mediated by administrators, headteachers and teachers. It uses the findings to reflect upon pupil responses to their schooling experience by drawing out some of the significant differences with regard to such culturally constructed concepts as the 'school', the 'teacher', and the 'class'. It also examines the interrelationship between the academic and the social/personal or 'affective' aspects of teaching and learning in order to illuminate the varying influences of organizational structure on the individual agency of teachers and pupils. The section begins with this chapter, which starts by examining the historical origins, ideological underpinnings, policy discourse and current schooling structures within the three countries.

The historical origins of the three systems

Comparative research into national education systems has had a long history of seeking to understand more fully the immediate observable similarities and differences between national structures, by looking at the historical and cultural origins from which they have sprung (Kandel 1933; Hans 1949; Archer 1984). Recently there has been a resurgence of interest in such studies as global pressures impact on policymakers and cause them to look for solutions to their own problems within competing national systems. Some studies use data from large international surveys of educational indicators which have been used by administrators to support the introduction of new policy initiatives. However, such data can be misleading unless they are interpreted with reference to the historical, cultural and ideological influences which have shaped them. For this reason the next three sections briefly outline the ideological and structural development of formal schooling, in each of the three countries studied, which has preceded the more recent changes since the 1980s.

England

The education system in England has grown out of a laissez-faire, liberal tradition which has been associated with voluntarism and local autonomy. It has drawn on a humanistic approach to learning which emphasized spiritual and moral values as well as individualism and early specialization. Thus it has promoted an individual, child-centred pedagogy which has historically regarded pupils as having individual needs and abilities, requiring different types of schooling. For the children of the wealthy classes independent boarding schools, known as 'public schools', were established where the focus was on the development of 'character' and personal qualities, and the pursuit of academic knowledge was underplayed. At the same time, charitable foundations established 'elementary' schools for the children of the working class and poor with the aim of giving them a basic, Christian education which would enable them to contribute positively to society.

As a result, the country's first major education act (Elementary Education Act, 1870) sought merely to 'complete the present voluntary system, to fill up the gaps' (Sharp and Dunford 1990). There was no intention to disturb the existing mix of provision provided by various religious and philanthropic organizations, nor disturb the independent sector which continues to be a significant feature of schooling in England today. However, it was the Education Act of 1944 which has probably had the most influence on the current structure of schools in England. It finally replaced the old arrangement of 'elementary' and 'higher' education with a continuous process conducted in three successive stages: primary, secondary and further education. It also removed the responsibility for education from individuals by making the Minister of State for Education ultimately responsible for the education of the people of England, with the local education authorities required to carry out their part 'under his control and direction' (MacLure 1979). Its other major influence was the endorsement of the earlier Norwood Report (1943) which argued that pupils could and should be split into three 'rough groupings' at the secondary level of schooling. A tripartite system was established which sifted and sorted pupils, into grammar schools for those 'interested in learning for its own sake', technical schools for those whose interests and abilities were 'in the field of applied science or applied art', and finally secondary modern schools for those more easily able to deal with 'concrete things than with ideas'.

However, during the 1960s and 1970s a more liberal and egalitarian view of the aims of education began to surface and with it the establishment, by many local authorities, of comprehensive schools, which took all children, without selection, from 11 until the end of their schooling. To cope with an increased diversity within the pupil population many curriculum initiatives were also established which sought to break the stranglehold of the universities and the grammar schools by creating a more child-centred view of pedagogy and assessment. This was encouraged, to some extent, through an influential speech made by the then labour prime minister, James Callaghan (Ruskin Speech 1976), which initiated the Great Debate on the future of education in England. This created a climate in which the control of education and schooling was opened up for general debate and saw the beginnings of a more widespread struggle for control over the aims and purposes of education.

France

Education in France has, historically, been organized according to the republican ideal. It has been characterized by the values of universality, rationalism and utilitarianism. The state has a duty to ensure a universal education which provides an equal entitlement for all. It is underpinned by an integrative notion of citizenship and nationality and based on rationalist traditions of knowledge which must promote national values and social solidarity. The French Revolution created the fundamental doctrine of free, secular education for all, but it took the successive laws of Guizot (1835), Falloux (1850) and Duruy (1863) to implement the Revolution's aims. However, primary education was somewhat neglected and only became part of the system with the introduction of the Jules Ferry laws of 1881–83, when free primary education became compulsory for all children aged between 6 and 12 years. Education was secular with one day set aside each week for religious instruction by the church. The Ferry laws centralized timetables, curricula and teaching methods. In 1889 this was extended to include the payment of teachers' salaries. Since the late nineteenth century the ministry of education has not only funded education but also controlled teacher appointments and the assessment system; prescribed curricula and school hours; and inspected school textbooks. However, by 1947 the Langevin-Wallon Commission had drawn attention to a tension between the highly centralized and controlled school environment and the pace of change within society. By 1959 the age for compulsory school attendance had been extended to 16 years, although at this time primary and secondary education were still conceived of as two separate tracks. It was only with the 1975 Haby law that the concept of primary education as the first stage leading to secondary education was introduced. Until this time the system had been divided into two distinct levels: primary education, which culminated in the *certificat d'études primaire* and took working class pupils who rarely transferred to the secondary level; and the secondary level, culminating in the *baccalauréat*, which was reserved for the élite and was not originally open to girls or to working class pupils. Gradually primary education was extended and stronger links were made between primary and secondary education in order to create one system with three levels.

Denmark

Denmark, along with other Nordic countries, has a strong tradition of communitarianism which places less emphasis on professional autonomy and relies more on a powerful folk tradition of local democracy and social partnership. It has traditionally seen education as a home and community enterprise in which individual schools are relatively independent but highly integrated with, and accountable to, the local community. The origins of the Danish *folkeskole* can be traced back to 1814 when the peasant school act (*almueskolelov*) was passed by parliament. This constituted the first universal, basic school act for 7- to 14-year-olds. During the course of the nineteenth century other forms of primary schools also grew up as alternatives to the state-maintained basic school and the previously existing, more academically focused, Latin school. In the cities the citizen's schools (*borgerskoler*) and in the countryside the influential 'free' schools (*friskoler*) emerged, together with the folk high schools for those over 18 years. The latter two had been greatly influenced by the writings of Grundtvig, the eighteenth century clergyman, poet and philosopher who emphasized the importance of oral tradition and the ideal of a liberal education (*folkeoplysning*), often translated as 'folk enlightenment' which combines education with companionship and personal development.

The 1903 education act brought together the *almueskole* and the Latin school and provided a unified system of education by establishing the present day *folkeskole* and *gymnasium*. This established a common core of education for four or five years which was followed by an eleven plus examination, which was used to divide pupils into two separate streams: a four year academic stream leading to the *gymnasium* and a two year practical stream preparing pupils for apprenticeship training.

In 1933 the national clerical inspection of the school was abolished and replaced by a system of local county inspection, and in 1937 a new act was passed which aimed to improve the status of practical, nonacademic courses. However, as the largely agricultural population of Denmark was dispersed across many islands, the changes did not have a full effect in some areas until as late as 1958. During the 1960s a major schools building programme was embarked on and it became the norm for all pupils to be taught together in mixed ability classes from 7 to 14 years. Pupils also began to continue their schooling for an additional two years until they were 16 years old. By 1972 the length of compulsory education was extended from seven to nine years and the 1975 education act formally established a system of nine years of basic education, with a voluntary preschool class and an optional tenth year. The *folkeskole* was given a new purpose, stressing democratic attitudes, the development of an enthusiasm for learning and close home–school cooperation. The previous streaming of children by attainment after grade 7 (14 years) was abolished and replaced by setting for the older classes in certain subjects such as mathematics, foreign languages and physics, which has since also been abolished.

National policy discourse and the aims of schooling

As recent studies have shown (Green *et al.* 1999), there is great deal of common agreement across Europe in terms of the general aims of schooling. All have a compulsory core of formal schooling for children of approximately ten years. This initially provides instruction in the basic skills of literacy and numeracy, and later helps to prepare students for employment or the upper-secondary stage of education. All also have a commitment to national cultural transmission and the social and personal development of individuals. However, the balance between the needs of the economy, social cohesion and approaches to personal development are often historically and culturally determined. Such structural and curriculum demands can be in tension and the policy responses of different national governments to such pressures have had a major impact on the work of teachers and the learning environments of their pupils. Within developed western cultures, the academic dimension of schooling is served by a largely common, subject-based curriculum. This is less true of the approaches used to support both social cohesion and individual personal development which are more varied and less easily operationalized. Within the three countries studied the different national approaches to these three elements of education and schooling have helped to define some of the differences which were uncovered.

All developed economies are currently struggling with common structural problems which include, changes in work patterns due to the emergence of new technologies; the effects of the liberalization of markets for goods, capital and services; the assimilation of economic migrants, widespread youth unemployment; ageing populations and shifts in social attitudes, particularly with regard to aspirations concerning educational attainment and qualifications (Green *et al.* 1999). However, despite this common agenda, there remain differences in policy emphasis between the three countries being studied which can be traced back to their historical roots. The national discourses currently used to describe these education systems serve to underline the continuing policy preoccupations of the different national governments.

England

In England the focus remains on the individual child and their innate abilities, and there is a continuing emphasis on the role of education in the economy of the nation:

> The basic principle underlying statutory [school] education is that it should provide a balanced and broadly based curriculum which is suitable to the child's age, ability, aptitude and to any special educational needs the child might have . . . The Department for Education and Employment's aim is: To support economic growth and improve the nation's competitiveness and quality of life by raising standards of educational achievement and skill and by promoting an efficient and flexible labour market.
>
> (NFER/QCA INCA Database 1998)

In 1988 a conservative government introduced the Education Reform Act. This was characterized by what has been referred to as 'the contradictory processes of decentralization and centralization' (Woods *et al.* 1997: 2). It removed much of the power that had rested with local education authorities by drawing some of it into central government by way of a highly prescriptive national curriculum, while at the same time devolving budgets directly to schools through the Local Management of Schools (LMS) initiative. National testing was established for pupils aged 7, 11 and 14 years, and these changes were further enhanced with a more rigorous system of inspection through teams of government-accredited inspectors working for the Office of Standards in Education (Ofsted). Boards of governors, consisting of voluntary representatives from parents, teachers and the local community, were also established for all schools. These were given a statutory responsibility to ensure the quality of education provision and the school's compliance with the requirements of the national curriculum and national testing. At the same time, a process of open enrolment encouraged schools to 'market' themselves to parents who were to be central in the choice of schools for their children. In an effort to provide parents with the necessary information to make these choices, the government controversially published league tables which listed schools according to their pupils' results in national tests. This gave rise to criticism that such tables were unable to capture the complexity of different school contexts and were therefore inequitable and divisive.

Despite some opposition in 1988, the majority of these policy changes were kept and extended by an incoming labour government in 1997. Additional assessment has been introduced for all 5-year-olds entering the school system and further curriculum changes have been put in place through the introduction of the literacy and numeracy hours in all primary schools. This has now been extended to the secondary sector, together with the establishment of a new curriculum subject: citizenship. Various funding initiatives have attempted to target moneys to areas of particular social and economic disadvantage and schools have been further encouraged to develop areas of particular expertise in such subjects as sport, technology and modern languages. Changes linking teacher appraisal to pupil performance, together with national, school and individual target setting all continue to put pressure on the outcome measures used to judge the quality of the education system.

Recent reform has, therefore, combined to increase central regulation over curricula and assessment while at the same time giving greater autonomy to schools with regard to budgetary matters. This has overturned a tradition of professional autonomy in matters of educational content and pedagogy and established a quasi-market which defines education as a consumer service. Support for a strong independent sector also continues to influence policy.

France

In France the emphasis is on the need for equity and a common experience, which remains central to education's fundamental purpose and is evident in official discourse:

> Every child and young person in France has a right to education and training, regardless of his/her social, cultural or geographical background . . . education's main objective is: to educate an entire age group to at least the level of the vocational aptitude certificate [CAP] or vocational studies certificate [BEP] and 80 per cent of the group to Baccalauréat level within ten years.
>
> (NFER/QCA INCA Database 1998)

Education holds a particular place in the French nation. As a basic element of the Republic, it has long been regarded as a separate institution with its own laws. Although change to the system has been continuous, it started to undergo more radical change at the end of the 1960s, and since the 1980s there have been even more important changes. These changes relate mainly to the concept of *massification*. The French system of education no longer has restricted access, but is open to all. *Collèges* and *lycées*, which were formerly open to only a minority of the population are now attended by nearly all of the 11–18 year age group. In 1962 just over half of children transferred to a *collège*, and by the late 1990s this figure had risen to nearly 100 percent. In recognition of a more diverse pupil population, the 1989 *Loi de l'orientation* began to relax the previously centralized system of control. Individual schools were required to initiate developments which would make them more responsive to the local area and its particular problems.

The administrative organization of the French education system has also changed. Since the acts of decentralization dating from 1982 (*Loi de décentralisation*). A centrally controlled national curriculum remains, along with centrally defined qualifications and control over the recruitment and remuneration of school staff. For teachers there is strong pedagogic 'framing' within the classroom and lessons are still modelled on the *cours magistraux*. However, schools now have significant autonomy in the setting up of individual school aims. Whether in the field of pedagogy or social and pastoral education, schools now have considerable room for manoeuvre and their objectives are stated and pursued through a *projet d'établissement*. As in England, extra financial help is available for schools in socially and economically disadvantaged areas and education is gaining a higher profile both among policymakers and parents. In theory, French state schools are mapped out in the *Carte Scolaire*. Each area has its assigned school or schools and parents cannot choose, although increasingly parents with the appropriate cultural and financial capital can manipulate the system. Taken together these changes have the potential to lead to an increasingly differentiated system. A growing awareness of social pluralism within French society has resulted in the recent policy changes which have begun to create the opportunity for some limited devolved power. Regionalization has involved both devolution and *déconcentration*, which has delegated powers to regional tiers of central government by making use of locally placed civil servants who may be better informed of local conditions than centrally placed bureaucrats (Lauglo 1990).

Denmark

In Denmark, there remains a dual focus on the personal development of individuals, linked to the need for cooperation and collaboration:

> As far as compulsory education is concerned, the general objective is to give the individual pupil the opportunity to develop as many of his/her talents as possible . . . The focus is on the development of personal qualifications: independence, independent thought, ability to co-operate and communicate, and a desire for learning throughout one's life span.
>
> (NFER/QCA INCA Database 1998)

Policy change within Denmark tends to be evolutionary, consensual and slow by other national standards. However, continuing calls for more equality in the 1970s did produce an overall plan (U-90 Plan) which recommended a 12-year comprehensive school for all, with a more 'socially relevant curriculum' and a more project-orientated and interdisciplinary pedagogical approach. Its ideas were not taken up at the time for fear of a lowering of standards. Later, in 1986, new principles were laid down which underpinned reforms in almost all sectors of education. These included curriculum changes which emphasized national historical and cultural perspectives together with the inclusion of values, and called for a reassessment of subjects to identify 'core fields'. The new principles relaxed central control over teaching methods and financial management, and enabled parents to make choices for their children between schools. The changes have been further strengthened by the most recent *folkeskole* act (1994) which has again stressed the role of interdisciplinary teaching and the inclusion of a more socially relevant curriculum. It has also abolished the last remnants of setting by attainment within the *folkeskole* and introduced the need for pupils to produce a final year project. Teachers have also been encouraged to ensure a differentiated approach to teaching and learning to match the particular needs of individual pupils.

In Denmark, therefore, the state continues to play a regulating and coordinating role, although recent changes have both retained local power, within a national framework, and encouraged school democracy and the importance of student rights within education.

Current schooling structures

Formal schooling within all three countries is divided into various levels or phases. In England and France, in common with the majority of schooling systems within Europe, a primary stage for pupils between the ages of 5 or 6 and 11 years of age is followed by a secondary phase at a different institution for a further four or five years. Within the Danish *folkeskole*, however, pupils begin at the age of 7 and continue within the same institution until they are 16 or 17 years of age. This has implications for both the role of teachers and the organization of learning. The focus of the ENCOMPASS study was on pupils aged 14 years and it is their phase of schooling which has been explained in more detail in the following section. However, for the purposes of clarity the whole of the required period of formal schooling has been illustrated in Figure 3.1.

All three systems have some provision for children before they enter formal schooling though this varies in length and availability. Most preschool children in France attend an *école maternelle*. The majority of Danish children attend a *kindergarten* and a preschool class before entering grade 1. The provision for preschool children in England is less widespread, although most will attend a reception class within primary schools from the age of 4 years.

All three national systems also include a small independent sector of schools which cater for between 7 and 17 percent of the school population. Although their structure and influence was beyond the scope of the ENCOMPASS project it is important to note that while the independent

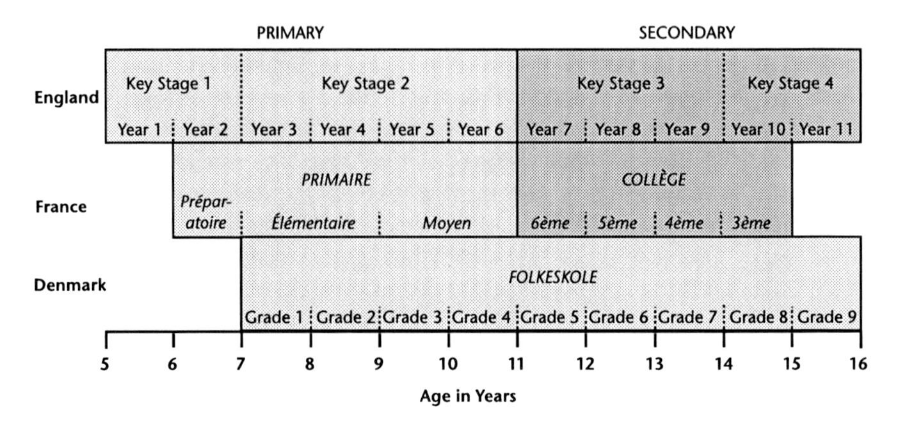

Figure 3.1 School systems in England, France and Denmark

schools in France and Denmark [*friskoler*] are funded almost entirely out of government funds, those in England are selective, élitest and able to charge high fees. All, however, have some degree of government influence with regard to their facilities and operation.

England

Formal schooling in England is split into two main levels: primary schools for pupils between the ages of 5 and 11 years, and secondary comprehensive schools for pupils between the ages of 12 and 16 years. Some state comprehensive schools also provide an additional two years of education (years 12 and 13) offering further advanced level study. The majority of schools are nonselective and comprehensive in nature, taking pupils of all abilities and offering them a 'broad and balanced curriculum'. Although pupil age has traditionally been an important criterion for pupil organization, it was only with the 1988 Education Reform Act that the terms 'year 1' to 'year 13' were established to emphasize the continuous and progressive nature of schooling. At the same time, the concept of 'levels of achievement' was formalized into four 'key stages' corresponding to the points at which pupils were subject to external, national assessment. Though comprehensive by name, many secondary schools group pupils by attainment for individual subjects and this is referred to as 'setting'. Within the primary sector pupils are taught by generalist class teachers who cover the majority of their curriculum needs. At secondary level their teachers are subject specialists who often combine this with the role of 'group tutor', looking after the social and emotional needs of particular group of pupils. More recently other types of secondary schools have been established, such as city technology colleges and city academies, which have been created in partnership with local business funding. These schools are nonselective and do not charge fees.

Evaluation of the pupils at the end of their statutory schooling is by external examination in each of their curriculum subjects: the General Certificate of Secondary Education (GCSE). Pupils sit written exams in up to twelve different subjects and final grades are awarded on the exam mark, plus differing proportions of coursework marked by their teachers and externally moderated. These examinations provide an important watershed for pupils because the marks they receive may be used to gain employment or move on to an upper-secondary level of study. If they plan to continue into higher education the marks they receive at GCSE level will also be used to predict their Advanced level examination grades at the age of 18. More recently, Records of Achievement have also been introduced for pupils to record their progress through school in a more inclusive way, including additional personal, social and physical achievements.

Both primary and secondary schools are monitored and evaluated by external teams of inspectors accredited by the Office of Standards in Education (Ofsted). Full inspections take place every four years and, following an inspection, schools are expected to produce a development plan to show how they will improve those areas which may have been found to be less than adequate.

France

The French formal schooling system is secular and divided into three levels: primary (*école élémentaire*) (6–11 years), lower secondary (*collège*) (11–15 years) and upper-secondary (*lycée*). The four years of French lower-secondary education are further sub-divided into cycles: the *cycle d'adaptation* (*sixième*), which since 1996 can take two years, the *cycle central* (*cinquième and quatrième*) and the *cycle d'orientation* (*troisième*). The first year at *collège* is aimed at introducing pupils to *collège* learning and the last cycle prepares them for the next stage of their education. *Collège* education is both a continuation of primary education, offering *savoirs de base* and *savoir faire de base* (basic knowledge and skills), as well as a preparation for upper-secondary level of schooling (*lycée*), thus giving access to a common culture (*une culture général*). In accordance with the principle that elementary and lower-secondary education should be comprehensive, offering equality of educational opportunity for all, grouping pupils by ability is, in principle, forbidden by law. The general aim is that all pupils should receive schooling as close as possible to the 'norm'. However, to adapt to the rates of learning of each child, the amount of time spent in each cycle can be extended (*redoublement*) or reduced by one year. It is, therefore, possible to have a difference of up to two years in the ages of the pupils in any one class. Generally speaking, such decisions are made by teachers in conjunction with parents. Teachers are subject specialists who have no formal responsibility for the pastoral care of their pupils.

On completion of lower-secondary education, all *collège* pupils sit a leaving examination (*diplôme national du brevet*) which was introduced in 1987. A pupil's overall mark in the exam takes into consideration their results in the written examination, as well as marks received for work completed over the last two years of *collège*. Unlike the GCSE in England, continuation of a pupil's schooling in the *lycée* is not dependent on their results in the *brevet*. Neither do the results achieved affect a pupil's option choices after the final year of *collège* (*troisième*). It also does not grant access to employment because, if pupils have not needed to repeat a year, they still have one further year of compulsory education to complete. It simply confirms that they have satisfactorily completed lower-secondary education. Under reforms proposed during 1999 it is intended that in future interdisciplinary projects will be introduced from the *quatrième* and that marks received for such projects will count towards the *brevet*.

On completion of their course of study at the *collège*, pupils must continue to attend school until they are 16 years of age. They generally do this by moving on to one of the three main types of *lycée*. This is the last compulsory school stage, taking pupils aged between 15 and 18 years. The main function of the *lycée* is to award the *baccalauréat*, which is a requirement for entry into higher education.

The directorate of assessment and planning (*Direction de l'Evaluation et de la Prospective, DEP*) of the national ministry of education was set up in 1987 to carry out all aspects of the evaluation of the French education system. The monitoring of schools is done through the inspection of individual teacher's work, which can by English standards be infrequent. Since 1989 compulsory mass diagnostic testing has also taken place in alternate years for pupils aged 8, 11 and 15/16 years to assist teachers in gauging pupil progress. End of year testing of selective samples of pupils during compulsory education is used in national and international surveys, and periodic mass diagnostic national testing is also organized every four or five years to measure the attainment levels of a representative sample of 15-year-olds.

Denmark

Primary and lower-secondary education in Denmark are contained within one system: the *folkeskole*. This provides nine years of compulsory comprehensive education, together with a voluntary preschool class and optional tenth year. The municipal *folkeskole* provides free, basic education to children between the ages of 6 and 17, although there can be some variation with some schools only taking pupils until they are 14 years. Pupils are divided into year groups by age and, as in England, progression from one year to the next is automatic. Groups of between fifteen and twenty children are divided into separate groups or classes (*klasser*) which each have a class teacher (*klasselærer*) who may be responsible for the same group of pupils for the whole of their primary and lower-secondary schooling. As well as having a responsibility to teach them several of their academic subjects, the class teacher has a clear pastoral responsibility, which includes creating a group unity within the class and liaising closely and regularly with the parents of their pupils. During the last three decades, parents and pupils have become increasingly involved in the management of the school through school boards and school councils.

In the same way that there is a requirement in English schools to conduct an act of daily worship which should be Christian in nature, there is a requirement in Danish schools to include religious education in the curriculum, although there is no requirement for an act of worship. Parents may withdraw their children from such lessons if they agree to personally assume the responsibility for the child's religious instruction.

Assessment is continuous and formative, although teachers are encouraged not to give pupils individual marks for their work until they reach grade 8 (14 or 15 years). Above this age, 'proficiency marks' must be given to pupils at least twice a year and discussed at the pupil–parent–teacher meetings. The final set of proficiency marks is given immediately before the national written examinations which may be taken by pupils prior to leaving the *folkeskole*. On completion of grade 9, pupils can present themselves for the *folkeskole* leaving certificate in Danish, mathematics, English, German and physics/chemistry. Those who complete an optional tenth year at the *folkeskole* can present themselves for examination in each of the above subjects for either the leaving certificate or the advanced leaving certificate. An obligatory project assignment has now been added for pupils in grades 9 and 10 for which assessment is given in the form of a written statement, as well as a final mark, if the pupil asks for it. The school issues a leaving certificate for pupils which contains information on their educational activities, their most recent proficiency marks and the results of any national examinations taken. The leaving certificate may also include a written statement and/or mark for the final project assignment if the pupil wishes.

Progress to the next level of education is by mutual agreement between pupils, parents and teachers and can be either academically orientated (*gymnasium*) where pupils are prepared for the national *studentereksamen*, or vocationally orientated. These programmes usually last approximately three years but they can vary from between two and four years. Having completed their upper-secondary, or youth education, pupils can either enter the workforce directly or continue into higher education.

There is no national school or teacher inspection service in Denmark, but schools are encouraged and supported in their own self-assessment by their local controlling municipality.

Summary

An investigation of the documentary evidence has highlighted not only many commonalities between the three schooling systems of England, France and Denmark but also some of their significant differences. In summary then, all three schooling systems have their origins in the nineteenth century. Through the twentieth century they have sought to progressively enlarge and extend the scope of such provision to ensure free state education for all children between the ages of approximately 5 and 16 years.

Ideologically the structure and operation of the three systems continues to be moulded by powerful historical and cultural antecendents. The system in England emphasizes morality, individualism, differentiation and early specialization, supported by regular external testing. In France the educational tradition is encyclopaedic and characterized by such values as universality, rationalism and equity. In Denmark by contrast, there is a strong tradition of communitarianism which places an emphasis on local democracy and social partnership, and the practical application of learning.

Finally, these differences are reflected in the organization of formal schooling, the provision of preschool places, the influence of the independent sector, approaches to pupil assessment and certification, and the inspection and external evaluation of the schooling outcomes. These differences have been illustrated in Table 3.1.

The next chapter moves from the national to the local level and uses

Table 3.1 Historical and structural differences in the three national schooling systems

Ideological basis	*ENGLAND (Liberal individualism)*	*FRANCE (Universalism)*	*DENMARK (Communitarianism)*
Provision of free, compulsory education	1870	1881–83	1814
Provision of a unified primary and secondary system	1944	1975	1903
Preschool provision	Minority	Majority	Majority
Independent sector	High fees	Low fees	Low fees
15–16+ certification	GCSE	*brevet*	Leaving certificate
Type of inspection	Ofsted	Diagnostic sampling	Self-evaluation

school documentation, interview and observation data to analyse the concept of the 'school' and its organization, as it is applied in the three national contexts.

4 School organization

Introduction

Having looked at the historical and cultural origins of the three schooling systems, this chapter begins to look at the meaning of the word 'school' in the three different national contexts. It will identify the differences and similarities within the ten study schools in order to analyse the context in which the target pupils' experience of schooling was set. The chapter draws upon data from headteacher, teacher and pupil interviews, as well as researcher observation and an analysis of school documentation. The chapter begins by making use of 'outsider' perspectives to illuminate the 'taken for granted', and then looks at the significance of individual schools as separate units and discusses the interplay of various partners with regard to power and responsibility. Finally, the differing approaches to the organization of the academic and affective components of teaching and learning are discussed with reference to the organization of pupils into class groupings.

The 'outsider' perspective

From the beginning of the project researchers in England worked closely with team members who were nationals from both France and Denmark to pose questions, design research instruments and analyse emerging data. This enabled the team to gain both 'insider' and 'outsider' insights into each national system as members of the extended team were asked to write about, and comment on, the schools and classrooms involved in the study, from a country which was not their own. The following three extracts illustrate those differences which, though very familiar to nationals, take on more significance when viewed from different national and cultural perspectives. These extracts also serve to highlight the underlying educational values which are a product of differing national contexts.

First a Danish researcher gives her impression of the French *collèges:*

> What first strikes a Danish visitor to a French school is its clinical and strictly functional environment, which seems to have little connection with young people's lives and their learning. Internally there is an impression of space with wide, bare corridors which are kept clinically clean. There is no evidence of learning outside the classroom. Nor is there any evidence of pictorial decoration or space for pupils to hang coats and leave personal effects. Classrooms, which are kept locked, are also strictly functional.
>
> The outside area provided for pupils during recreation, which includes a covered section for inclement weather, is very limited in size. Pupils are sometimes reduced to standing or sitting in groups as there is insufficient space for physical games. Pupils are not allowed access to the interior of the school during recreation. They are also not allowed access into the staff room. Before lessons pupils line up in class groups, either in the recreation area or outside the relevant classroom, and await their subject teacher.
>
> Lacking a home base French pupils appear not to belong anywhere. There is much movement in between lessons from one similar classroom to another. Pupils are obliged to carry their school bags and outdoor wear with them during the school day. Pupils do not have the opportunity to create their own physical space where they can express and stamp their individuality.

The significant issues to note here are the description of the physical environment, the perceived separation of learning from the pupils' social lives, the paucity of external facilities and the lack of a 'home base' for pupils in which to express their personalities.

Next, a French researcher comments on his impressions of the English comprehensive schools:

> A French visitor to an English secondary school is immediately struck by two impressions, both of which relate to the English school context.
>
> On entering a school the visitor comes upon an entrance hall of varying proportions and modernity, which serves to express the school's individual identity. The history of the school, the portraits of its senior members of staff and the school's main claims to fame are presented at a glance. English school entrance halls are like miniature museums in the way in which they summarise the past and outline the school's individuality. English schools display their identity, show that they have a past, give evidence of their existence as a social

> organisation and thus stake their claim to an individual reality. The individuality of the school is further enhanced by not only the display of the names of former headteachers but also often those of former headboys and headgirls. These displays emphasise the importance of 'belonging' to a school.
>
> The second impression given by English schools to the French visitor is the feeling of space. English school buildings may be dilapidated and not adapted to pupil needs but the school grounds are always impressively vast with good sports equipment and extensive playing fields. This feeling of space is important as it gives firstly the impression that schools are places designated as much for living as for learning. Secondly it gives the illusion that schools are not enclosed places bounded by four walls, but that they are places open to their surroundings. This impression is particularly strong in rural schools where the school's boundaries are not always immediately apparent to the visitor's eye.

Again the significant points to notice here are the establishment of a school identity and the importance of 'belonging'. This is closely related to the provision of sports equipment and playing fields which serve, for the French researcher, to extend the schools' boundaries into the local community and blur the division between the two.

Finally, an English researcher discusses her impressions of the Danish *folkeskoler:*

> When visiting a Danish *folkeskole,* the English visitor is reminded more of a large English primary school than a secondary comprehensive school. The average size, in terms of pupils is about half that of a typical comprehensive school in England. Pupils often live within easy walking or cycling distance and so there is less need for them to arrive by public transport or private car. School buildings are relatively compact, with only one or two storeys. Located close by there are usually supervised after school facilities for the younger children to use when they finish school at about midday.
>
> Close to the main entrance there is usually a suite of administrative offices which are well staffed, well equipped and easily accessible for pupils, parents and teachers. Teachers' staff rooms, communal areas, corridors, and outside facilities for pupils all contribute to the high standard of the physical environment. Schools in urban areas have conditions which are less spacious and well equipped but these also give the impression of being comfortable and well cared for.
>
> It is perhaps within the classroom that there is the greatest noticeable difference for the English visitor. Each class group has their

> own teaching room in which pupils have collaborated with their class teacher to create a comfortable, individual learning environment. Classrooms, which in England would need to accommodate around thirty pupils, would be used by classes of often less than twenty pupils. This gives the feeling of relative space and allows for a more relaxed approach to teaching and learning. As pupils stay in their own classroom for the majority of their lessons there is none of the noise and confusion associated with the changeover of lessons in large comprehensive schools in England. Pupils also take turns to tidy and sweep their classrooms at the end of the school day.

Here there is an emphasis on size, stability, the relatively high standard of the physical environment and the creation of a personalized space for individual groups of pupils.

These three extracts highlight, from a largely social and anthropological perspective, important elements of schooling within the three countries and help to provide a context against which the following data analysis can be referenced. The strong identity of the English schools and their influence beyond the school boundaries; the functional nature of French schools and their separation of the academic from the affective; and the role of the class teacher and the emphasis on a social space and group cohesion within Danish schools, will all be investigated further in later sections of this chapter.

The school as a unit

There were considerable differences in the three countries in the extent to which lower-secondary schools promoted an individual identity. At one end of the scale, the schools in England displayed strong identities as individual units. At the other end of the scale were the French *collèges*, which prioritized the class as a unit of identity rather than the school itself. In between were the Danish *folkeskoler*, which were in the process of developing individual identities, although the class was still the main unit of organization.

The English schools stood out from the other two systems because of the importance which was given to their individual identity. Local Management of Schools (see Chapter 3) had empowered schools by taking away responsibility for the financing of school budgets from the local authorities and giving it directly to each school. The quasi-market system under which the English schools operated had led to an economic need for schools to market their individual identities and reputation in order to attract clients (pupils). School reputation was the key to marketing success in the English study schools and considerable effort was put into the creation and marketing of a school's image, 'The need to maintain the reputation of the school . . . in terms of ensuring that the image of the school is all that one would want it to be' (headteacher, Lady Margaret School). The English schools also marketed their reputations in terms of a collective identity and a caring, happy ethos in the school prospectus, '[We have] a sense of collective purpose . . . a very strong sense of the collective' (school prospectus, St Theresa's), and in headteacher discourse, '[We are] very much a cooperative, integrated, caring community, which shows a great deal of affection for its members and compassion as well' (headteacher, St Theresa's), and again, '[We are] a happy and safe environment, children enjoying school . . . I think that the whole ethos of the school, in terms of having a place to which the children want to come, having a place where the children enjoy their school life, that message gets through' (headteacher, Lady Margaret School).

The reputation of the English schools was also strongly linked to the identity the school could present as academically successful. Thus the local and national press statistics for academic achievements of pupils in national assessments could affect the reputation and identity of the school, 'There are good lead line figures and that obviously helps the school's reputation no end' (headteacher, Lady Margaret School). School uniform was another means by which school reputation and identity were fostered. Not only was the uniform itself important but also how it was worn, 'The pupils wear a very identifiable uniform and they wear it well. The school has worked hard to make sure that children dress appropriately, and that means that when children are queuing up at the bus stop . . . [our] pupils look more presentable than do those from other schools' (headteacher, Lady Margaret School). School identity and reputation were also cultivated in whole school assemblies, which took place at least once a week, and were celebrations of individual pupil achievement. These had a clear collective function for staff, 'that gives a strong sense of togetherness and actually makes staff . . . you know, we are buoyed up by it' (headteacher, Westway). Such occasions were also a means of communicating the school ethos to pupils, 'People are clear about what we are about as a school, the kids are, because they hear the message so often, it permeates a lot of what we do' (headteacher, Westway).

In addition, since schools in England had responsibility for teacher appointments and the selection process is determined by interview, the criterion of the candidate's suitability for a particular school ethos could be addressed. The headteacher at Westway explained that the teacher selection process at his school was often finally decided in response to the question, 'Would the candidate fit in? Could the applicant become an Westway person?' As comprehensive schools, the English schools were unable to select pupils. However, as the headteacher at St Theresa's commented, the first year pupils could be 'trained' into the school ethos. Competitive sports between schools, school drama and music productions encouraged collective identity both within the school and within the wider community. Ironically, in trying to establish an individual school identity in a competitive market the English schools tended to present similar images, as they were all promulgating common English educational values of care, understanding, happiness, enjoyment of learning, discipline, academic excellence, smart uniform and the importance of the arts.

Although local community power was strong in Danish education, individual school identity was not strong. Both in Denmark and France the underlying aim of egalitarianism, that is, of providing the same education for all regardless of differences between socio-economic status, ethnicity and achievement, mitigated against the promotion of individual school identities. Danish and French schools needed to present an image of uniformity in order to ensure pupils' equal entitlement to education. However, in Denmark there was some tension between the traditional image of consensus and homogeneity, and a movement towards a more consumer orientated philosophy of education which encouraged an individual school identity. In what ways could the *folkeskole* be described as having individual identities? Regulations regarding school catchment areas had been relaxed so that parents could choose schools outside their area, and school 'reputation' had some conceptual significance. It was important to headteachers.

The headteacher at the Province school described the school's reputation as 'being efficient' and some headteachers were starting to use the media to further their school's reputation. School reputation, unlike in England, was not related to high marks and examination results but to school atmosphere, the quality of school life for pupils, the quality of the relationship between teachers and pupils and the quality of learning, 'What matters is how you feel in the school and how the teachers are. Are they good and do you learn something and how well do you feel in school' (pupil, Denmark). Individual school identity was also developing as a result of a new requirement for schools to draw up individual school plans based on locally perceived social and pedagogical goals. Furthermore, in each of the four Danish study schools there were events and activities where each school could draw attention to its collective identity. For example, whole school excursions, sports events and annual festivals such as carnival and the Lucia procession, as well as a school newspaper. However, the architecture of Danish schools was not generally designed to include an area where large assemblies of pupils could be held, as was the case in England. School uniform did not exist, though school shirts and headgear were worn for external sporting events.

In general, the French *collèges* were not preoccupied with establishing and managing an identity or reputation. Reputation was related, in the main, to the factual socio-economic status of school intake and area, 'The area has a role to play, you must realize that everyone knows that the intake is mostly middle class' (headteacher, Cathédrale). The headteacher at Montand *collège* perceived its poor reputation to be a consequence of the local area, 'It's due to the set up of the town, in that the town is almost divided into two. There's the middle class bit at the bottom, the centre is more proletariat and it's working class at the top. We are associated with the proletariat part, the bit with the bad reputation.' Related to the local area was the reputation a school had by virtue of its pupils' behaviour. Cathédrale had a good reputation because, as the headteacher put it, 'There aren't any problems', Montand had a very poor reputation because of long standing rumours, 'That there are strange goings on, that pupils fight, that scores get settled, that there's extortion and drugs. People get their opinions from these rumours' (headteacher, Montand). Although academic success, in terms of the proportion of pupils acceding to a *lycée général*, was also a factor in a school's reputation, it functioned at the level of rumour and was rarely managed.

The concept of 'school ethos' did not exist in the *collèges*, 'I think the pupils are happy and proud to be here, but it's not something we promote . . . we don't really put forward the idea of pupils identifying with Cathédrale' (headteacher, Cathédrale). However, there was evidence of a movement away from the traditional *collège* homogeneity towards the creation of an individual school identity at Montand and Berbere, schools which were situated in low socio-economic areas. Local problems had stimulated these schools to respond to government reforms which gave schools more autonomy and encouraged them to be more responsive to their local environments by putting in place a school project (*projet d'établissement*) and curriculum innovations. As in Denmark, the headteachers of these schools were starting to use the media to create a school image. The headteacher at Montand regretted the absence of an English style school ethos (*la culture de l'établissement*) which he thought would have helped to promote a school identity.

Thus the concept of 'school' as a unit with an individual identity differed in England, France and Denmark. School identity was strongest in England and weakest in France. School identity could also have been linked to the degree to which the schools were related to, and integrated within, a community. English headteachers gave an impression of strong school community links and a responsibility for pupils which extended beyond the school gates; links which were governed by time and function as well as place, 'We are responsible for our children until they arrive home . . . on their way to and from school' (headteacher, St Theresa's). Westway school had a duty team of eight to ten teachers who not only controlled school exits but covered locations in the community such as housing estates and the tube station for up to an hour after school had finished. The wearing of uniform worked both ways, English pupils had some responsibility for the school's reputation and the school took responsibility for pupils while they were wearing those uniforms for school purposes.

Relations between the relatively weak unit of the French *collège* and external agencies in the community have traditionally been of minor importance, reflecting the compartmentalization of French education as a whole, although innovations were taking place in the two *collèges* situated in low socio-economic areas. Responsibility for pupils in all three *collèges* ended abruptly just outside school gates.

Relations between schools and the local community were strong in Denmark. In terms of school responsibility for pupils, Denmark was again somewhere between England and France. As in France responsibility was officially based on the criteria of place and school hours. However, in practice responsibility extended beyond these criteria to issues of safety or unsuitable behaviour such as drunkenness, violence and vandalism, 'Of course we can't catch the person if it happens outside school, but we can try to influence them' (*klasselærer*, Denmark). This perhaps reflected the closer relationship which Danish teachers had with the parents of their pupils.

Power and responsibility between partners

There were important differences between the three countries in the degree of power and the range of responsibilities that were invested in central government, local government, the school's headteacher, its teachers, parents and the pupils themselves.

The school as a unit of control

Despite a general move towards decentralization, central government still had strong control over French schools. Responsibility for the management of schools was shared between a partnership of local authority (*département*) and school personnel. Secondary schools were no longer national institutions but 'local public educational institutions' (EPLE). Although the headteacher has responsibility for the general direction of the school, a *conseil d'administration*, which consisted of a mix of representatives from the school staff, local administrators, parents and pupils also had power within the school. However, a '*conseil*' was much more restricted than its Danish and English equivalents. It was limited to the organization of pupils into classes, the organization of teaching time and timetables within the prescribed limitations of central government, and the organization of extra curricular activities. Another of the *conseil d'administration*'s roles was to define the school project. Unlike an English board of governors or a Danish school board, there was little budget autonomy and no school autonomy over staff, whose appointments, pay and promotion remained the responsibility of central government.

In England power resided in central government and the school itself. As a result of the Educational Reform Act of 1988, the role of local government had been eroded and English schools had become more directly under the control of central government. In some areas, however, English schools had also moved towards more autonomy. Governing bodies had been introduced to be responsible to the government for the statutory requirements laid upon them, as well as having some decision-making powers in respect of staffing and budg*et al.*location. English governors' committees covered all areas of school life. For example, each school in the English sample had a committee for pastoral education, curriculum and staffing, finance, equal opportunities, special education, health and safety, accommodation, and so on. These committees were required to produce a school policy plan in each area, which was then assessed in the inspection process. Each school also had a development plan put in place by the headteacher and agreed by the governors. There was some democratic participation in school development plans in some English schools. Parents at St Theresa's were consulted by questionnaire on what they perceived were the school's weak points. However, the management structure of the English schools was less democratic and cooperative than that of the Danish schools and it differed from the French schools in that it was more complex and hierarchical. Unlike in both French and Danish schools, management terms were used in English schools. Quoting one of the English headteacher's descriptions of his school's management, but equally applicable to the other two English schools, the school was organized on the basis of 'clear line management structures' with levels of 'senior managers' and 'middle managers'.

Danish school management has traditionally been decentralized, democratic and cooperative. Local partners and pupils both had an important part to play in decision making. The municipal councils had overall responsibility for the schools in their area and worked within a general national regulatory framework. The councils provided a financial framework, opened and closed schools, appointed and dismissed staff, and approved curricula within the guidelines of central government. Danish schools were managed by school boards (*skolebestyrelse*) whose responsibilities were laid down by the municipal council within a national framework. The school boards included a majority of parent representatives as well as representatives from the teachers and pupils. The school board supervised the activities of the school within a tradition of negotiation and consensus. It had some control over the details of the curriculum and school projects which had to be approved by the municipality, as well as approving the school budget, making recommendations on staff appointments, drawing up school rules and approving teaching materials.

The role and power of the headteacher

English headteachers in the study appeared to have more power than their French or Danish colleagues. The main duties of the French headteacher included representing the school externally and presiding over the school 'board'. In addition, and depending upon how the deputy head and head had decided to allocate tasks, French headteachers could be responsible for timetabling and driving forward the school project (*projet d'établissement*). However, French headteachers had little authority over teachers:

> You sometimes have to remind them that they don't only have rights, they have responsibilities too . . . that's the head's job. You have to get them to work together on a shared plan and that's the role of the head, even if it's not easy, in the end they'll have to knuckle down, and we can apply pressure on them, the number of hours per class that we have for example. They'll have to do it, that's certain.
>
> (headteacher, Cathédrale)

Danish headteachers perceived that they had a supervisory rather than directorial role in school, putting into practice what the board and school staff had agreed upon in some schools, and in other schools what the municipal council had recommended. However, some headteachers perceived a development of the role into one of mediation between the school and the municipal authorities.

One of the main differences between headteachers in England, France and Denmark, which might have affected pupils, was the degree and type of contact between heads and pupils in the three countries. Both English and Danish headteachers had greater contact with pupils as their role involved teaching. All three English headteachers were proud of their teaching time and the contact that it gave them with pupils, 'So that I know what it's like to be teacher in the classroom at this school and I can't really manage the school unless I understand that' (headteacher, Lady Margaret School). This headteacher had the heaviest teaching load and taught for about 20 percent of the teaching week. The English headteachers were keen to portray their involvement with every aspect of school life. It was important to English headteachers that their traditional pastoral and teaching role should still be in evidence to pupils and not become totally overshadowed by their increased managerial role. All three English headteachers took part in several assemblies a week. The headteacher at St Theresa's estimated that he spent 30–40 percent of his week with pupils. The English headteachers also emphasized their visibility in the school, 'I like to be in contact and visible in a positive way' (headteacher, Westway) and their accessibility, 'The door is always open . . . I think I'm very accessible' (headteacher, St Theresa's).

Danish headteachers, too, felt that they had an important role to play with pupils through teaching and particularly with the affective dimension of education. They also emphasized their visibility and openness to all. Danish headteachers liaised with partners in the educational process and this function of 'being open to the different parties in and outside the school' was often seen as the primary one in the Danish headteacher's role. The degree of contact between the different partners varied. The headteacher of the North School attended all parents' meetings held in her school during the autumn term in order, as she put it, 'to get to know them' (parents, teachers and pupils). The headteacher of the inner city school set aside an hour a day at lunchtime for parent consultations. The headteacher of the Periphery School prioritized making herself both visible and approachable for both pupils and parents, by walking around the school talking to everyone at the start of the school day. She felt that it was important to know all the pupils' names and had regular meetings with pupils who needed help with their schoolwork and/or needed to have a 'talk'. This particular headteacher's teaching duties were restricted to supply cover. Another Danish headteacher placed more emphasis on meetings with all teachers. The headteacher of the Province school saw himself primarily as the 'head of teachers'.

French headteachers were more removed than Danish and English headteachers, both from pupils and from teaching and learning within their schools. They had no teaching duties and did not always have a teaching background. The French headteachers' contact with their pupils was very limited, 'I don't have any daily contact' (headteacher, Montand). Where there was contact it was mostly with pupils from difficult home backgrounds.

The management role of teachers

There were also differences in the way in which teachers in the three systems contributed to school management, with English and Danish teachers playing a fuller role than their French colleagues. English teacher participation depended upon the teachers' position in the hierarchical management structure of the school and whether or not they were part of the governing body. Danish teaching staff were involved in school management through their participation in the pedagogical council, the existence of which was a legal requirement and functioned to advise the headteacher. Examples of issues that were discussed included problems within the school, the coordination of teaching and learning, and planning the school year. A more extended discussion of the differing role expectations of the three sets of teachers can be found in Chapter 5.

Parent power

In contrast to parents in England and France, Danish parents too were more directly involved with the organization and management of their schools. As well as strong parental input at the level of the *skolebestyrelse*, Danish parents were in close contact with what went on in the classroom and would attend up to three parents' meetings a year to discuss the academic and social progress of their children. Class teachers sent home regular newsletters and most class groups elected parent representatives to ensure a good flow of information between the class and other parents. Parents were encouraged to involve themselves actively in their children's education. The class teacher was someone with whom they had an on-going relationship, and someone whom they could contact by telephone out of school hours. Although French parents had representation on the French school board, their role was limited due to the comparatively weak decision-making role of the school board itself. The role which French parents have in career decisions made about their offspring is however stronger in France than in England as French parents can and do appeal against teacher decisions.

The role of parents in English school management was limited to elected individual parents on the governing body. The degree of representation of such parents was questionable, 'They don't have a mechanism for feeding back and getting information from the parents at large on a week to week and month to month basis' (headteacher, Lady Margaret School). English parents could also take part in parent–teacher associations (PTA) but these functioned more as a forum for debating issues, fund raising and generally supporting the school rather than having a decision-making role in school management. Other involvement of English parents was limited to gaining information about offspring through reports and at parents' evenings.

Pupil power

As with parents, it was pupils from Denmark who had the most voice. Pupils from the Province school, for example, had played an active part in the setting up of the school's development plan. The pupils' council, the parents and the teachers, had worked out separate proposals and the three sets of ideas had then been integrated by the teachers into the final plan. The Danish pupils' council played a stronger role in decision making than its French and English equivalents, 'The board listens very carefully to them [the pupils] . . . and if they have any ideas . . . the board willingly takes up the issue, if it's something at all possible' (*klasselærer* representative on school board, Denmark). Examples of areas in which pupil councils had been effective in the Danish schools were: the development programme of the school, the setting up of a library workshop area, a homework club, the playground and the canteen. However, the Danish pupils felt that the impact of their voice was very much dependent on the support the teacher, appointed or selected for this role, gave in guiding pupils through the decision-making process.

English pupils played a weaker role in school management. A pupil 'school council' existed in each English school, made up of elected pupil representatives from each tutor group, but its role was mostly limited to one of feedback. There were other channels through which pupils could express their opinions. St Theresa's had set up a consultative group of pupils, based on a representative sample of gender and low, mid- and high levels of achievement, which met with the headteacher once a month specifically to discuss teaching and learning issues. The headteacher at Westway had put in place the use of a confidential post box (also in use in some Danish schools) for pupils to express their opinions.

French pupil representatives in both the *conseil d'administration* and the *conseil de classe* (an association of teachers which meets three times a year to discuss the progress and possible school and career path of individual pupils) had a fairly superficial role, they were heard rather than listened to. The function of French pupil representatives was more one of communication than decision making, 'They're meant to relay information between the subject teachers and the class' (*professeur principal*, France).

The strength of the relationship between educational partners in the management of lower secondary schools in the three countries is summarized in the following table:

Table 4.1 The relative influence of different school partners

	Central government	*Local government*	*School*	*Parents*	*Pupils*
England	Strong	Weak	Strong	Weak	Weak
France	Strong	Strong	Weak	Weak	Weak
Denmark	Average	Average	Strong	Strong	Strong

The relative autonomy which schools in the three countries had over finance, staffing and curriculum issues can also be represented in the following way:

Table 4.2 The relative autonomy which schools had over finance, staffing and the curriculum

	School autonomy for finance	*School autonomy for staffing*	*School autonomy for curriculum*
England	Strong	Strong	Weak
France	Weak	Weak	Weak
Denmark	Strong	Strong	Strong

Thus the main contextual differences in school management for English, French and Danish pupils was that pupils (both directly and through their parents), teachers and parents all played a stronger role in decision making within the Danish schools. It was also the case that Danish and English headteachers had more regular contact with pupils than did headteachers in France.

Differing structures for the academic and the affective

A major area of difference in school environment for English, French and Danish pupils was the way in which schools in the three countries were organized with regard to the academic and affective elements of their schooling. In this respect, school organization was related to a deeper national understanding of the concept of 'education'. All three countries share a basically similar understanding of the term which includes first a pedagogical or taught element, second an intellectual or cognitive element and third a nonintellectual and noninstructive element. However, a major problem of comparative education is equating concepts and finding mutually acceptable terminology. This is particularly true in the domain of nonintellectual, noninstructive education for which the term 'affective' education is used in England, 'the aspect of the educational process that is concerned with the feelings, beliefs, attitudes and emotions of students, with their interpersonal relationships and social skills' (Lang *et al.* 1998: 4). In England 'education' encompasses an 'academic' element (a combination of the first and second concepts) and an 'affective' element (the third concept). There is also a strong tradition in the development of the individual and the inclusion of a spiritual domain.

In the French system the following two terms are used which roughly equate to 'academic' and 'affective': *l'instruction* which is the combination of the pedagogical and intellectual concepts and *l'éducation* which refers to the noninstructive and nonintellectual concept of education. However, more weight is given to pedagogy in the French pairing of pedagogy and cognition than is the case in the English pairing, and less weight is given to the nonintellectual and noninstructive concept in French education. The Danish conceptual understanding of 'education' is very different. The term *undervisning* refers to the pedagogical and didactic aspect of education (which, in common with the French concept of education, is more encyclopaedic and knowledge-based than it is in England) while *dannelse* consists of *both* intellectual learning *and* the noninstructive and nonintellectual concept of education. Academic and affective education are generally not conceived as separate in Denmark. These conceptual differences are reflected in school organization.

In France the academic and affective needs of the pupils are dealt with by two separate groups of staff in the following way (see Figure 4.1):

'Affective' education (*la vie scolaire*)	**'Academic' education**
Conseiller principal	Subject teachers
Surveillants and/or	*Professeurs principaux*
Aide éducateurs	Librarian
Emplois jeunes	Careers adviser
Appelés du contingent	(*conseiller d'éducation*)
Stagiaires	

Figure 4.1 The organization of the academic and the affective in French schools

Thus, *la vie scolaire* was concerned with pupils' *éducation* as opposed to their *instruction*. The difference with England was that there was a very strong division between the two systems:

> A child has two lives at school. There's the world of teaching and intellectual learning (*le travail pédagogique de son instruction*), but there's also the child's general education and learning how to behave (*son éducation et son comportement*) . . . school is a micro world and in this micro world we are responsible for the lives of adolescents and future adults. Our role is to teach them how to become adults. All the staff have this responsibility some in their role as subject teachers (*en les instruisant*), some as educators (*en les éduquant*).
>
> (conseiller principal d'éducation (CPE), Cathédrale)

Two differently qualified types of staff occupied the two different roles in the French system. In England the role of the subject teacher and group tutor combined to straddle both the academic and the affective. Furthermore, each system in the French schools had a certain amount of autonomy '[*La vie scolaire*] it's a system within a system' (headteacher, Cathédrale). Leadership and administration was a third separate system within the French schools.

In the English schools the academic and the affective (or pastoral system) had a certain organizational separation, but were regarded as complementary

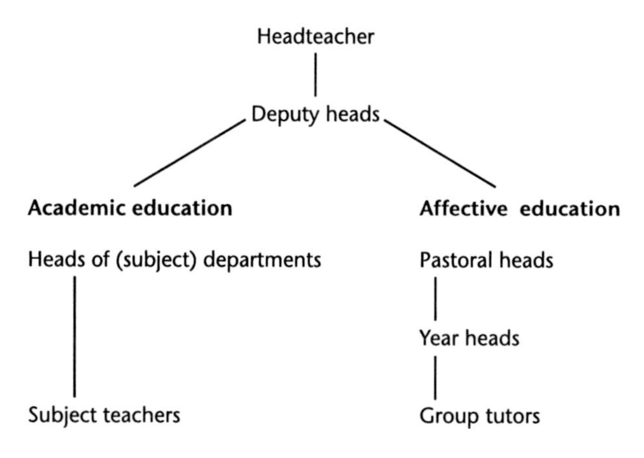

Figure 4.2 The organization of the academic and the affective in English schools

because they were both handled by teachers in their roles as subject specialists and group tutors (see Figure 4.2).

While the English pastoral system existed as a separate system with the aim of providing a support system or 'safety valve' for pupils and to 'make sure they're as happy as they can be and that they turn into decent adults' (language teacher, Westway), academic and affective education were perceived as inextricably connected. This was partly due to the fact that English teachers were legally required to include an affective element in their subject teaching by 'promoting pupils' spiritual, moral, social and cultural development through their specialism'. However, it was also because the majority of subject teachers were also group tutors. As a result, their separate but related role as group tutor was clearly related for many teachers with their subject teaching:

> It's to support pupils' learning. It functions as a sort of academic guidance system, it helps pupils with their personal self worth, it helps in situations of bereavement, where families have medical problems and helps with families that have different values. However I wouldn't separate it from my maths teaching.
>
> (head of year, Lady Margaret School)

and mutually supporting:

> I try to sort of say, you know, 'And what did you do in the holiday?' And if they went away, ask where and who with and what they got up to, or sometimes I say. 'Did you have nice weekend?' Or I ask if someone's injured, 'How did you do that?' Most of the kids I've ever spoken to, have taken it as that you're interested in them, and they like it I think. They wouldn't necessarily smile and say, 'Oh hello'. But

> I think they like it and certainly that's part of good teaching and learning, to know.
>
> (language teacher, Westway)

However, it was observed that attention to the affective was being given a lower priority in the English group tutor's role, 'We are now emphasizing the academic tutoring role . . . It's a move away from the traditional pastoral bit to a bit more focused . . . I'm the person that oversees that child's learning' (headteacher, Westway).

In Denmark, where academic and affective education are seen as an integral part of school life and the curriculum, school organization was not compartmentalized into two systems. From the level of the school board to the individual teacher, affective education in Denmark was seen as an essential part of learning. All teachers had an implicit responsibility for the affective aspects of pupils' learning as part of their subject teaching, 'It's a responsibility that we all have . . . there's nothing in print' (*klasselærer*, Denmark). In addition the majority of teachers also had the role of class teacher (*klasselærer*), responsible in a more codified way for the academic and the affective dimensions of learning for a particular group of pupils (see Figure 4.3).

Academic and Affective

Headteacher

Deputy headteacher

klasselærer

teacher

Figure 4.3 The organization of the academic and the affective in Danish schools

Thus the three models of school organization suggest that there is a continuum between the three countries in the way in which the academic and affective aspects of education are dealt with. France is at one extreme with its separation of the affective and academic into distinct systems within the school and two separate groups of staff. Denmark is at the other extreme. In Denmark the two systems were not perceived as separate but were embodied in the role of subject teachers, in particular in the role of the class teacher. England came between the two. There were two parallel systems within English school organization but the two structures co-existed in the roles of particular staff and most subject teachers incorporated some affective education into their subject teaching. This continuum is expressed in diagrammatic form in Figure 4.4.

France	England	Denmark
Intellectual | Affective	Intellectual | Affective	Intellectual
Teacher | Non-teaching staff	*Teacher*	Affective
		Teacher

Figure 4.4 An academic/affective continuum

School structures and staff roles in each country were seen to be related to national concepts about education, so that ultimately the type and quality of pupil relationships with teachers were strongly dependent on the national context. The common ground between the three countries was the realization that whatever school structures were in place there was a greater need for academic and affective education to be combined, and that there should be an increase in the sharing of information about pupils between staff, particularly in schools that were set in the more economically deprived areas with high proportions of ethnic minority pupils.

The concept of the 'class'

The last contextual element at the school level which is connected to pupil experience is the way in which pupils were organized into classes in the three countries. As pupils spend most of their time at school in class groups this area is fundamental to understanding national differences between pupils' school experience. The way in which pupils were organized into classes was, again, strongly linked to national values about the school as a unit, and how academic and affective education was organized in each country, as well as to national values about education as a whole.

It was suggested that although the school itself was the main unit of identity in England it was the class group which had this function in France and Denmark. The term 'class' had different significance in the three countries. The concept of the class was at its strongest in Denmark, as the Danish class had longitudinal as well as subject continuity. The concept of the class was also strong in France where the class had subject continuity but only for the duration of one year. The class was a structurally weak concept in England as there was neither longitudinal continuity nor for many subjects was there subject stability. The relative structural stability of the class in the three countries had important consequences for social continuity and the opportunities for pupils to engage in social networking.

In the Danish system, because pupils generally remain with the same class (*klasse*) or group of pupils for up to nine or ten years with the same class teacher (*klasselærer*), the class was relatively more important than the school. The main criterion for selection of Danish pupils into classes was age, the second criterion was residential location. Class heterogeneity was the norm and class size was small; it tended to be about 19 pupils. The ideology behind this organization of pupils was that the *klasse*, which is a concept combining a group of pupils, their class teacher and the classroom, provided pupils with *tryghed* (in other words, feeling socially comfortable and secure). An often articulated principle in Danish education is that children cannot learn unless they feel safe and secure socially. The long-term continuity of belonging to one class group, working in groups with classmates who lived in the same local area and had the same teacher, was perceived by Danes as the way to maximize learning. Danish pupils were aware of the importance of close relationships, 'if you get on with people in class then it's easier to learn ... you're not so worried about saying what you think' (girl pupil, Denmark).

The class was also an important unit of identity in French schools. The French class had subject continuity in that most subjects were studied with the same class but, unlike Denmark, only for one academic year at a time. The guiding principle for pupil organization throughout the French educational system was not pupil age but that of a standard level for each year which pupils had to reach before acceding to the next year or level. Year repetition operated for pupils with inadequate achievements in key subjects. The underlying ideology behind the organization of pupils into classes in France was that of egalitarianism through heterogeneity, 'It's absolute heterogeneity . . . we, that is everyone, are completely against homogenous classes' (headteacher, Berbere). Thus where subject options existed, as at Montand, pupil choice was limited. This was because it could create differences in level between classes, which would ultimately be unegalitarian as élitist pathways (*des parcours nobles*) and 'sink groups' would result. This would mean that more pupils would leave *collège* before *3ème*, having reached the school leaving age without completing their lower-secondary education. It was also thought important that the class should work together as a cohesive unit. French pupils were aware of class heterogeneity, 'Those that work hard and those that don't work hard are mixed up' (pupil, Berbere), 'The teachers deliberately don't separate the boffins from the thickies, they get put in the same class, then they can go on being together' (girl pupil, Montand). Middle class parental pressure at Cathédrale swept aside the traditional discourse and strategies of French egalitarianism, 'Here, if we've understood the system right, you get to Cathédrale and you choose German as your first language, then you're sure of being in a top class. If you do Latin as well as German, then that's really it' (boy pupil, Cathédrale). The headteacher at Cathédrale was opposed to what he called, 'flagrant injustice', as 'the choice of German as first language is strongly linked to parental social class'.

The notion of the class was at its weakest in England. Classes were formed first on the basis of pupil age for the relevant year. Second, they were selected on the basis of performance level. In the three English study schools the pupils were organized into 'sets', 'streams' and/or 'bands' for certain subjects, such as mathematics, foreign languages and sciences. The most extreme example of this was at Lady Margaret School. The school was divided into an upper and lower band with seven sets for all subjects except technology, physical education and a second foreign language, where pupils were taught in tutor groupings. The composition of the classes or sets was reviewed each term, but was decided initially on information from pupil performance in national assessments, primary teachers' subjective and objective assessments, cognitive assessment tasks and internal school tests. The consequence for pupils in all three schools was that the school day was socially fragmented as the composition of each class could vary according to subject and level of attainment. Pupils moved from the large social group of one class to another.

Behind the criterion of achievement level in the allocation of pupils into English classes was the discourse about meeting pupils' individual needs, 'It's about meeting the kids' needs and it's also about a different approach and style to learning' (headteacher, Westway). There was variation in the use of subject setting in the English schools. It was at its strongest at Lady Margaret School and weakest at Westway where the English department had refused to set pupils in the belief that homogeneity reduced learning for lower achieving pupils. Class homogeneity also had implications for pedagogy. Some teachers felt compelled to adapt their teaching style to the level of the set, 'I'm just much more formal, much more precise as to what they have to do. I would be far less ambitious with discussing things with the class . . . of middle to lower sets' (teacher of history, Lady Margaret School). Some teachers thought that the social class status of pupils was undermining the English criterion of performance level:

> It's [setting] a process of social selection, that's what's going on. The less motivated go down to learn less, that's what it comes to, and the more motivated go up into classes where there will be less disruption. I'm not meaning to be cynical but effectively that's what's going on. It's not done by ability, we call it by ability, but it's not by ability.
>
> (language teacher, Lady Margaret School)

> Your middle class children in this school are in the top sets and your working class children are in lower sets . . . I can go into a Year 10 or 11 class, and I can teach a top set, and it's like teaching in a different school. It's like a different plant to teaching a bottom set. Top sets, they're all there, and saying, Oh yes, so-and-so-and-haw-hee-haw-hee, *and* OK can we do some more homework?. . . . And you know,

> bottom set, it's sort of, Why do we 'ave to do this. My dad said it doesn't matter', you know.
>
> (geography teacher, Lady Margaret School)

Teachers at Lady Margaret School were also critical that pupil movement between sets and bands was not as fluid as it should have been, 'Children get trapped one side or other of the band decision'.

Setting, and its associations with inequality, was also a topic which featured strongly in English pupil interviews. Pupils in top and bottom sets were the ones who were the most pressurized by the system. Pupils in top sets were concerned about slipping down, and pupils in the bottom sets were dissatisfied with their position at the bottom. Inevitably, it was pupils in top sets who appeared the most satisfied with the system:

> It's a lot easier to work in sets. It's like you might get something wrong, but your neighbour won't. Your neighbour might get something else wrong, which you wouldn't, so you can share ideas. But if you're like in a mixed ability group, it's all one way, sort of thing. So if your neighbour's always got something wrong, then you always have to correct it.
>
> (high achieving boy, Lady Margaret School)

The organization of pupils into homogenous classes for different subjects and in different years also varied in complexity and openness in each English school. Pupil confusion about setting reflected the school's degree of openness about setting. At St Theresa's and Westway where homogeneity was more covert, pupils were unclear about which classes were set, 'I'm happy with my tutor group [in fact a homogenous class] because it's meant to be the top one. I think it's because we might have got the results from the SATs in Year 6' (boy pupil, St Theresa's). There was confusion about the criteria used in selection, whether it was ability, 'I think maths, they changed the groups because of the ability of people' (girl pupil, St Theresa's), or performance, 'It's like how well you do, how well you know French and everything, and then they judge. They put you into like, you've got four, I think it's four or five different groups, like the first one's for the lower people, then it goes up higher' (girl pupil, Westway). Or, indeed, whether any criteria were used at all, 'People say it's if you're brainy, or if you're not so brainy, and all that lot. But then some other people just say it's because they put you in a different group. They had too much in that group and you had to go in this group' (girl pupil, St Theresa's). Some pupils at St Theresa's and Westway were also unsure about their position in the setting hierarchy, 'I think for maths, I think I'm in third group, or second, I'm not sure' (boy pupil, Westway). Pupil understanding of setting was much clearer in the more overt setting environment of Lady Margaret School. Pupils in the top sets in particular had a clear understanding of the system, 'If you're intelligent you're in J, K, L, M, and if you're not so like, N, O, P, and then, if you're really not intelligent, then you're in S, T' (girl pupil, Lady Margaret School), 'J is the top and then it goes down depending on how bright you are' (boy pupil, Lady Margaret School). They were also more aware of the criteria used, 'I think at the beginning of Year 7 they look at what you've done in your school before and your SATs results . . . If you're in J, you start off from in Set 1 and then depending on the tests through the year you can get put down or up' (boy pupil, Lady Margaret School).

Despite some intra-country differences, the existence and type of selection used in the organization of pupils into classes in the three countries is summarized in Table 4.3.

Table 4.3 Pupil organization by academic performance in England, France and Denmark

	Overt selection by achievement	*Covert selection by achievement*
England	Yes	Yes
France	No	Yes
Denmark	No	No

Summary

It can be seen, therefore, that the study has identified important differences at the level of the school between the three countries. School identity was important in England but less so in Denmark and France. Democratic cooperation between different partners was fundamental to Danish school decision making but of less importance in England and France. The integration of the academic and affective domain was also fundamental to Danish education. It was important in England too but to a lesser extent, whereas in France the tradition was that the academic domain was separate and dominant. The principles by which pupils were organized into teaching groups were seen to reflect national values about the enhancement of learning. Selection by achievement was important in England. Selection existed in France although it was ideologically incorrect. In the Danish *folkeskole* selection, in so far as it existed, was based on chronological age and social factors.

These various national differences with regard to the importance of school identity, the extent of democratic cooperation with partners within the community, the integration of the academic and affective elements of teaching and learning, and the basis for organizing pupils into their class groups is summarized in the following way in Table 4.4.

Table 4.4 School level characteristics

	School identity	*Democratic cooperation between different partners*	*Integration of affective and academic education*	*Pupil organization by achievement*
England	Strong	Average	Average	Strong
France	Weak	Weak	Weak	Average
Denmark	Average	Strong	Strong	Weak

Thus the context of education at the school level provided many contextual dissimilarities for pupils in England, France and Denmark. Terms such as: 'education', 'school', 'headteacher', 'teacher', 'tutor', 'class' and 'pupil', whose meanings are often assumed within a given national context and which in general discourse are also often assumed to have cross national comparability, have been shown to vary in significance from one national context to another. The next chapter will now look in more detail at what is meant by a 'class teacher' in the three national contexts and how this influences teacher values and classroom practice.

5 Teacher perspectives

Introduction

Previous chapters have outlined how differing historical and cultural perspectives within the three countries have influenced the present day policy, structure and operation of the education systems at both a national and school level. This chapter looks more closely at the values and concerns of the teachers who, as the ultimate implementers of education policy (Croll 1996), have a major influence on pupil experience and classroom practice. Interview data from a selection of teachers closely involved with the study have been used to investigate teachers' working conditions, teaching priorities and issues of pedagogic practice. These are then related to their national context to try and tease out commonalities and differences in approach and to seek to understand the impact of global pressures. To what extent can we see evidence of commonalities across national boundaries, with common pressures creating a more similar teaching and learning environment for teachers and pupils? To what extent are the priorities and pedagogies of the teachers concerned being influenced by current policy initiatives?

The chapter begins with a brief outline of the various routes to teacher qualification currently operating within the three systems. From the general interview data, a composite 'model' is then constructed for each national context. This helps to provide a context for an analysis of teachers' aims and priorities, their attitudes to the academic and affective elements of teaching and learning, their pedagogic practice and their approach to the extent of their responsibilities. Finally, the findings of the study are summarized, giving an overview of the tensions which were present in teachers' work and the impact that this had for their current practice.

Initial teacher education

The initial professional training of the three groups of teachers displayed many similarities in both length, structure, content and level of training. All involved three main areas of study: theoretical perspectives on teaching and learning, one or more subject specialisms and a school-based teaching practice element.

Within the English system there are two major routes into secondary school teaching: the concurrent, four year undergraduate course which gives both a first degree and Qualified Teacher Status (QTS) (Bachelor of Education), and a one year postgraduate course (Post Graduate Certificate of Education (PGCE)), which consists almost entirely of professional preparation. Since the mid-1970s university departments have taken responsibility for teacher education, and students at the secondary level have been required to specialize in one main subject area. Entry to the undergraduate route is normally at 18 years, after students have completed their Advanced level examinations at school, whereas entry to the postgraduate route is normally after the student has successfully completed an initial Bachelor degree. All candidates must show evidence of an acceptable level of attainment in English, mathematics and science, and all candidates must be interviewed before they can be accepted onto a recognized course. This reflects the view that the profession relies not only on academic abilities but on a combination of academic and personal qualities which allow prospective teachers to develop appropriate relationships with their pupils in order to facilitate learning. Since the mid-1990s there has been an increased amount of school-based, teaching practice and extra efforts to widen participation through the introduction of some entirely school-based courses for older students. With the establishment of the Teacher Training Agency in 1995, a national curriculum for teaching training, together with a checklist of exit competencies for newly qualified teachers has also been introduced.

In contrast, the training backgrounds of French *collège* teachers is not uniform due to a major reform of teacher training at the beginning of the 1990s. Currently teachers come from three main sources. Teachers trained prior to 1990 come from the *Ecoles Normales*. They specialize in one subject and their qualifications include a degree (*licence*), optional Masters degree (*maîtrise*) and a teacher training qualification (*Certficate d'Aptitude à la Profession d'Enseignant*). The latter was a two-year course, which consisted of a first year of theory with a competitive examination at the end, and a second, practical year where the trainee teacher received instruction and support from the '*centre pédagogiques régionaux*'. A smaller number of teachers within the *collège* system have a two-year university qualification (*Diplôme d'Études Universitaires Générales*) followed by training for two years at the *Écoles Normales Primaire*.

They have been up-graded to *collège* level teaching to cope with staff shortages. These teachers have two main teaching subjects. However, since 1991 many teachers have been trained in *Instituts Universitaires de Formations des Maîtres*. These were established to gain parity between primary and secondary teachers and create an all-degree profession, similar to changes in the English system during the 1970s. A fourth type of teacher found within the French *collège* system is the *professeur agrégé* whose extra subject expertise entitles them to fewer teaching hours and higher pay.

In Denmark teachers for the *folkeskole* system are educated in independent colleges of teacher education (*lærerseminarium*) which are separate from the university system, although they confer a qualification which is equivalent in scope and level to a Bachelor degree in England. There is a national curriculum for teacher training but individual colleges may focus on particular areas of strength. Courses last for four years and include a total of 24 weeks of school-based teaching practice. Until recently student teachers went into schools in small groups to work together under the supervision of a qualified teacher. They were not expected, as they would be in England, to take full responsibility for a class of children before they were fully qualified. As well as a common core of subjects providing students with a broad professional competence, students must also study a total of four other school curriculum subjects, either Danish or mathematics plus three others chosen from a spread of disciplines. In theory a teacher's certificate qualifies the graduate teacher to teach all subjects to all grades in the *folkeskole* (grades 1 to 10) and to become a *klasselærer*. In fact the teacher is generally considered competent to teach only those subjects which they have specialized in, especially with regard to the older pupils. In practice the authorities responsible for the appointment of teachers will take the final decision about competence: the municipal school councils, the school board and the headteacher. Twenty-five percent of study places are awarded on the basis on the school leaving examination (*studentereksamen*) alone, whereas the remaining 75 percent are awarded on a combination of factors including the result of the *studentereksamen*, practical work experience, folk high school attendance, travel abroad and experience of working with children.

Differing constructs of the 'class teacher'

Teachers within all ten study schools were interviewed as a representative sample of their national colleagues. Although teachers in all three countries had similar roles and responsibilities with regard to their teaching, there also emerged three distinct, national models which differed in important respects in line with the differing organization of state-funded schooling. These models can serve as useful templates against which to discuss the more complex findings illustrated by the discourse of individual teachers. The three case studies below illustrate some common themes which were context specific to the national situations in which the teachers found themselves:

The French model: The 'autonomous subject specialist'

Monsieur Leprof: *'It is important that the pupils* know *something . . . his or her socialisation is not my priority,* all *that matters is my subject.'*

Monsieur Leprof teaches in a French *collège* for 11–15-year-olds, although some of the pupils in his classes are in fact one or two years older than the rest of the class. He is very clear about his teaching contract and appreciates that he can increase his earnings by carrying out extra duties to his 18 hours of contact time. He hopes with length of service that he will be able to group his teaching hours together and get an afternoon or two away from school.

Monsieur Leprof enjoys his subject and likes the autonomy of his own classroom. He considers that his main priority is the academic progress of his pupils and is clear about where his role ends, and that the social and personal aspects of pupils' learning are the concern of his non-teaching colleagues. He appreciates the support he gets from these staff.

He considers that it is important for all pupils to receive the same knowledge and experience and is against selection, despite some difficulties in teaching heterogeneous groups. His own specific objective is to get as many of his pupils to the correct academic level for the following year, however, he knows that some of his colleagues have wider objectives.

French teachers in the sample demonstrated a more restricted perception of their role in line with their civil service status. Typically they maintained a certain professional distance from the parents of their pupils. Their focus was their subject teaching and their aims concentrated around encouraging pupils to be inspired by their subject and ensuring that they got as many pupils as possible to the correct level for the following year. They were generally clear about where their professional role ended and where the school's non-teaching staff should take over with regard to the social and emotional needs of their pupils. They appreciated the support they got from these staff. Most teachers spent approximately 30 hours per week in school, although only 18 hours of these were involved in classroom teaching. For anything over their contracted hours, which included time for preparation and planning, teachers would receive extra remuneration. Some teachers had the role of *professeur principal* for which they received additional remuneration. There was no special time set aside for this role, which was normally carried out during one of the subject teacher's lessons, in a session referred to as *l'heure de vie*. The role was officially seen as one of intermediary between home and school but, by the teachers, it was mostly perceived as an administrative role. Its function was seen as that of introducing and reminding pupils of the school rules, liaising with other teachers and guiding pupils in their school trajectory.

However, this traditional role was changing, first, due to policy initiatives and, second, due to the changing demands of the school population in difficult areas. Some teachers were beginning to have a more extended concept of their role, which included an affective dimension. However, they were generally in favour of the national curriculum, which they did not consider to be over-prescriptive and which they considered provided all pupils with the same knowledge and experience. In line with the French principle of equality, they were generally not in favour of selection.

The English model: The 'subject specialist and group tutor'

Mrs Dixon: *'They think I'm a bit strict [in my subject lessons] but the very same kids can also sit down and have a good laugh with me [outside lesson time]. As a tutor, you need to be sensitive to children's needs, as very distinct from academic needs.'*

Mrs Dixon teaches in a state comprehensive school which takes pupils from 11 to 18 years of age. She teaches 29, 45 minute periods a week to classes throughout the school. She enjoys being able to teach her subject not only to the younger pupils in Year 7 but also to Advanced level students in Years 12 and 13. She has six 'free' periods a week when she can catch up on preparation, marking and any pastoral issues she may need to deal with. However, this is never enough time to complete all she has to do and so she works every Sunday and most weekday evenings during term time to catch up. She appreciates the close working relationships she has with colleagues in her subject department, supporting each other with regard to curriculum planning and staff development.

As well as being a subject teacher, Mrs Dixon is also a group tutor for one of the six parallel Year 8 classes. As well as registration, both mornings and afternoons, this role gives her responsibility for the personal and social problems of her group. However, lack of time means that this role is largely administrative.

Mrs Dixon enjoys both the subject and pastoral sides of her role but she does experience a tension between the two. She considers that she must take a different approach to pupils when they are in her teaching groups. Here she needs to maintain a strict discipline and ensure that they cover the necessary work to enable them to achieve well in their regular tests. However, when she deals with the same pupils in her tutor group she considers that she needs to be more approachable and sympathetic to their worries and concerns both inside and outside school.

At secondary school level the teachers in our sample were 'specialists', teaching classes of pupils throughout the age range, their particular curriculum subject. They worked with other teachers within the school who taught the same subject and with whom they had regular 'department' or 'faculty' meetings. To a certain extent this allegiance to a subject gave them a specific identity which could also influence their approach to classroom practice. They were supervised by a department/faculty head who was usually part of the school's senior management team.

In addition to their subject teaching, the majority of teachers also had a responsibility as 'tutor' for a particular group of pupils. This role was largely pastoral and required them to look after the social and emotional needs of their tutor group. They also served as the initial contact with parents and home. Contact with their tutor group was usually for a short period, about 10 or 15 minutes at the beginning of each morning and afternoon session. This was when they took the class register, handed out notices and dealt with any matters concerning the behaviour of their tutor group which had been brought to their attention by colleagues. For many teachers this left little time or space for engagement with issues to do with the affective aspects of teaching and learning. Evidence from the project suggested that this role, rather than concentrating purely on the affective domain, was beginning to be reconceptualized as primarily a learning support role. In practice the short periods of tutor time at the beginning of both the morning and afternoon sessions were usually taken up with registration and administration with little time to explore issues or build relationships. Some teachers accepted this situation, others considered it a missed opportunity. Group tutors were often responsible, in a curriculum sense, for the personal, social and health education (PSHE) of their group. This should have given them more opportunity to explore the social and emotional issues which occupied their particular pupils but increasingly this time was constrained by a highly prescriptive curriculum, which included study skills as well as issues to do with personal development. Tutor groups were of mixed ability, but the pupils usually spent most of their time grouped by attainment in subject lessons. Teachers found themselves under increasing pressure to raise standards and meet government targets. This, together with an intense inspection system, left many of the sample feeling overworked and stressed.

Most teachers within the Danish sample were *klasselærer*, and had a special responsibility for a particular class of pupils, together with organizing the team of teachers who taught them. This involved a combined academic and pastoral responsibility for a single group of pupils often for the entire period of their schooling (grades 1 to 9/10), although there was flexibility within the system for a change in grade 5 or 7 if the teachers wanted it. These two elements of the teaching role were not divided, as in England and France, but were considered to be intimately related in all that they did. The classes in the study

The Danish model: The 'class teacher'

Hanne: *'The class teacher should be engaging, able to understand their pupils' concerns and problems and live and grow together with their pupils . . . the better children get al.*ong with each other the more power and energy they are able to use on learning. Learning will be hampered if you feel socially insecure.'

Hanne teaches at a *folkeskole* which takes pupils from 7 to 16 years of age. She has been the class teacher of her 7th Grade class since they began at the *folkeskole* over six years ago. She teaches ten lessons a week to the class in Danish, geography and biology. She also teaches history, social studies and art to classes higher up in the school. She has 18 pupils in her class and feels that she knows both them and their families very well.

She considers her role as *klasselærer* to be an integral part of her extended role as teacher and considers that her responsibility to her pupils and their families extends outside the school premises into the community. Her approach to teaching is that she should include the knowledge and experience which pupils bring with them to school and that she should encourage them to work together effectively. The need to get them to respect decisions made in class by the majority is an important element in creating future democratic citizens.

Hanne wants her pupils to enjoy coming to school and she is open with them and allows them, especially on activity camps and outings, to get close to her and understand her attitudes and values. She supports the new act of the *folkeskole* and considers that it is only a statement of what good teachers have been doing for a long time. She likes the idea of cross-curricular themes and pupils working collaboratively on projects. She wants her pupils to reach a high academic standard but also thinks that it is important for her pupils to be excited and engaged by her teaching. She emphasizes the need for the pupils to learn to communicate, to express themselves, and to become independent and responsible.

normally consisted of approximately 18–20 pupils of mixed ability and a great emphasis was put on the cohesion of the group and their ability to work together both academically as well as socially. Use of the 'hour of the class' as either a separate, timetabled period or integrated into other lessons, enabled the class teacher to build up close relationships between themselves and their pupils and to investigate issues of concern within the class group. However, similar to their English colleagues, there was pressure for *klasselærer* to use this time to catch up on missed teaching. Policy initiatives meant that teachers were under pressure to develop cross-curricular project work and provide for a differentiated curriculum within their mixed ability groups. Class teachers often worked in teams of three or four teachers who, between them, covered the spread of the curriculum. It was a general organizing principle that children in the first five or six years of their education should be taught by as few teachers as possible. Teachers who had specialized in specific subject areas would then enter the team for the older classes. However, the class teacher had specific responsibility for links between home and school. Typically they also spent some of their time teaching additional subjects to pupils in classes throughout the age range as part of other class teams. This helped to integrate the various groups within the school. Teachers generally felt free to interpret the national curriculum framework in a way that supported the needs of their pupils by introducing themes which had a direct relevance to their lives outside school.

Teaching aims and priorities

Teachers within all three systems spoke in similar general terms when asked about their aims and priorities for their pupils. All were concerned that pupils should achieve academically, that they should grow and develop as individuals and that they should acquire the skills and abilities which would enable them to take their place as future citizens and workers. However, these aims were often expressed in terms which showed the differing ideological influences within the three systems:

> I think the main political aim is to raise academic standards . . . but personally I would say the development of the whole child, which includes fulfilling their academic potential, but also their development as a sound human being and their personal development – [to ensure that] they're not scarred in any way by their school experiences, or undermined, or they don't come out with an overriding sense of injustice, or failure, or loss of confidence.
>
> (teacher of humanities, England)

> I'm a maths teacher so my aim is to structure their thoughts, not only in maths. At secondary level, maths is a means of getting them to learn how to reason but it is a skill that will also help them in their future lives as citizens. I would say that my main aim as a maths teacher is to help pupils to develop into citizens who know how to reason and how to think.
>
> (teacher of mathematics, France)

> It's important that the children like being here, otherwise they won't learn anything. But it is also important that they learn something and

> have a positive experience of being together. I think it's important that they treat each other in a proper fashion.
>
> (*klasselærer*, Denmark)

These quotations illustrate the importance of the development of the 'whole child' and the individualist nature of the educational process for English teachers, the emphasis on intellectual and cognitive development for French teachers, and the importance of the 'group' and collaborative working in the development of future citizens for Danish teachers. However, there were other aspects which were more nationally context specific and related to the underlying aims of the national education system as a whole.

In England there was an emphasis on the need to enable pupils to reach preset targets in their learning, which had increasingly become a measure by which individual teaching was being judged:

> My priorities are to do what I'm paid to do. To give the taxpayer and their parents, you know, no cause for concern about their children's results. That must be number one. You know, I must be professional, I'm paid to do a job and, you know, I must always be thinking about targets for children. What is the likely result of the children's work?
>
> (teacher of geography, England)

> Uh, a difficult question. I suppose really, what I'd say was very important to me is that they learn to enjoy a language, and they learn to see it as not just grammar but as a way of life . . . But, obviously, I am pressurised by exams and things. I do feel that I want to do well and I do want them all to reach a high standard
>
> (teacher of modern languages, England)

French teachers, in contrast, often cited the more characteristically French aim of the transmission of communal knowledge so that all pupils would have the same basic level of education. This embodies ideas about egalitarianism, French identity and social cohesion and was expressed in the following way:

> That all the children of one generation should share the same knowledge base, at least up to 3ème.
>
> (teacher of French and Latin, France)

> That every single pupil should participate, in other words, despite the fact that there may be some brilliant pupils in the class, they must all make progress in the same way so that they can all get there.
>
> (teacher of technology, France)

> I think an important part of education is to pass on common references to all social classes. I strongly support a national curriculum. The national curriculum is a norm. The norm isn't an objective, it's something that provides a structure. Teaching pupils the basics of the national curriculum is a means of socially integrating them.
>
> (teacher of history and geography, France)

French teachers were also more concerned than their English and Danish colleagues with an emphasis on structure, system and stages. Each stage in the system was seen as a rung in the ladder to get to the next stage. For example, lower-secondary education was seen as, 'a springboard for the *second cycle*' (teacher of French). There was also a concern, shared by their Danish colleagues, that their pupils should learn how to reason and become future citizens 'the main aim is to produce citizens who can reason and think' (teacher of mathematics, France).

While recognizing the need for their pupils to achieve academically, Danish teachers, all of whom had class teacher responsibility, also put a great deal of emphasis on the development of social skills and the need to engender enjoyment, self-motivation and independence in learning, by learning how to learn:

> [It is important] . . . that they learn to respect each other. That they take responsibility for what they are doing and that they do what is important in the learning context, whether I am watching them or not, either because they like it or because they have to. It is also crucial that they learn to co-operate.
>
> (klasselærer and teacher of maths and Danish, the Periphery School, Denmark)

> [It is important] . . . that the pupils become as academically able as possible, within their own capabilities. They must also consider that it is worthwhile going to school. It is a mixture of academic and social learning.
>
> (klasselærer and teacher of Danish and English, the North School, Denmark)

> Firstly, that everybody is happy and confident to go to school. Secondly, that the children learn something and, finally, that the school provides an enjoyable social atmosphere.
>
> (klasselærer and teacher of Danish and geography, the Inner City School, Denmark)

> that the pupils learn the rules of democracy, that they learn at their own level, that they learn to be independent and take responsibility

> for organising their own work. I want each of them to learn how to appropriate knowledge, and how to solve a problem and work with it, to learn the learning process
>
> (klasselærer and teacher of maths, biology and science, the Province School, Denmark)

However, there were also common themes which crossed national borders. Teachers who taught in schools with more disadvantaged intakes laid great emphasis on social priorities and the need to give their pupils the skills necessary for their future lives, rather than concentrating on purely academic aims:

> I have spent a great deal of time on the social side of things. Sometimes you're more of a social worker than a teacher. That's what I've found recently with the children we've been getting. We spend an incredible amount of time on the social aspect.
>
> (klasselærer and teacher of Danish, the Inner City School, Denmark)

> What is it that really counts in education? Is it to get a qualification called the *Baccalaureate* or is it to give a person a sense of job fulfilment? To arrive as an adult who is happy with himself and will have expertise in some things. In my opinion, I can honestly tell you that I don't care if a child gets the *Bac*. So what if some people are more suited to a vocational qualification in catering or building, as long as they are happy in what they are doing? I would rather get my bread from a good baker who has a vocational qualification than get it from a bad baker who has got a *Baccalaureate* but got totally turned off in the process.
>
> (teacher of history, France)

Issues of equity also emerged across national boundaries where school intakes were socially and financially disadvantaged, especially in those schools with significant ethnic minorities:

> If you've got the chance to have parents who support you, who give you life skills as well as help you academically then there isn't a problem. But that isn't the case with these pupils. There's little support at home, you see children still in the streets at midnight, they don't open their school books at home. They get average marks of 3 out of 20, they say that they're not interested in school, and that they don't want to stay in this country anyway. In my opinion, what we have to do is to limit the damage that has been done. We have to at least develop their common sense.
>
> (teacher of design and technology, France)

An English teacher talks about his commitment to after school 'catch-up classes':

> That's why, obviously, most of us go home late . . . it's all about our intake. Most of them sometimes just cannot find the time to do it [homework] at home, or the space to do it at home, or the help to do it at home. So it's two things. The first one is about academic improvement, so we help them to do it here. But, secondly, sometimes it is just to keep them out of trouble . . . I will run maybe detentions after school, but sometimes you just have kids here for an hour and a half who just want to stay and help me do something, or do their work.
>
> (teacher of English, England)

The headteacher of a Danish school in a poor city suburb speaks of the need to prepare pupils, whatever their background for active citizenship:

> In general, I think it is important that the *folkeskole* is for *all* children in Denmark. That it is a school system where the parents *want* to send their children. I think a good *folkeskole* is the foundation of a society . . . if you want to give power to the people who have few privileges it is very important that you educate them as well as possible . . . kids who can't read become citizens with very little influence.
>
> (headteacher, Denmark)

Aspects of the 'academic' and the 'affective'

As we have seen in Chapter 4, one of the major structural differences within the three systems was the management of the 'academic' and 'affective' domains of teaching and learning, where 'academic' was used to describe knowledge content and 'affective' included those areas of social, spiritual and emotional aspects of teaching and learning. Within the English system, subject teachers often had a separate, but complementary, responsibility as 'group tutor' which included the personal and social well-being of a particular group of pupils. Within the French system these two aspects of schooling were managed by completely different groups of staff: teachers concentrated on the academic, whereas the *conseiller principal d'éducation* and their staff were responsible for the pastoral care of pupils. In Denmark both aspects of education were seen as so intimately connected that it was impossible to split them. However, evidence from the teachers uncovered a more complicated picture when these three different systems were operationalized.

In England the aims of the pastoral system were similar in all three study schools. It was there to provide a safety net for pupils and to act as a bridge between issues which affected their lives outside the classroom and their academic performance. It was characteristic of most English teachers, in common with Danish teachers but very unlike French teachers, that whatever the school context, the affective domain was important. Most English teachers considered that their role as a group tutor could complement their role as a subject teacher, 'I view the children (in my tutor group) in a more sympathetic light, and balance perhaps their backgrounds' (teacher of science), though others experienced a tension:

> I view my role as a tutor fairly separately from my role as a teacher. In my role as a tutor I certainly am a lot gentler than my role as a teacher, so that the door is always open [as a tutor] and they don't view me as being so disciplinarian that they can't feel that they can approach me any time on any issue. So I do play my role as a tutor somewhat differently.
>
> (teacher of humanities, England)

However, it was also observed that, in an effort to raise standards there was evidence of a re-focusing of the group tutor role to include more academic support and personal planning. Tutors were being required to monitor the progress of pupils using computer data in order to set targets, which would then be discussed with individual pupils.

In addition to their pastoral role, group tutors were often required to teach a curriculum subject known as personal, social and health education (PSHE) to their tutor group. This involved study skills, as well as issues to do with individual personal and social development and provided teachers with an opportunity to relate to pupils on a slightly more informal level with a more individualistic and flexible curriculum which could include the worries and preoccupations of their pupils:

> Kids, their general idea of PSHE is to have fun. It's a chill out zone. It's time to relax. And it will tend to be that because, again, PSHE is not about drumming home this and that. It's about your skills as a form tutor, I think that's why it is so important in the lower school.
>
> (teacher of English, England)

> they [year heads] give us a guideline which we can follow if we want to, or follow if we're stuck, or follow if we haven't got ideas of our own to bring in. But very often you can use it as a basis on which to tack on your own things.
>
> (teacher of humanities, England)

Despite the administrative separation of the cognitive and pastoral roles within the French system in theory, French teachers have long been required to cover some aspects of the affective domain within the taught subject of civic education. This consisted of knowledge-based education about the rights and responsibilities of citizens. In the more pedagogically innovative schools in disadvantaged areas, teachers of other subjects were also starting to include aspects of affective education. First, they encouraged group and team work, and pupil responsibility in project work. Second, depending upon individual personalities and again particularly in disadvantaged areas, some teachers were taking on a more active role in the development of their pupils as people. Several teachers referred to the increasing demands made on the affective dimension of their role. However, many teachers in all three French schools resisted this trend:

> I'm rather against teachers having responsibility for the personal and social education of their pupils. I think that in France teachers are being made more and more responsible for it. I feel that more and more is asked of teachers. As soon as there is a problem, the solution is always to pass it on to the teacher.
>
> (teacher of French, France)

Most French teachers restricted their aims to the traditional, instructive and cognitive, although, as a teacher of English was aware, 'There is another dimension to the pupil which completely escapes us'. This was partly because of the traditional view of the teacher's role in France which recognized that the skills and resources were not necessarily available:

> In France, education means mass participation. Okay, it's the same education for everyone, so social and personal development isn't something that concerns us . . . Although there are ministerial directives about looking for better strategies with pupils, but we don't have the means to do that sort of thing . . . We neither have the time nor the locations to deal with pupils in that way . . . to have more personal discussions with them, it just has not been provided for.
>
> (teacher of mathematics, France)

Most full-time French teaching staff, like their English colleagues, had a second role as *professeur principal* with a particular class. However, as the term implies, the role has had little to do with affective education or individual pastoral care. It was mostly perceived as an administrative role, to introduce and remind pupils of the school rules and study methods, as there was little time or space in which they could deal with individual problems. Sometimes, as with English group tutors, there was a conflict between the role of tutor and the role of subject teacher, 'the problem with individual pupil relationships is that we do not have enough time . . . there's the syllabus to get through'.

However, more important was seen to be guiding pupils in their school trajectory and liaising with other teachers with regard to pupils' academic progress. In this sense, the role of the group tutor in England appeared to be taking on some of the aspects of this French tutor role. There was some evidence within the French schools set in more disadvantaged areas that there was an increasing recognition that a more involved role was needed with a changing school population:

> We look at relations between kids, fighting, insulting, knowing when they are insulting, that it's not just a way of talking, how to speak to adults. At the beginning of the year it was, 'Don't spit on the floor', but now it's more like how to become a responsible teenager. I teach them how to respect each other, because there are many different nationalities, different colours, different ages . . . I have some that are three years older, that have repeated.
>
> (teacher of modern languages, France)

> You have to be ready to listen to them. Sometimes there are things which have nothing to do with their life at school. But who else can they talk to?
>
> (teacher of history, France)

For Danish teachers the tension between the cognitive and the affective domains of teaching and learning was both structurally and personally less of an issue. All teachers considered these aspects of teaching to be interrelated and part of an integrated educational process. As one new class teacher put it 'It's, you know, kind of part of the Danish education tradition that we don't just teach but also help in bringing up the children'. They were supportive of the role of the designated class teacher (*klasselærer*) who had the major pastoral responsibility for any one particular group of pupils. This function was considered so important within the Danish schooling system that class teachers were often encouraged and facilitated to remain with the same group of children throughout the whole of their time at the *folkeskole*. This enabled them to build close relationships, not only with their pupils, but also with the parents and families of their pupils. As one class teacher explained, 'The children have to learn what they are supposed to' but that at the same time the class teacher has to be 'sensitive to and able to understand the problems of the children'. The class teacher had a total of 75 hours a year to discharge the very wide range of duties for which they are responsible but there were growing concerns that it was unreasonable to expect such a complicated and time consuming function to be carried out by one teacher alone. As a class teacher put it, 'you have to be an octopus, mentally as well as physically. But you should also be capable of doing other things than just teach. You need to be a human being, someone who can get close to the children'. Pupils also, in practice, sometimes had difficulties in approaching their class teacher with problems, often choosing another subject teacher of their own sex. This could lead to procedural tensions, as this teacher explained:

> It is sometimes a problem that we are in a team where we teach the pupils in many lessons. You sometimes have to touch on an issue which is not really yours because it is the concern of the class teacher – sometimes you feel that it is a problem that you could help to solve – but the procedure must work the other way round [in other words, be referred back to the class teacher].
>
> (klasselærer, Denmark)

The current role has therefore been the focus of considerable research and there was a growing trend, as in the case of one of the study schools, that teachers were being actively encouraged to take on the role as a job share, with one male and one female teacher.

Pedagogy and assessment

All three groups of teachers worked within a centrally determined national curriculum. However, the extent to which they felt constrained by this differed. English teachers considered that a highly prescribed national curriculum combined with 'high stakes' national testing gave them little flexibility. Whereas their French colleagues did not seem to feel constrained to the same extent and felt more free to be creative:

> The syllabus isn't a constraint at all. It's true that we're very lucky and I don't know how long it will last. You can shut your classroom door and you're free to do what you like. My classroom is like a cocoon or the maternal breast for me. I feel good in my classroom.
>
> (teacher of French and Latin, France)

This could have been the result of a combination of the infrequency of inspection and the traditional autonomy of the French teacher whose system lacked the pressure of national testing. Where French teachers did feel constraint it was usually because they felt responsible, not so much to central government, but to their professional colleagues:

> We feel responsibility to the colleagues who take over from us . . . each year we have different pupils. I hand my pupils over to another teacher who has to follow the required syllabus.
>
> (teacher of mathematics, France)

The absence of national testing and the progressive and longitudinal nature of the *klasselærer* role, which saw one teacher remain with a class of pupils through the whole of their lower-secondary schooling, meant that neither of these pressures applied for Danish teachers. The current act of the *folkeskole* states that teaching content should be selected and organized to give pupils the best opportunity to learn and that individual teachers must determine their working methods and content, as far as possible, in cooperation with their pupils. This meant that the national curriculum was seen as a loose framework within which both individual municipalities, schools and teachers could have a great deal of flexibility. Within this framework, teachers often chose to base the content of their teaching on the experiences of their pupils. A geography teacher who was able to spend time on a project dealing with the recycling waste said, 'We had some good discussions about what we throw away, what we do with the rubbish at home, how much water we use, *et cetera*'. The project finished with pupils making paper out of recycled waste products.

Teachers in all three countries wanted their pupils to enjoy their subjects and to be well motivated to learn. This was a more pressing concern for teachers in all three countries with more difficult intakes, who tried to make their lessons more interesting and meaningful to their pupils. There was a recognition by some teachers that some subject areas were more open to this type of interpretation than others:

> I think I'm lucky to be a history teacher. It can't be easy to get pupils to laugh in maths. But in history there are often anecdotes . . . For example, I was asked, 'Sir, was medicine effective in the Middle Ages?' I replied, 'Look, I'll tell you what it was like. Imagine you've got the plague and I'm going to look after you'. So I got my coat, which is black, and put it on back to front and it so happened that day that I had a football rattle handy. So, as in the Middle Ages, I made a lot of noise and recited some charms. 'But Sir', they said, 'That's not possible'. I told them that that was what happened and I asked them if they thought that was effective. I try to introduce humour because then they get to like the subject, and I'm the gainer as they are happy to come to my lessons and are prepared to work knowing that they might get some interesting anecdotes thrown in.
>
> (teacher of history, France)

Language teachers, both foreign and mother tongue, also appeared to have more scope to involve pupils by using examples from their current interests and concerns:

> [I] try and stimulate pupils to learn more than just the basics, to have an interest in languages obviously, and other cultures, and they're

> taken on trips and have quite a lot of opportunities to do things like that.
>
> (teacher of modern languages, England)

Another approach was to relate teaching to the circumstances which pupils would face in their working lives:

> My aim is to face children with challenges that they would meet in the work place. That is to say that when they are faced with a problem they have to choose the best solution between several alternatives . . . Everyone contributes their ideas, we look at each idea and throw out those that are not realistic. The ideas are evaluated according to our budget and the equipment we have . . . With the equipment we've got in this workshop, without bits of wood, how are we going to resolve the problem? Is the first idea a realistic one? Yes or no? We don't know. There's lots of brainstorming, it's the only way. And every idea is listened to, but we can only carry out one idea, so there is bound to be some resentment, and those pupils have to be convinced and brought round. It's just like adult life.
>
> (teacher of design and technology, France)

Danish teachers were particularly keen to use examples from their pupils' lived experiences in their teaching, and to enter into discussion with them about news items in the media or issues of international importance. However, the requirement for differentiated teaching contained in the most recent act, which was welcomed by some teachers as an endorsement of current good practice, was less well received by others:

> Now textbooks are overshadowed and I must find things myself – this needs more preparation than previously. The pupils have to work much more independently and you have to focus on individual pupil's work rather than on the class as a whole.
>
> (klasselærer, Denmark)

Within the English schools, there was evidence that outside pressures had limited teachers' abilities to use a creative approach to pedagogy, as this teacher explained when talking about the effect of national testing:

> And yes, it can stultify, it can stifle creativity in a way. When I teach A level, for instance, I'm a geographer, we do two residential courses on Exmoor and Snowdonia and the children go there and they are inspired. And we do wonderful geography and we work from nine in the morning 'til ten o'clock at night, doing geography, and they love

> it, and it's really good. But when we get back into the classroom I have to sort of stop that and I have to start dictating notes. Because they need to have the notes, they need to be spoon fed the notes, to learn by heart, to get the A level grade.
>
> (teacher of geography, England)

Teachers in all three systems used a mixture of formative and summative assessment to help pupils understand how they were progressing. However, English teachers were required to have a more active interest with regard to summative assessment, in line with national and school target setting, and Danish teachers were actively discouraged from giving their pupils marks for their work until grade 8.

English teachers spoke of a mixture of the regular marking of workbooks and national and school assessments, combined with an awareness of pupils' oral and written contribution in class. The relationship of the teacher with the pupil as an individual was important in making these judgements and ensuring that individuals were working to their potential. As one teacher said:

> I think the more you get to know pupils, the better it is, both in personal terms and in straightforward class teaching terms. It's helpful to have an insight into where they're coming from.
>
> (teacher of humanities, England)

Some teachers in England involved pupils in group or class discussions at the end of particular projects to assess the value of the work done and there was some evidence of the use of pupil self-assessment. Some teachers expressed a concern with the amount of testing their pupils were subjected to and the lack of time for a more informal, one to one formative model. They also recognized that the pressure of assessment and testing impacted differently on different pupils and, for some, could be demotivating:

> I think the brighter pupils do like tests, and they love getting results and they get a real sense of achievement when they do well. But for some pupils, tests are something daunting and they feel as though it's a punishment rather than a chance to show off.
>
> (teacher of modern languages, England)

The formative element of assessment was often stressed by French teachers. They pointed out that the objective behind marking pupils' work was to assist pupil learning, 'I correct the pupils' exercise books, so that the books are a tool in their learning. Their exercise books allow them to work individually' (teacher of history). This teacher continued by explaining that he wrote, 'Look at this again' on work which showed that a topic needed to be gone over again. Error analysis was held, particularly by maths teachers, to be very important for pupil learning, 'Errors have an important role to play in children's learning'. Other teachers complained that pupils did not pay attention to teacher annotations to their work, that pupils were only concerned with the mark itself. Many French teachers decried the importance that pupils gave to their marks, though given the emphasis in the system to marks in pupils' termly reports and given that pupil progress to the following year depended on the pupil's average mark for the year, pupil concern with marks was not surprising.

French teachers agreed with their English colleagues that, for low achieving pupils, marks could be demotivating and that consistently low marks ceased to have an effect. Teachers from schools in more competitive, middle class areas drew attention to the pressure their pupils felt due to high parental expectations.

Compared to their English and French colleagues, Danish teachers, together with the Danish school system, took a much more formative approach to assessment. The official documents stated that:

> As part of the teaching, there shall be a regular assessment of the pupils' profit from the teaching. The assessment shall form the basis of the guidance to the individual pupil with a view to the further planning of the teaching.
>
> (Act of the *folkeskole* 1995: 13(2))

When tests were used it was stressed that they were for pupils to compare their present with their past achievement, and not to compare the work of one pupil with another. Much of the focus for assessment was to inform the twice yearly, parent–teacher–pupil discussions, where pupils' individual progress is discussed, together with plans for further development. Individual face to face assessment, self-assessment and group assessment were all used by teachers to help pupils discover what they had learnt and to know what they needed to develop. Within the study group, because of the increasing age of the pupils, some teachers were beginning to give their pupils marks if they asked for them, but there was a recognition that it was the higher achieving pupils who were keen to know how they had done, 'It is never the one who gets 6 who asks'. These marks were rarely made public and teachers made efforts to give the marks to pupils personally, so that their significance for the individual could be explained. There was some concern among teachers in the study school with a large ethnic minority that some parents from other cultures were very ambitious for their children and were keen to see evidence of progress through high marks. Much time was also spent correcting pupil's written work. Comments tended to focus on what had been achieved and where there was room for improvement. Most teachers would discuss these comments personally with each pupil and ask them to comment on whether they considered them to be justified.

Teacher collaboration

The current structure of the systems in England and Denmark gave more scope for teacher collaboration than the more traditionally autonomous role of the French teacher. The departmental or faculty structure in English schools meant that subject specialists regularly worked together on curriculum issues, while year group heads worked with group tutors on pastoral issues. However, there was also some evidence that current policy was creating increasing pressures on this 'middle management' level school organization:

> I don't think it'll be any secret in this school that the senior management team devolve all responsibility to middle management. And middle management would be expected to face up to all issues, all national issues within education, including targets . . . grades . . . school rolls. All curriculum developments, they're expected to be on top of all that, and to make sure that everybody in their department is teaching at strength, and that the children . . . doing their subject get high exam results. And if they don't, then they will be called to account to explain why.
>
> (teacher of geography, England)

French teachers, with their relatively autonomous role, tended to work alone. There is no head of department, as in an English school, and teachers in the most socially advantaged area provided hardly any instances of teachers working together, as one teacher said:

> I don't actually work with the other maths teachers. We work in the same place but we don't work together . . . we each work on our own.
>
> (teacher of mathematics, France)

However, in the two smaller French schools, which were dealing with a more disadvantaged intake, there were examples of teachers working together:

> In English we're always comparing, how do you teach this notion. We work together and I think it's a small school so all the teachers know each other very well. There's a lot of work done in common. It's not necessarily about subject work but . . . in English there are only three of us, and then my student teacher, and we all work together in a group
>
> (teacher of modern languages, France)

> Here we all get on well, so it's easy to get together about work. One way of putting it is that we harmonise our work
>
> (teacher of French, France)

This collaboration had also extended to their work with non-teaching staff, as the headteacher of Mazarin described it, 'When it comes to things that concern the whole school we really work as a team'.

In Denmark, the latest school act had extended the need for teacher collaboration from one which centred on curriculum issues to one which also included the pastoral care of the pupils and the class group as a whole. Class teachers organized meetings with the team of subject teachers responsible for their class to coordinate teaching content and to discuss pupil learning and behaviour, as well as issues to do with the social life of the class. There was also a requirement in the act for teachers to approach their teaching from an interdisciplinary perspective. This was welcomed by many teachers, but there was some resistance with regard to the amount of time taken up with meetings, and it could sometimes be dependent on the relationships of individual teachers:

> I think that we have so much work to do that it [collaboration with other subject teachers] gets a lower priority. It also depends on the people you work with. My colleagues are teachers who like to close their classroom door behind them. Sometimes I have experienced excellent collaboration with the class teacher of the parallel class, sometimes I haven't.
>
> (klasselærer, Denmark)

> I work extremely well with the maths teacher. We plan almost everything jointly and sometimes even swap lessons – she has mine and I have hers. But it is rather difficult with the other subjects. Some colleagues apparently don't feel the need for more extended teamwork.
>
> (klasselærer, Denmark)

Extent of the teacher's responsibility

One area where there was a distinct difference between the three national contexts was the extent to which teachers considered that their role extended outside the classroom. For French teachers this was more clearly defined in that they considered that their role was confined to the classroom and were often only on the school premises when they needed to teach classes. As we have seen, it was left to other, non-teaching staff to deal with administrative and behavioural matters.

The school uniform in England which was an outward representation of the school reputation meant that there was an implicit responsibility for English teachers when pupils were on their way to and from school:

> Certainly on the buses going home, the school is very careful to make sure that behaviour is good. The staff actually go – there are staff who are on duty watching them get on the buses, to make sure there are no problems . . . and in terms of walking to and from school, generally speaking, they're told about certain rules, they must keep to certain footpaths, they're supposed to set a good example.
>
> (teacher of modern languages, England)

> Outside the school gates, for instance, after school we will always have about five or six teachers on duty . . . we will patrol that area . . . once you have your school uniform on we can still tell you what to do outside school . . . Wherever you are, if you're wearing our uniform, we have the right to tell you what to do.
>
> (teacher of English, England)

Both English and Danish teachers considered the boundary of their responsibilities to be more fluid and both groups considered their role to extend beyond both the classroom and school boundaries. Both were required to have formal responsibility, on a rota basis, for pupil behaviour at break times, and both English and Danish teachers considered that an involvement in, or knowledge of, pupils' home situations could be beneficial to their academic and personal development.

Although English teachers considered that their role extended to knowledge of their pupils' home circumstances, there was also some recognition that pupils had a right to privacy:

> On the other hand, I think there is a limit to how much I should know as a teacher as well. Because there is personal privacy, and a child actually might not want me to know if there's major problems at home. In which case, I think the child to a degree has got their own personal privacy to protect, if you like. Even though I might be trying to peer into it, for the sake of their learning and their academic life . . . I think there is a hazy edge to it.
>
> (teacher of humanities, England)

Danish teachers, on the other hand, considered that there was a community responsibility for their pupils which extended well beyond the school gates. Although the schools officially had no responsibility for pupils' safety outside school, teachers did feel involved and would sometimes include discussions within lesson time about incidents which had been reported to them or contact parents:

> If something happens outside school, like some pupils are teased or bullied on their way home by other pupils at the school, then we would intervene. We would contact the parents or work as an intermediary to get the parents to talk together.
>
> (klasselærer, Denmark)

Teachers also felt it was their responsibility to intervene directly if they came across pupils acting inappropriately, including behaviour such as vandalism or drunkenness, outside school. As one teacher said, 'I would stop a pupil on the road if he were riding his bike dangerously'. Another teacher agreed that:

> If an accident happened to somebody in this street [outside school], then I would regard it as our responsibility – or at least mine – or not responsibility, but I would feel a duty to help. If I came across some acts of hooliganism around the school area at night, I would also intervene.
>
> (klasselærer, Denmark)

However, this view of their extended community role could sometimes come into conflict with other cultures. One teacher, in an area with a large immigrant population, considered that she had a moral responsibility not to turn a blind eye to customs which she considered unjust or inequitable. She had had long discussions with some Muslim girls about their insistence on wearing headscarves. She explained:

> We should respect all religions and cultures, but I don't want to be respectful of what I don't agree with – if you see what I mean. I don't accept that you can beat women and children, or that you choose to sell your children. No.
>
> (klasselærer, Denmark)

Pupil and parent influence

Another area of difference was the extent to which pupils and parents were involved in decision making (Chapter 4). We found a continuum, with French teachers and schools requiring least input from pupils and their parents, and Danish teachers and schools regarding pupils and parents as partners in the educational process who needed to be engaged and encouraged to take part.

English teachers generally felt that they had the support of parents but would usually only have direct contact with them at parents' evenings, twice a year. Very occasionally they would need to contact parents if there were a problem which needed to be addressed, either academic or pastoral. However, there was some evidence that parents were becoming more demanding in relation to their own children and were keen to know what could be expected of them academically. The management structure of English secondary schools tended to protect class teachers from more direct criticism from parents:

> There are awkward parents, parents who write to the chairman of the governors, perhaps, all the time, you know, complaining. We tend to get shielded from that so we don't know. There are parents who write to the headteacher, or year heads. I think heads of year probably deal mainly with parents.
>
> (teacher of geography, England)

> I dare say though that, if you asked a year head, you might find there's a different response there. Because I tend to see parents who are electing to come in, whereas a year head would sometimes be ringing up parents to make an appointment over bad behaviour, who maybe don't want to come in. And so that might be a very much stormier relationship than I've ever experienced with a parent.
>
> (teacher of humanities, England)

Danish teachers spoke of a more direct involvement with both parent and pupils with respect to curriculum, as well as social matters:

> I ask for their [the pupils] opinion a great deal . . . ask for their attitudes . . . I use a lot of time on what I call dilemma questions, using actual events from outside school. They are very good at it. Good at putting questions to me like, 'But you just said . . .'
>
> (klasselærer, Denmark)

Some class teachers sent weekly newsletters home to parents to explain what was being covered in the next week's work and what involvement, if any, was to be expected of them. A yearly parents' evening was also used by class teachers to open up for discussion curriculum and social matters, 'What would you like your children to deal with in relation to certain subjects?' However, teachers also pointed out that it was they who made the final decisions.

There was also some evidence that teachers in all three countries, while recognizing the importance of parents, expressed a professional distance to protect themselves from what they saw as an increasing demand by the individual consumer, expressed here in its clearest terms by a French teacher:

> The first parents' evening is to explain our approach to pedagogy, but we do not give away too much. The reason for that is because some teachers regard pedagogy as a professional secret.
>
> (teacher of English, France)

> When parents feel powerless in relation to their children, they tend to take their children's side in opposition to the school and teachers . . . Sometimes they have unrealistic expectations for their own child without considering the impact on other pupils.
>
> (klasselærer, Denmark)

Summary

In summary then, evidence suggested that the different national structures within which the teachers worked gave rise to different approaches to teaching and learning, related to the purposes and priorities of the national schooling systems. The French teachers worked within a centrally controlled framework which identified the texts, timing and pedagogical approach to teaching and tended to conform to a model of the teacher which emphasized the academic and intellectual. The Danish teachers, on the other hand, worked within a system which assumed a holistic approach to teaching and learning and included the personal and social development of pupils. It relied very little on external control and gave teachers and pupils a great deal of pedagogic freedom. For teachers in the English study schools, the academic and affective were also combined but a different schooling structure, which perceived them as separate strands, led to a tension between the two.

Evidence also suggested that national policy change had created new ways of working. English teachers were struggling to hold onto their commitment to the affective and pastoral, while at the same time being set ever increasing targets for the achievement of their pupils in national testing. Pressures from *massification* and the increasing variation within their student population were causing French teachers to reassess the role of the affective and pastoral within teaching and learning. Meanwhile in Denmark a concern with low levels of pupil achievement and the accommodation of an increasing number of immigrant children had brought pressure for a more differentiated approach to pupil learning and a reassessment of the role of the class teacher.

These changes had also created tensions for the teachers in all three national contexts, codified in Table 5.1. Despite the fact that such tensions have been represented by means of two columns, they are not meant to represent a typological 'either/or'. Teachers in all three contexts recognized not only the existence of these tensions but also the variability of their nature. As such, they represent axes along which individual teachers moved depending on both external as well as internal stimuli.

Table 5.1 Some current tensions within teaching

Academic focus		*Affective focus*
Concern for the 'learner'	*versus*	Concern for the 'emerging adult'
Subject knowledge	*versus*	Personal development
High academic achievement	*versus*	Achievement for citizenship
Discrete subjects	*versus*	Cross-curricular projects
Individual achievement	*versus*	Group cooperation
Common levels of achievement	*versus*	Differentiated teaching
Individual autonomy	*versus*	Collaborative working

In general terms, French *collège* teachers could be characterized more easily with reference to the academically focused ends of the axes. They perceived the pupil as 'learner' and promoted a common core of learning for all pupils through a subject orientated curriculum interpreted by autonomous professionals. Their Danish colleagues, on the other hand, included a strong emphasis on the more affectively focused aims. Generally they worked collaboratively, recognizing the importance of an affective component to learning. They engaged with the 'emerging adult' through a more holistic and democratic approach to knowledge, which included both personal and social development and was more concerned with cooperation than individual achievement. For teachers in the English study schools a professional proclivity to engage more fully with the affective component of their work was at odds with a managerially driven policy model which sought to be effective in terms of a narrowly defined measure of pupil achievement more in keeping with the academically focused ends of the axes. An emphasis on accountability had added to the administrative demands of their work, while a concern with target setting, for themselves and their pupils, had also reduced the time and space for a more personally satisfying approach to pedagogy. A crowded, and sometimes contradictory, policy agenda continued to create competing demands at both ends of the axes, and this presented teachers with daily dilemmas in respect of their professional practice.

Within these general national differences the study schools also provided some evidence of commonalities across the three countries. Younger, or more recently trained, teachers tended to be more positive towards recent policy changes, they accepted the need to work more closely with colleagues and create a curriculum that would equip pupils for the changing work environment. They were also generally more satisfied with their role and more accepting of the new challenges being placed upon them. Teachers in areas of social and economic deprivation were also, generally, more ready to fit their teaching around the lived experiences of their pupils. Subject specialisms, in

England and France, could also have an impact on the ability of teachers to adapt their teaching to the needs of their pupils, with teachers of modern languages and the humanities especially proactive in this respect.

Chapter 6 completes this contextual section of the book by using classroom observation to relate issues of national structure, school organization and teacher agency to classroom practice.

6 Classroom contexts as a reflection of national values

Introduction

This chapter explores the differences between classrooms in the three countries, differences which affect pupil experience on a day to day basis. These are then related to the underlying cultural values concerning education which were explored in Chapter 3. The evidence presented here underlines one of the central messages of the book; that neither the act of teaching nor the learning experience of pupils can be decontextualized from the school and country in which it is set.

Data for this chapter are based on both actors' perspectives and classroom observations carried out by researchers from all three national contexts. Insider and outsider perspectives were again employed to help 'make the familiar strange' and draw attention to those aspects of national practice which were contextually relevant. Classroom observations were carried out opportunistically within the ten study schools and concentrated on classes where either target pupils or other members of their year cohort (13- and 14-year-olds) were being taught. Qualitative analysis of the pupil questionnaire, individual pupil and group interviews, as well as teacher interviews, is used in this chapter to relate what was observed in classrooms to the actors' experience of the classroom context.

Lesson observation and the classroom environment

Despite often strong intra-country differences, inter-country comparisons can make apparent the particular classroom characteristics of a country. There is a growing body of research which explores qualitative differences in classroom practice between contrasting countries (Osborn and Broadfoot 1992; Planel 1996; Pepin 1999; Alexander 2000). For both pupils and teachers, classrooms represent the 'work face' of school. Classrooms are social and cultural arenas where pupils negotiate with each other and with the teacher, independently, in pairs, in groups and as a whole class. Pupils come into contact, and sometimes conflict, with the values of the national and institutional context in the personified form of their teacher. Pupils also have to relate to the expectations of individual teachers and pupils. Culture in the classroom for the purposes of this study can, therefore, be regarded as 'the forms of behaviour, forms of language, patterns of speech and choice of words, understandings about ways of doing things and not doing things' (Woods 1990: 27).

Classrooms are thus amphitheatres of social action where performances of social and cultural drama are played out on a daily basis. A comparison of the similarities and differences between English, Danish and French classrooms and classroom processes throws light on the context of pupil experience in the three countries as well as giving further insight into the underlying social and cultural values of the three countries. The following three case studies begin to illustrate the differences which can be found within the three national contexts in relation, in this case, to the teaching of mathematics:

Excerpt from a mathematics lesson, France

(The lesson was a review of homework. The teacher's objective was that pupils should understand and be able to use two different algebraic methods to solve the same equation, which was written up on the blackboard: $A = -3(-5)-(-2)+(-3)+(+7))$

The teacher elicits process from a pupil, '*Je transforme . . . sous forme de d'addition . . . Chantal tu me rappelles ce que je fais.*' Chantal supplies the answer. The teacher replies, '*Oui je transforme une soustraction en addition opposée.*' She writes, $A = -3+(-5)+(+2)+(-3)+(+7)$. Teacher, 'What do I write here Isabelle?' Isabelle mutters an answer. The teacher helps Isabelle 'I don't change anything because I've already got an addition. We don't make changes just for the sake of making a change'.

The teacher continues to work through the equation with the class. Before coming to the final answer she analyses the errors pupils had made in their homework. She names the pupils who had forgotten to do the '*addition opposée*' and those who had changed everything.

The teacher then turns to the second method. She returns to the problem on the board and reminds the pupils of the rules. She writes them up on the board and says them aloud. The pupils join in, in chorus, as she says and writes, 'A plus in front of a minus becomes a minus, a minus in front of a plus becomes a minus, a plus in front of a plus is a plus, a minus in front of a minus becomes a plus'.

The teacher then elicits another version of the same in a less mathematical form. The pupils join in, in chorus, as she starts off, 'The friends of my enemies are my enemies, the enemies of my enemies are my friends'.

Excerpt from a mathematics lesson, England

(The lesson was a review of simultaneous equations. The teacher writes up another example $2x + y = 40$)

The teacher asks, 'Any offers to have a go?' A boy volunteers and suggests multiplying the top line by 2 (he remains at his desk to do so as do all the pupils during the lesson). The teacher praises his suggestion and gives an explanation as to why it is an appropriate method. The teacher, with help from individual pupils, works through the example on the blackboard.

Teacher, 'Do you want another one?' She writes up another example. The teacher continues, 'Any offers to have a go?' She turns down the offer from a boy who has previously made suggestions. Teacher, 'Someone else, I think we should have someone else, Lawrence?' Lawrence declines to offer a solution. A girl makes a suggestion (the only girl to participate orally in the class). Another boy makes a different suggestion.

Excerpt from a mathematics lesson, Denmark

(The lesson is a review of a test which the pupils have previously completed.)

The class work through the calculations and problems of the test. The pupils are concentrating and attentive (though one boy is restless and is asked to calm down or remove himself from the room). The teacher and class discuss together the possibility of solving the test items in different ways. Realizing that some of the pupils had guessed at how to arrive at an answer the teacher comments, 'Guessing is better than nothing'.

The teacher asks the class how she can help them improve. This develops into a constructive dialogue. One boy suggests that calculators should not be used. Other suggestions are made. Another boy discusses his preference for different types of problems and calculations. A girl realizes she is having problems with percentage calculations. The teacher refers her to the text book for assistance, but will help if the girl still doesn't understand.

No clear signal is given that the class has ended. Pupils pack up and slowly leave.

An analysis of such observations indicated that there were significant differences in classroom contexts between the three countries which, in turn, could be ascribed to differences in underlying educational values. The French extract points to the pace of learning in French classrooms, the teacher's dominant role, the emphasis on the use of rules and precise terminology in learning, the relative lack of private assessment and the public highlighting of individual pupil errors, and finally the use of individual pupils in a whole class learning situation. The teacher's language was less formal in the English classroom, the teacher played a less dominant role, pupils could choose whether or not to participate and there was evidence of positive assessment. The pace of learning was even slower in the Danish extract. Danish pupils were given more responsibility and they were treated as more equal partners in the learning process.

These differences have been analysed using the following headings:

- the concept of the 'class';
- classroom interiors;
- approaches to pedagogy and pupil groupings;
- teacher control;
- pupil autonomy within the classroom;
- methods of assessment;
- definitions of learning;
- the place of adolescent culture.

The 'class'

As was seen in Chapter 4, the concept of a 'class' had the most structural continuity (in terms of pupils staying together as a group for most or all of the time), and heterogeneity (in terms of the mixed ability composition of the class) in Denmark, and the least structural continuity and heterogeneity in England. Underlying the importance given to heterogeneity in Danish and French class composition were values of egalitarianism and equal entitlement.

An important difference was found to exist between the three countries in the degree of social networking between pupils that arose. English pupils were provided with the most opportunities for socialization due to the different class groupings for different subjects and the possibility for change within a school year. Some English pupils welcomed the opportunity to widen their social networks, 'I'm pleased they've done that [made different groups for science, maths, technology and PE] because there's always a chance to be with other people and not the same class all the time' (girl pupil, St Theresa's). In comparison, although Danish pupils had remarkably unshifting and stable class groups, this continuity, combined with smaller classes and smaller schools meant there was much less opportunity for social networking. Friendship groups were a high priority for English, Danish and French pupils but it is not clear if the relatively fragmented class experience of English pupils and its concomitant high level of social networking was conducive to learning. There was also more opportunity for social networking within the English class itself. For example, in the weak framing of the English tutor period, the physical space of the classroom was almost ghettoized as a result of pupil friendships. An English boy describes the seating pattern in his tutor period classroom in the following way, 'That area's for the hard working people and that area's for the in-between people and that area's for the people who say they're hard'.

In the French context there was little opportunity for friendship groups to operate during classes, 'In maths we work as a class, the teacher's quite strict [the maths teacher's strong framing did not allow friendship groups to surface] it's for things like history that we can be in groups, because we're allowed to help each other ... we can whisper together [the history teacher's weaker framing allowed a measure of friendship grouping to function]' (boy pupil).

In the organization of pupils into classes all three countries mixed boys and girls in the class grouping. Gender was, however, an important factor in pupil seating in the classroom. Teachers from each country reported that they generally allowed pupils to choose their own seating arrangements initially and then when necessary moved individuals to maximize learning. In all three countries, in situations where pupils could choose who to sit with, or work with (or which friends to be interviewed with), single sex groups tended to predominate but there were always some mixed sex pairs and groups. However, observations did tend to indicate that gender differentiation in lower-secondary education was less pronounced in French classrooms. A French history teacher commented that gendered seating patterns only became pronounced in *4ème* (approximately 14 years):

> Distinctions start to be made between girls and boys between *5ème* and *3ème*. A time will come when the class is going to divide into two. In *6ème* no differences are made. They sit next to a boy or next to a girl. Things start to change in *4ème*. You often see them in *4ème* preferring to be by someone of their own sex. *4ème* is where gender becomes important and in *3ème* it's even stronger.
>
> (teacher of history, Montand)

In both the organization of pupils into classes and in pupil seating, friendship groups were often an important factor. In composing classes teachers in all three countries would cooperate to split up friendship groups which might have a negative affect on individuals or on the class itself. A French girl at Cathédrale observed, 'They try not to put all the same friends in one class'. Similarly within the class, teachers tried to maximize learning by controlling the seating arrangements of friendship groups. An English boy at Lady Margaret was aware that, 'The people you sit with can change the way you work. Teachers arrange the seating to avoid naughty ones together. At first you're annoyed, but then you think it's quite sensible. If it's you that's been moved you don't like it'. Class groups, particularly in England and France, often temporarily divided up friendship groups but pupils did not report problems in any of the three countries in establishing friends in different classes.

Classroom interiors

Classroom design was found to be related both to the concept of the 'class' in each country and to underlying national values about learning. In Denmark, where learning is thought to involve the whole person, the class group were allocated specific classrooms where pupils spent most of their day. Pupils regarded the classroom as 'their' space and they were often required to be responsible for its cleaning. Danish classroom interiors were physically adapted to the needs of pupils as people, their comforts and tastes. Easy chairs, coat hooks, hi-fi equipment, drinks, candles in the Christmas period were part of the classroom interior. Pupil desks and seating also conformed to a high standard of design. Seating arrangements were facing the front but in rows or semicircles. The same high standard of design and attitude to pupils with needs as people continued in school corridors and entrance halls. Pupils were free to come and go between the two.

French classrooms were in complete contrast. One of the characteristics of learning in France is its compartmentalization. One manifestation of this compartmentalization was that French classrooms were strictly geared towards pupils as pupils. At the time of fieldwork pupils had no homebase classroom or area (although since the 1999 reform *Le Collège des Années 2000* French schools were obliged to provide first year *collège* pupils with a class homebase which included the provision of lockers). French classrooms were always kept locked. Classroom interiors were designed to be functional rather than stimulating. Wall displays, where they existed, were knowledge based with little input from pupils. Classrooms were always large and well lit. A common seating arrangement in French classrooms was a double 'horse shoe' pattern. All French pupils could see the front even if not directly facing it. In another example of the compartmentalization of French learning, there was a clear separation between classrooms where learning took place, and corridors which were unadorned and physically run down in old school buildings, or unadorned and clinically clean in new buildings. Corridors had a strictly functional role of access and transfer.

England, where the compartmentalization of learning and the view that learning involves the whole person, is somewhere between the two extremes of Denmark and France, classrooms were sometimes adapted to pupils as people and sometimes to pupils as pupils. English tutor groups (class groups who remained together for non-key subjects) were associated with a tutor room (the subject classroom of their tutor). This room acted as the English pupils' homebase, where they would gather twice a day and to which they often had access during school breaks. Although adapted to the tutor's subject teaching, and thus containing both teacher and pupil wall displays from other classes, there was often a section of wall display given over to notices for the tutor group. Corridors and entrance halls continued the display of pupil learning and pupil achievement beyond the classroom. Seating arrangements in English classrooms were sometimes planned around large rectangular tables with some pupils not facing the front of the classroom.

English and Danish classrooms tended to be better resourced than French classrooms. There was a greater provision of computers in Denmark and England and music was better resourced in England than in France. This was reflected in national differences in pupil response, which placed a greater value on learning resources in the Danish and English context than in the French.

English and Danish educational values about individualism and empiricism were reflected in the classroom interiors which took into account the significance of pupils as 'whole persons'. In contrast, French classroom interiors were more related to values of intellectualism. The strictly utilitarian classrooms showed the importance of cognitive learning.

Approaches to pedagogy and pupil groupings

While whole class teaching occurred in all three countries there were important qualitative differences to be found. Whole class teaching did not have the same meaning in the three countries. Danish and English teachers tended to deal with the class as a group of individuals while French teachers were more likely to treat the class as though it were one person. The excerpts from three maths lessons at the beginning of the chapter show first how the French mathematics teacher sought to use Chantal and Isabelle as vehicles for the class to work altogether as a class through a mathematics problem. Chantal went to the board and demonstrated the next step in the maths operation. The whole class was expected to participate in the thinking process with her in much the same way that professional musicians make use of an individual music student to demonstrate a particular point in a master class. Second, the French class was heard to chorus replies as though it was one person. However, Danish and English classrooms showed more instances of teachers working with individuals. For example, the English mathematics teacher respected a pupil's decision not to participate and the Danish mathematics teacher encouraged individual suggestions and likes and dislikes. It was also common for English teachers to work with individual pupils in a private and not public sphere within the whole class teaching context. Even if the teacher dialogue was audible it was clear that the class was not expected to listen, it was a private teaching moment, albeit in a whole class teaching context.

Group work was common in Danish and English classrooms, but rarely observed in French classrooms and this was generally supported by pupils' perceptions of pedagogy and pupil groupings. In English classrooms group work was particularly common in music, drama and personal and social education. English teachers taught pupils group working skills by allowing them to form their own groups and by encouraging them to listen to each other and allocate tasks within the group, 'If you're working as a team, one can grease the tins while the other uses the mixer' (food technology teacher, Lady Margaret School). Some English pupils had internalized group working skills as can be seen in the following case study of a music lesson at Westway, which also demonstrates the degree of pupil autonomy, pupil–teacher relationships, assessment and the importance of practical learning in English education:

Excerpt from a music lesson, England

Music room is modern and well equipped. It has small practice rooms with keyboards and recording facilities giving off it. Written above the entrance to one of the practice rooms, 'The cooler or padded cell – for problem pupils'. A notice above the blackboard lists the sanctions used in the Expressive Arts: detention, extended detention, curriculum manager's detention, letter home. There are keyboards around two walls of the room, with chairs, and a selection of percussion instruments. The music teacher is young and casually dressed. He reminds the class of the topic, 'This is an important time . . . it's the last day of your music exam . . . I'll give you two thirds of the lesson to refresh your memories about your composition and get it up to standard. You've got to sort it out to get the best mark you possibly can.'

The teacher speaks fairly quietly and unassumingly. He tells the class he will give them the privacy of their own rooms to work in, 'In a minute you can go into the same rooms you were in yesterday . . . you can't choose the percussion instruments, I'll give them to you'. He reminds the class they have to compose a piece using only a pentatonic scale (he illustrates this with the black notes on a keyboard) and rhythm groups. Group by group pupils are directed to their practice rooms. While pupils organize themselves, the teacher deals with a boy who refuses to cooperate. The pupil is eventually removed from the lesson.

Five girls work together. One plays the base notes on the keyboard and provides the basic structure of the piece. Another girl plays the treble. Three girls are on different percussion instruments. The girls play their piece several times, offer suggestions and try to influence the rest of the group. The girl on base complains that one of the percussion instruments is too slow. The girl on the treble points out that she should be at the same beat as one of the other percussion girls (she uses the term 'speed'). They try the same piece again. It is much improved with two of the percussion girls playing in time. The piece starts off

Excerpt from a music lesson, England – continued

with a base motif. It is joined by one percussion instrument, the tune on the treble, and finally the two girls playing percussion on the same beat. The treble repeats the tune, this time in harmony of thirds. The piece winds down, getting softer, losing instruments and finishes how it started with the base on its own. It is difficult to understand the group dynamics. Sometimes without a noticeable signal the girls run through the piece again. The teacher moves from one room to another, listening, giving advice and generally sorting out problems. The three percussion girls use their own notation to write down the rhythm. Girl 2 pauses before writing, and comments to Girl 1, 'You're the same as me.'

Girl 1	X	X		X
Girl 2	X	X		X
Girl 3	X	X	X	X

Later on the teacher returns to the girls' group and they perform their piece to him while he assesses it. Pupils coming in seeking the teacher are motioned away. The girls achieve the top assessment mark and are clearly delighted. One girl is heard to say, 'I'm happy now'.

Group work was observed in Danish classrooms and pupils were clearly accustomed to, and skilled at, working in groups. An important educational objective for Danish teachers is that pupils should learn to work together. Many Danish lessons followed the same model seen in English classrooms of pupils working and discussing ideas in groups prior to a class presentation of their ideas. For example this biology lesson at the Province school:

Excerpt from a biology lesson, Denmark

The theme of the lesson is ethical issues: is it a human right to have handicapped children? The class is asked to return to the groups they were working in before. Some pupils are not sure about who they were working with. The teacher assigns to groups those who cannot remember.

There is some noise and movement. The class is quickly calmed down by the teacher, 'Jacob, I'm quite aware that you are not listening to what I am saying'. To another pupil, 'Morten, go and get the book you were using, what you're doing now is disturbing everyone.'

A pupil takes the lead in one of the groups, 'Shouldn't we concentrate on the questions?' The groups discuss the issues and make use of a textbook (*Into Life . . . Ethics for Young People*). Some pupils take notes.

The teacher interrupts the group work with questions, 'What is a good life?' Pupils voice their opinions. The teacher personally addresses some of the quieter pupils, 'What is your opinion?', 'What would you say?'

One of the members of a group presents their views to the class.

Danish pupils' group working skills included peer assessment. In an observed Danish lesson Danish pupil groups creating text with computers were asked to exchange disks for peer evaluation by another group. Criticisms were noted in a window pupils created next to the original text. A pupil who was asked about the value of this activity replied in English, 'Constructive criticism is good, it helps us to get on.'

Paired work, although common in England and Denmark, was positively discouraged in the French classroom. On some occasions in England paired work arose as a necessity due to an insufficiency in the number of textbooks. In Denmark pair work was so favourably regarded that some teachers expressed a wish to see national assessments carried out on pairs of pupils on the basis that this was closer to the realities of adult working life.

The degree to which teachers in the three countries used whole class, group and paired pupil teaching strategies brought out deeper cultural differences. The teachers' approach to whole class teaching in England and Denmark suggested that individualism (in the sense of teachers seeing pupils as individuals) was more highly valued in England and Denmark than it was in France. The Danish approach to group work and the French approach to whole class teaching suggested that collective learning was more highly valued in Denmark and France than it was in England.

Teacher control

Earlier in the chapter we argued that teachers in England and Denmark played a more significant role in school management than did teachers in France. We also showed that the responsibilities of teachers in England and Denmark extended beyond the school boundaries. However, it was teachers in France who exerted the most control over pupils in the classroom. In the classroom French teacher control extended from the pace of learning to pupil posture (French pupils were often reminded to sit up straight) and pupils' physical mobility. French pupils were not expected to leave their seats during a lesson unless specifically asked to do so. As a French music teacher reminded her pupils: 'No, no, you're not allowed to go for a walk to the waste paper basket'. For French pupils silence in class was the norm but interviewed pupils occasionally mentioned individual teachers who might allow pupils to whisper to each other in their classes. In Danish and English classrooms there was more occasion for noise, with higher levels of group working. However, the small group sizes in Danish schools tended to keep noise levels lower and it was pupils in England who referred to noise levels as a distraction which could make concentration difficult.

Danish and English teachers exerted less control over pupils' movements in and out of the classroom and Danish pupils were observed to leave classrooms without referring to the teacher. There was also less control in Danish and English classrooms over pupil posture. Neither a Danish pupil with his feet on a table during a lesson nor a Danish pupil wearing roller blades in class provoked teacher comment. There also appeared to be less control over pupil behaviour and noise levels. English pupils were observed applying make-up, throwing books and whistling during lessons. In England tutor period was the class time in which the least teacher control was apparent. These were often used to encourage social interaction, 'We're all talking, everyone just laughing and messing about. Well, not like, being bad or anything, they're just talking while Sir's like taking the register. We have about 15 minutes of talking before the bell goes' (boy pupil, Westway). However, both English and Danish teachers exerted strong control over pupils in the classroom when the learning objectives required it, 'Most of the time people are chatting, but in something like history, geography or French, you've usually got to be qui*et al.*l the time' (girl pupil, St Theresa's). English and Danish teachers were prepared to vary their approach and give pupils more autonomy according to the learning task of the lesson rather the French approach of applying strong control according to place (at all times in the classroom but rarely outside of the classroom where non-teaching staff were responsible).

Through the medium of control over pupil dress and appearance, English teacher control extended in terms of place, not only beyond the classroom and into the school site but also beyond the school and into the community, and in terms of focus it extended beyond the pupils' learning to the whole child. On the other hand, pupil dress and appearance aroused little teacher interest in France and Denmark, French and Danish teachers seemed more interested in what was *in* their pupils' heads and not what was *on* their pupils' heads. A Danish pupil was observed during a science lesson, wearing a cap back to front at a provocative angle. The teacher, when questioned by researchers, did not see this as an issue. A French girl was seen in school with her hair dyed bright red. When questioned, her subject teachers and her *professeur principal* were not concerned, first because it was not their responsibility but that of the *conseillère d'education* (head of *la vie scolaire)* and second because it was a non-issue. However, in England, pupil dress and appearance seemed to threaten both teacher and school discipline. This was because control over pupil dress and appearance in England was indirectly linked to pupil learning through the emphasis given to school identity. 'Smartness' affected a school's reputation, which in turn affected pupil intake, and ultimately the pupils' performance in learning. As pupils were told at a school assembly, 'You have to be tidy and a credit to the school. Shirts must be tucked in. It looks scruffy if you have your shirt tails hanging around your knees . . . It is for your benefit that the reputation of the school is high' (head of Year 9, Lady Margaret School). It was thus at Lady Margaret School, the English school that fostered the most academic image, that the dress code was the most severe. Dress rules permeated all lessons. Part of Lady Margaret School's teachers' class routine at the start and end of all classes was to check pupils' uniforms. A teacher was observed to enter a tutor period ordering a pupil to, 'Tuck your shirts in properly please'. This discourse included sports clothes. A sports teacher monitored each girl leaving the changing room, 'Sandra, tuck your shirt in', 'Anna, tuck your shirt in'. The pupil strategy to avoid detection was to fold the shirt under so that it gave some appearance of being tucked in.

Thus, in the classroom, French teachers were more authoritarian than English or Danish teachers. In both Denmark and England there were underlying values of empiricism in learning, allowing pupils more autonomy and opportunities to find out for themselves, and underlying values of individualism, acceptance that pupils were individuals and behaved differently, without necessarily challenging the teacher's authority. However, unlike England, where teacher control extended beyond the classroom over the whole child, Danish and French teacher control was more directly concerned with learning. This was linked to underlying values of intellectualism in Denmark and France.

Pupil autonomy in the classroom

As was suggested earlier, Danish pupils had more say in school management and decision making than English or French pupils. Futhermore, the corollary of strong teacher control in the classroom is weak pupil autonomy. Thus pupil autonomy was at its weakest in France, where teacher control was particularly strong, and at its strongest in Denmark. This generalization holds true despite individual teacher variation within each country and variation according to curriculum subject. Thus French classrooms were characterized by lack of pupil consultation, pupil opinion or pupil choice. The following case study of a music lesson at Cathédrale illustrates the lack of French pupil autonomy, as well as providing an insightful comparison with the English classroom context of a music lesson described earlier:

Excerpt from a music lesson, France

The topic is, 'Learning a new note on the recorder: B flat'. The music room resembles an ordinary class with the exception that it has posters on the wall depicting the composition of a symphony orchestra and there is a record player at the front. The pupils sit in tables facing the front.

The teacher shows the pupils how to produce a B flat on the recorder. They play several together at approximately the same time. Each pupil has a piece of music in standard notation. The teacher checks they know the meaning of some musical terms. The teacher asks, 'What does *coda* mean?' A pupil replies, 'We go back to the beginning'. The teacher checks they can read the music. As a class

Excerpt from a music lesson, France – continued

they read out the notes, 'La, si, la, la, mi . . .' The class plays the tune while the teacher sings out the names of the notes. The piece is played again this time with a taped orchestral accompaniment, complete with seagulls. It is quite a stirring little number with a catchy tune. During the course of the lesson the teacher has to ask pupils not to move their feet about in time with the music as the vibrations make the record player jump. Some pupils ignore the directive. The teacher points out that some pupils have forgotten how to play a B flat. The class practices B flats together again.

The teacher asks the pupils to look at the notation, 'Who knows what that's called on top of that note?' Pupils hands go up. Teacher reprimands a pupil for calling out an answer, 'There's no good in speaking without putting your hand up first'. The teacher selects a pupil and she repeats his correct answer, 'It's called a pause . . . it means you don't go straight on'. She asks them to write down the term and its definition in their exercise books.

French pupils were allowed considerably more autonomy in foreign language lessons. Inspectoral directives to place more emphasis on communication in foreign language lessons had resulted in pupils being able to make more spontaneous contributions and express their opinions more freely. Furthermore there were opportunities for pupil discussion as demonstrated by this excerpt from an observation of an English lesson in one of the French schools:

Excerpt from an English lesson, France

A text is introduced concerning the assassination of John Lennon: Jean, who often makes contributions in English (complete with errors) says without elicitation, 'I cried when John Lennon was *assasiné*'. The teacher corrects the past participle. Jean's contribution sparks off a conversation on the lines of, 'When were you born?' This in turn leads to a discussion in both French and English about the difference in tense between the two languages in the previous English sentence. One boy thought that in French the past tense was used if you were talking about a dead person's date of birth. This causes some merriment and provides a moment of relaxation. The teacher continues to use the John Lennon passage and asks pupils, 'Write down where the preterite is linked to tense and time markers'. Some pupils seem to have forgotten the meaning of a 'tense and time markers'. Jean obligingly contributes with a little song, 'Yesterday, when all my troubles were . . .' The teacher is distracted by Mark who is murmuring to a neighbour, 'Mark, you know what I'm going to have to do at the end of this lesson . . . concentrate'. One of the pupils is heard to say, 'God this is a pain'. Fortunately the teacher does not hear.

The relative invisibility of teacher control in Danish classrooms is linked to assumptions about strong pupil autonomy. Examples of pupil autonomy were pupils clearing away science equipment without teacher instruction and leaving the classroom only when this task had been completed after the bell had rung; and pupils continuing with their work during a teacher's 20 minute absence from the classroom. Pupil autonomy in Denmark was linked to Danish values of education: that learning is a social act with individuals sharing their thoughts. In a biology lesson on heredity, the teacher's stated objective was not only that pupils should learn about genetics but that they should practice making up their own minds, that they should learn to develop their own opinions and learn to distinguish between personal opinions and generalizations. Danish pupils were also respected as individuals who had a right to have a say in their learning, and whose opinions were sought. In a Danish mathematics lesson pupils were asked to contribute to how they thought their learning could be improved. Furthermore, Danish pupils had more opportunities for making their own choices, choices over not only with whom to work and how to work, but what subject they could study, as this fieldnote excerpt demonstrates:

> After the break the teacher tells the class that she is going to have two more lessons with them this day because some of the teachers are attending a course. They can decide if they want to continue working on biology or to go on with their maths. The teacher does not require a decision to be made then and there. (The pupils later decided to have biology.)

Pupil autonomy in English classrooms was in between that of French and Danish classrooms. English pupils were sometimes able to choose with whom they wanted to work. They could choose whether or not to make an individual contribution (as in the example of a maths lesson at the beginning of this chapter). When working in groups (as in the example of the English music lesson) they were given considerable responsibility and control within the boundaries of the task they had been set. However, English pupil autonomy did not extend into major decision-making areas about working methods and timetabling.

Although pupil autonomy was less strong in England than in Denmark, its existence in both countries was linked to educational values about individualism and the importance given to the pupil voice. It was also connected to values of empiricism in learning in both countries; the idea that it is important to allow pupils a degree of autonomy in order to learn and find out for themselves.

Teacher–pupil relationships

The distance between teacher and pupils was at its greatest in France. There was more inequality between teacher and pupil status in France than in England or Denmark and more formality (pupils used the *vous* form to address teachers, teachers used *tu* to pupils). The non-involvement of teachers in France with the affective domain of children's learning led to a relationship which was mainly restricted to the intellectual development of pupils. Furthermore, interactions between French teachers and pupils were mainly restricted to the classroom context. The role of the French teacher prioritizes subject expertise and pedagogic skill at transferring knowledge to pupils. Knowledge equates with power in the French classroom. The assessment used, as will be demonstrated in the next section, helped to maintain distance and control.

The teacher–pupil relationship was at its least distant and unequal in Denmark where pupils addressed their teachers by their first names. This reflected the more extended relationship between teacher and pupils. The relationship was also extended over time as pupils could remain with the same teacher for nine or ten years. In comparison with the French context, the teacher–pupil relationship was based more on negotiation than dominance. Danish teachers treated their pupils were more respect. Interactions were more relaxed and flexible.

English teacher–pupil relationships had more in common with those in the Danish context than in the French. There was more negotiation between teacher and pupils rather than overt dominance, as demonstrated by this excerpt from a mathematics lessons at Lady Margaret:

> Maths teacher refuses to help individual pupils with their work unless they tuck their shirts in. Helen says she thinks it is unfair to get detentions for not having your shirt tucked in because it can come out by accident. She asks the teacher if his shirt ever comes un-tucked. There is a good humoured exchange. Helen relents and tucks in her shirt.
>
> (excerpt from a mathematics lesson, England)

As in Danish classrooms, there was a more easy going familiarity than could be found in French classrooms, as this fieldnote illustrates:

> Jane from another class comes to return a dustpan and brush, borrowed earlier by a boy. Teacher gives her a friendly greeting, addresses her by her name. Jane puts away the cleaning equipment and says to the teacher, 'I've just got to have a word with Susan'. Jane goes over to a group of girls and engages in animated chat. The teacher smiles.

> Jane finishes her conversation and says a cheery goodbye. The teacher responds in kind.
>
> (excerpt from a technology lesson, England)

English teachers were more flexible than French teachers. In the same way as English teacher control varied with the task, so did the degree of formality with pupils:

> The second stage of the lesson is in a completely different mode. Pupils move around equipping themselves with pencils, scissors, glue. They leave the room to seek more scissors in other classrooms. There is considerable noise as pupils chat to each other. Pupils work mostly in pairs. The teacher's role changes, as does her relationship with the pupils. The teacher perches on a bookshelf (there is very little room in the classroom). She talks to the two boys in front of her. There is so much noise in the room it is not possible to hear what they are talking about. It does not appear to be in German, nor about German. A girl hauls out a meat cutlet from her bag, to show her friends what she has brought in to cook in food technology. The teacher is slightly horrified and suggests she put it in a fridge as soon as possible so that she does not get food poisoning.
>
> (practical task in a German lesson following on from a formal task in grammar, Westway)

English teachers often tried to meet their pupils half way and take the pupil perspective into consideration. The teacher of mathematics in England introduced the lesson to the class with, 'It's stinking horrible simultaneous equations today', giving some attention to what learning was like from the pupils' point of view. The traditional distance between French teachers and pupils is related to French values of egalitarianism and intellectualism. In French education it is considered more egalitarian to disregard individual differences and the affective domain. Furthermore, intellectual development is valued in French education above personal development and personal relationships. English and Danish education give more emphasis to individualism and personal relationships.

Methods of assessment

Assessment played a more dominant role in French and English classrooms than in Danish classrooms. In French classrooms assessment was summative and delivered to individuals in a very public context. It was often severe by English and Danish standards. Furthermore, it was often negative. However, in the French context, where assessment is restricted to the academic aspects of the pupil role and not aimed at the whole person, negative assessment could motivate pupils. The negative aspect of French assessment reinforced teacher dominance and control and the distance between teacher and pupils:

Excerpt from a music lesson, France

Known as an *interrogation* (oral assessment) each pupil has to play the same tune in turn on their recorders accompanied by the teacher on the keyboard. The rest of the class listen and occasionally make comments. A boy plays. He has problems with the time of the piece. The class laughs. The teacher asks, 'How long does a dotted crochet last?' He makes no reply. She writes a mark down in her book.

A girl asks to be *interrogée*. She plays but makes an error and asks if she can start again. The teacher points out, 'You're losing marks doing that'. However, the girl starts again. She has difficulty getting the notes out but her fingers are in the correct position. The teacher make a tutt-tutting noise and asks the class what her problem is. A girl answers, 'She's blowing too hard'. The teacher makes no further comment to the girl whom she was assessing and writes down a mark.

Another girl plays. Her recorder is out of tune. Teacher sighs at the end but says nothing. She writes down a mark.

While the teacher chooses another pupil the class gets restless. The teacher restrains them, 'Watch out your marks are going to go down' (a threat that she will lower all the marks if they are disruptive). She uses the same tactic later with an individual pupil who is whispering, 'Mamadou, your marks are going to be affected too'.

With some pupils who are having real problems the teacher leaves the keyboard and stands closer to the pupil giving individual instruction. For example, with a boy at the back, she asks him to play 'si', then 'la' several times to get the notes right. The whole class watches. The teacher points out, 'You're not covering the holes enough . . . If you paid more attention in class . . .' She writes down a mark.

French assessment also often involved the manipulation of collective peer pressure in order to motivate individual pupils.

> When a boy is asked to take 9 away from 15, he gets it wrong. The teacher reprimands him for listening to what somebody else had said and not working it out for himself, 'You're repeating again what someone has just whispered to you, you're an idiot'. The boy gets flustered and tries another answer which is also incorrect. The class laughs. The teacher points out his error and then encourages him.
>
> (excerpt from a mathematics lesson, France)

Assessment was not so public or referenced to other pupils' attainment in Danish classrooms. Danish pupils were encouraged not to take formal summative assessment into consideration in their work:

> The class ask the teacher if they are to get back their exercises and if she has remembered to give them marks. To this she replies that it is not only the marks that are important, they must look at her comments, because they will tell them what was good and what could be done better. The class returns to the text. After ten minutes the issue of the marked exercise is returned to. The teacher tells them they will have to wait. The class is very anxious to get their marks. The teacher repeats how difficult it is to give marks and that marks will not really tell them how well they are doing.
>
> (excerpt from a biology lesson, Denmark)

English assessment was very varied. It was less criterion referenced than French assessment and less formative than the assessment observed in Danish classrooms. On the whole assessment in England and Denmark was related to values of individualism. English and Danish pupils were encouraged to set themselves individual targets that related more to individual performance. French assessment could be characterized as more summative and criterion referenced with the class playing a part in normative assessment too. French assessment was more related to values of collectivism and egalitarianism.

Definitions of learning

The strongest contrasts between the types of learning observed in classrooms were those between English and French classrooms. Learning in Denmark could be characterized as containing elements that were associated with both England and France. Learning was more compartmentalized in French classrooms. It was often decontextualized from day to day experience. Texts were often used without contextual settings. Learning was often carried out through an impersonal and distant teacher–pupil relationship. The cognitive domain of rational thought was often emphasized:

> Teacher asks the pupils, 'Where is the marker of the preterite? . . . in the verb ending? . . . in the radical?' Pupils respond, 'It's in "did" '. The teacher agrees, 'That's right the auxiliary verb carries the preterite.' The pupils are asked to write this down using the notation of *øV* 'zero verb' to indicate that the main verb has not changed.
>
> (excerpt from a structural analysis of English past tense sentences, France)

This illustrates the high expectations which teachers in France had of their pupils' intellectual skills and knowledge, making utterances such as, 'The preterite is in the negative form, the verb is zero and the verb is regular'. Learning in English classrooms was less directly cognitive. Practical activities and learning through empiricism were often given more dominance. Comparisons of music lessons in the two countries provided the most contrast between the two national approaches. French teachers of music used a more cognitive and knowledge-based approach, pupils learning musical techniques and music theory, whereas English teachers requiring pupils to compose music, make music and develop non-standard methods of music notation. The teaching of foreign languages also makes interesting comparisons because of the assumptions that English and French teachers made about pupil learning. Cognitive elements were reduced to a minimum in the teaching of foreign languages in English classrooms. Teachers avoided structural linguistic terminology. Pupils were reminded that 'verbs' were 'doing words' and the term 'preposition' was often completely avoided and referred to as a 'little word'. Language use came first, structural understanding came second. Pupils were encouraged to discover grammatical rules for themselves. A warm teacher–pupil relationship was also considered to have an important role in the learning process in England:

Excerpt from a top set German lesson, England

Teacher: 'We're going to look at something very important in German'. She makes small 'Shh' noises from time to time to control the class and get everyone's attention. She elicits four sentences from the class, asking, for example, 'What is "I do my homework"?' She writes them on the board, 'Where's the verb in this sentence? Where's the doing word?' A pupil says, '*Mache*'. The teacher praises him and she underlines the verb in the sentence on the board – *Ich* mache *meine Heimaufgaben*. She then asks, 'Whereabouts is it in the sentence, where's its place?' Another pupil replies, 'It's second'.

She moves on to another sentence on the board, '*Um zehn Uhr gehe ich ins Bett*' and points out that although the verb is the third word it is the second element as *um zehn Uhr* is one idea. She explains, 'In your books you've written, "*Ich gehe ins Bett*" where the verb was the second element. Now we have to swap the words round to get the verb in second position'. She explains that this does not happen in French.

Pupils are attending and participating. The teacher gives them another example. 'If I gave you another sentence, "*Ich esse mein Mittagessen um zwei Uhr*", what does that mean? . . . David?' David replies, 'I eat my lunch at 2:00'. She continues, 'Right, we'll all do it together . . . What's at 2:00? . . . Neesha?' Neesha gives the answer, '*Um zwei Uhr*'. 'Good', says the teacher, 'Four words

Excerpt from a top set German lesson, England – continued

left . . . Which comes next? . . . Ruth?' Ruth replies '*Esse*'. The teacher praises her and writes up, '*Um zwei Uhr esse ich mein Mittagessen*'. 'Okay?' she asks the class. The pupils nod their heads.

The teacher moves on quickly to the second learning objective of her lesson. She says, 'That's the main thing . . . there's one more thing'. She points out a sentence on the board, '*Ich stehe um sieben Uhr auf*' and asks the class, 'What's happened here?' She gives praise and repeats a pupil's response, 'Good, we've split it up . . . All these little words like "*auf*" need to go at the end'. She elicits more phrases from pupils that they already know, to give more examples of the pattern.

This short instructive and cognitive phase where the whole class worked together and pupils appeared to be concentrating and participating was followed by a longer stage of pupils carrying out a practical activity to practise what they had learnt. They were given a sheet of words and groups of words from *Zigzack Neu* (Rogers, Briggs and Goodman-Stephens (1993) 1: 27, published by Thomas Nelson & Sons:

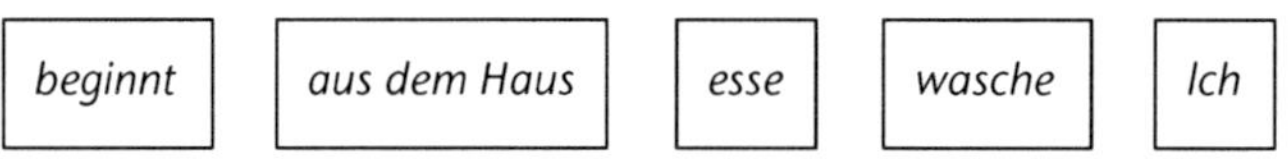

The class had to cut out these words and stick them down into their exercise books to make correct German sentences. Before doing so the teacher gave the pupils more help. She asked them to identify all the verbs on the sheet and underline them. She then read them all out to check that everyone had done so correctly and repeated the main point of the lesson, 'Each of your sentences has got to have one of those words in it and they must be the second idea'.

In Danish classrooms there was less evidence of compartmentalization than in the other two national contexts and cross-curricular teaching was common as teachers usually taught several subjects. An illustration of this is a biology lesson which was observed at the Province school where the teacher related the ethical issue of handicapped babies to chromosomes, heredity and the environment. However, in between she also integrated some maths and had discussions about spellings.

As in England, learning through empiricism was valued in Danish classrooms. Danish pupils in a biology lesson on respiration at the Periphery school were observed measuring their pulse rate before and after running. Discussion work was also frequent. However, Danish teachers resembled French teachers in the high expectations which they had of their pupils. A Danish teacher of Danish was observed to keep up an oral question and answer session based on a literary text with individuals in the public sphere for forty minutes without changing the activity. As in French learning there was a strong reliance on the study of texts and strong emphasis on cognitive skills and retention of knowledge (Laursen 1999).

Thus there were parallels between learning in England and Denmark. There was a strong practical component in the two countries which was related to values of empiricism. This was combined with an informal teacher–pupil relationship which was associated with values of individualism. Despite differences between France and Denmark, with learning in France often taking place in a context of a distant pupil–teacher relationship, often compartmentalized and with teacher instruction playing a more dominant role, there were also parallels between French and Danish learning. An important element of learning in both France and Denmark was the emphasis given to intellectualism and knowledge. Educational values of intellectualism in France and Denmark underlay this common approach to learning.

The role of adolescent culture

There was a difference in the three countries in the degree to which adolescent or youth culture was considered to be related to learning and was accepted in the classroom or school context. In France and Denmark youth culture was allowed in schools when it was seen to be unrelated to learning, for example, where it took the form of different styles of dress and appearance. However, where adolescent culture might be related to learning, it was not taken into account by the school. Thus art work in Danish classrooms and corridors reflected the national heritage culture and not adolescent culture, and literary texts studied in Denmark and France were more likely to be taken from the national or western cultural heritage.

By contrast the attitude to adolescent culture in England was more complex. Adolescent culture in the form of dress and appearance was perceived to have an indirect and negative effect on learning in the English context of strong school identity. English pupils could not display adolescent culture in their dress and appearance. However, other expressions of youth culture, such as literature and music, were seen as related to pupil learning and were acceptable. Thus popular youth culture dominated English pupils' compositions in music, and in a Westway music lesson the teacher played a recent Number One hit on the keyboard to illustrate types of musical sequences. English teachers used adolescent culture to motivate and involve pupils in learning.

The French and Danish teachers' use of national heritage culture is a reflection of egalitarian values in French and Danish education, the notion that all pupils have an equal right of access to the culture of their country. The inclusion of adolescent culture might be seen to discriminate between pupils and deny those from more disadvantaged homes equal access to the national heritage. The multicultural discourse of English education is thus more open to certain forms of adolescent culture.

Summary

In this chapter, which completes the contextual setting underlying pupil experience, important differences were found in English, French and Danish classroom contexts. Once again educational terms, such as 'class', 'classroom', 'pedagogy', 'teacher', 'pupil', 'assessment' and 'learning' varied in their significance in the three national contexts. Such differences are summarized in Table 6.1.

As Alexander (2000) has pointed out, differences in classroom contexts can also be shown to relate to differences in national education values. Denmark and France shared values of egalitarianism, collectivism and intellectualism. Danish and French values concerning egalitarianism and equal entitlement underpinned the lack of selection and the stronger heterogeneity in the Danish and French concept of the 'class'. The exclusion of adolescent culture from French and Danish classrooms, where it was perceived to be related to pupil learning, was also underpinned by values concerning egalitarianism and equal entitlement. However, egalitarian values were stronger in France with the more distant teacher–pupil relationship and the limitation of the relationship to the academic domain. Danish and French values about the importance of the collective underlay the importance given to the structural continuity of the class group as well as the French concept of whole class teaching where the class functions as one. Conversely, Danish values about the importance of the collective were seen in the importance given in Denmark to learning through group work. Danish and French values about intellectualism underpinned the cognitive and knowledge-based approach to learning. Both Danish and French teacher control was more concerned with intellectual rigour than pupil dress and appearance. However, intellectualism was stronger in French classrooms, whose very design reflected the importance of a cognitive and abstract approach to learning with distractions kept to a minimum.

England and Denmark shared values concerning the importance of the individual, though this included a communitarian dimension in the Danish context. Individualism underpinned pupil autonomy, teacher organization of pupils, classroom interiors, assessment, learning styles and teacher–pupil relationships. Although pupil autonomy was stronger in Denmark than in England, both countries shared values about the importance of the pupil voice and individual opinion. In the teacher organization of pupils, both Danish and English teachers' whole class teaching included a more individualized approach. The Danish classroom context also valued long-term class continuity as a key requirement for individual pupil well-being and learning.

Table 6.1 Differences in classroom contexts

	ENGLAND	*FRANCE*	*DENMARK*
The 'class'	Structural discontinuity; Homogenous, strong opportunities for social networking	Structural continuity; Some homogeneity and some social networking	Structural continuity; Heterogeneity, limited social networking
Classroom interiors	Reflect some compartmentalization; Pupils seen as pupils and 'whole persons'	Reflect strong compartmentalization; Pupils seen as pupils	Reflect weak compartmentalization; Pupils seen as 'whole persons'
Pedagogy and pupil groups	Whole class and individual; Some group and pair work	Whole class and collective; Rare group or pair work	Whole class, individual and collective; Strong group and pair work
Teacher control	Varied with task; Direct and indirect role with learning; Extended	Strong; Direct role with learning	Varied with task; Direct role with learning
Pupil autonomy in the classroom	Varied with task	Weak	Strong
Teacher–pupil relationships	Varied with task; Extended pupil role	Formal; Restricted pupil role	Informal; Extended pupil role
Assessment	Summative and formative; Frequent, often positive	Summative, criterion referenced; Frequent, often negative	Formative, informal; Frequent
Definition of learning	Empirical	Cognitive and intellectual; Compartmentalized	Cognitive and empirical; Not compartmentalized
Adolescent culture	Some aspects associated with pupil learning	Acceptable when not associated with pupil learning	Acceptable when not associated with pupil learning

Classroom interiors in Denmark expressed a concern for the individual, for the pupil as a person. Danish assessment in particular, with its emphasis on formative assessment emphasized individualism. Learning styles in England and Denmark were related to teacher–pupil relationships and gave more weight to individual pupil differences. The teacher–pupil relationship in the two countries, but particularly in Denmark, was less distant, more informal, more equal in status, more personal and more individualized. This was highlighted by the use of first names for both pupils and teachers. Denmark and England also shared a concept of learning that was based on empiricism and the need for experiential learning which was relevant to pupils' lives. There was less teacher control, allowing pupils more opportunities to be autonomous and find out for themselves. In both countries classroom interiors were also designed to stimulate pupils.

The Table 6.2 presents the underlying values that have been distilled from the classroom contexts of each country:

Table 6.2 Differing national educational values

ENGLAND	*FRANCE*	*DENMARK*
–	Egalitarianism	Egalitarianism
–	Collectivism	Collectivism
Individualism	–	Individualism
–	Intellectualism	Intellectualism
Empiricism	–	Empiricism

When the three countries are compared in terms of the values that underlie the classroom contexts it can be seen that there is some overlap between France and Denmark, and England and Denmark. Individualism and collectivism, and empiricism and intellectualism, values which had appeared as opposing pairs in the comparative contexts of England and France in other studies (Broadfoot *et al.* 2000) have been shown to exist side by side in Danish culture.

Part 3 which follows discusses pupil experience and pupil perceptions in the light of the cultural context and educational values we have outlined in Part 2.

PART 3
Pupil Experience and the Development of Learner Identity

7 Constants and contexts in pupil experience: young learners' views of schooling, teaching and learning

Introduction

This third section of the book moves to examine the views of the young learners themselves and to emphasize the significance of a more holistic understanding of the cultural context in which motivation and learning are situated. By giving a voice to young learners in early secondary education it also moves to highlight the differences between the intended consequences of education policy, the implemented policy and the experienced consequences of the policy, between the intentions of policymakers and teachers (as highlighted in Part 2 of the book) and what pupils actually experience in the classroom. This part of the book draws upon data from questionnaires, and individual and group interviews with pupils. First, in Chapter 7, we examine the perspectives of the 12–14-year-old pupils in the three countries on the purposes of the schooling and on themselves as learners. Chapter 8 considers, through a series of in-depth learner profiles, how individual learners in the three countries constructed an identity as learners and adolescents, and how they negotiated pathways that lead to success or relative lack of success on the dimensions of academic achievement, peer status and social conformity. In Chapter 9 we consider the influence of important intra-national factors in the three countries, particularly those deriving from differences in socio-economic status, gender and ethnicity. We pose the question of how and what we can understand from these issues about the extent to which young peoples' experience of secondary education may be becoming more similar or moving towards convergence in the context of Europeanization, globalization and the internationalization of adolescent/peer culture.

International differences in pupil experience

In this chapter, then we focus particularly on young peoples' perceptions of their schooling, of their teachers, and of learning, comparing and contrasting pupil experience in the three countries and posing questions about the universality and specificity of pupil experience within different national contexts. Our previous studies (see Chapter 1) had led us to hypothesize that, although students in the three countries would be likely to share many concerns associated with their age and with global youth culture, they would also have very different attitudes to and expectations of themselves as learners, of their teachers and towards school. Thus the broad aim of the study was to explore the social reality of schooling for students and the relative significance of the factors that influence the development of learner identity in the three national settings.

In the questionnaire part of the study, when the 1800 pupils (600 in each country) were asked to agree or disagree with a set of statements about school, the impact of universal concerns with the economic function of education made itself felt very strongly (see Table 7.1). In spite of different national emphases on the link between school and the economy, almost all pupils perceived the economic function of school and its link to jobs as strongly important.

Table 7.1 My feelings about school (i): Here are some statements of what you might think about your school. Please show how much you agree or disagree by filling in the appropriate bubble

	Strongly agree/agree (%)		
	Denmark	*England*	*France*
1 On the whole I like my teachers	64	69	63
2 School gets in the way of my life	21	30	31
3 I enjoy school	67	54	56
4 I really enjoy most lessons	63	52	54
5 I want to do well at school	92	96	96
6 I feel as though I'm wasting my time at school	10	7	13
7 The best part of my life is the time I spend in school	11	17	18
8 I'd like to leave school as soon as I can	17	23	17
9 School is the first step on the way to my career	85	91	85
Totals	**n = 610**	**n = 577**	**n = 444**

Over 85 percent of children in all three countries saw school as 'the first step on the way to my career'. Roughly two-thirds in all three samples felt very positive 'on the whole' about their teachers. However, the Danish children emerged as the most positive overall in their feelings about school. They were the most likely to enjoy school and lessons and the least likely to want to leave school as soon as they could or to see school as getting in the way of their lives.

In the QUEST (Quality in Experiences of Schooling Trans-Nationally) study, in some respects the English children were the least enthusiastic about school. They enjoyed school and lessons the least and they were the most likely to say that they would like to leave school as soon as they could. However, the gap between English and French children in terms of positive and negative feelings towards schooling and teaching had narrowed compared with our findings at primary level (Osborn *et al.* 1998). French children felt equally as strongly as English children that school got in the way of their lives. In the earlier study of primary schools, French children had shown far more positive attitudes to learning, teaching, and schooling than their English counterparts. Now, at secondary school level, French secondary pupils who completed the current questionnaire and interviews were far more negative about their teachers and schools than their 10- and 11-year-old compatriots at primary level. This suggests that perhaps the transition to secondary school and entry into adolescence might have engendered a change in French children's relationship to school, just as it has been shown to do in England (Rudduck *et al.* 1995).

Difference in perceived functions of school

Table 7.2 shows pupils' responses to a series of statements about the functions of schooling. All pupils were broadly in agreement that one of the functions of school is to teach you to learn new things and to be aware of your own strengths and weaknesses. Their general agreement that school is also concerned with 'helping you get qualifications' reflected global concerns with the economic functions of education and its links to careers and the jobs market.

However, in many respects the differences between the responses of pupils reflected the differences in the aims of the national systems discussed earlier. There was a stronger emphasis placed on the personal development function of school by pupils in England. Of English pupils, 58 percent felt that school teaches you to understand other people's feelings compared with 44 percent of French pupils and 33 percent of Danish. By contrast, in Denmark the national emphasis is more on democratic discussion leading to consensus and on encouraging pupils to fit in with the group (Kryger and Reisby 1998). Perhaps this is why fewer Danish pupils (45 percent) felt that school is a place where you learn to obey rules. The findings suggest that group norms are more

Table 7.2 My feelings about school (ii): Here are some statements of what you might think of school in general. Please show how much you agree or disagree by filling in the appropriate bubble

	Strongly agree/agree (%)		
	Denmark	*England*	*France*
1 School teaches you to understand other people's feelings	33	58	42
2 An important thing about school is meeting up with your friends	66	79	86
3 School helps you to sort out your life	65	67	58
4 School helps you to become mature	57	76	75
5 School is boring	36	36	27
6 An important thing about school is learning to cooperate with others	91	84	78
7 School is all about getting jobs when you leave	75	70	84
8 An important thing about school is that it helps you to get qualifications	80	95	75
9 An important thing about school is learning new things	94	95	97
10 School makes you aware of your own strengths and weaknesses	78	79	86
11 School is a place where you learn to obey rules	45	78	80
12 School is a place where you can express your own ideas and opinions	59	73	48
13 School is a place where it is difficult to succeed	25	20	43
Totals	**n = 610**	**n = 577**	**n = 444**

internalized in Denmark so that there is no apparent need to simply obey an externally imposed disciplinary framework. For French pupils (79 percent) and English pupils (78 percent) however, school was seen as a place where there was a high premium on obedience to institutional rules.

The results of the questionnaire present a picture of secondary school as a hard and often difficult experience for French pupils. They saw school as a place where it is difficult to succeed (43 percent compared with 25 percent of Danish pupils and 20 percent of English), where rules are of paramount importance, and where there is little room for expressing your own ideas and opinions. The emphasis in England on individualism and on differentiation was reflected in English pupils' perception of school as a place where you can express your own ideas and opinions (73 percent) but, as for French pupils, this was less important for the Danish (59 percent), possibly for the reasons cited above, the emphasis on collectivism and consensus reflected in the national goals of the system. The social function of school as a place where it is possible to socialize and meet your friends was clearly more important for English (79 percent) and French (86 percent) young people than for the Danish (66 percent).

In Tables 7.3 and 7.4 the pupils in the three systems were asked to respond to a series of statements about teachers by indicating the extent to which this applied to 'most of your teachers/many teachers/only a few teachers/hardly any teachers'. Danish pupils were the most likely to see most or many of their teachers as helpful with problems and worries, building friendly relationships and building self-esteem. Danish teachers seemed to avoid suggesting that pupils were not good enough in their work. Danish pupils also saw many of

Table 7.3 Teachers (i): Please read the statements below about teachers and mark a bubble in each row to show whether you think this applies to: most of your teachers/many of your teachers/only a few of your teachers/hardly any of your teachers

	Most/many teachers (%)		
	Denmark	*England*	*France*
I believe teachers:			
1 Are there to help pupils pass exams	75	71	65
2 Are there to help pupils learn	92	92	84
3 Aren't really interested in pupils as people	33	24	57
4 Make all the decisions about what happens in lessons	71	79	72
5 Give challenging work	66	74	64
6 Really want their pupils to do well	85	79	74
7 Live in a different world from their pupils	49	35	40
8 Encourage pupils to say what they think in class	62	65	47
9 Will have a laugh with pupils	47	43	23
10 Make pupils want to work hard	49	73	39
11 Are understanding about pupils' problems and worries	54	45	34
12 Give pupils a say in how they learn	67	36	37
13 Are only interested in their own subject	46	51	51
14 Will be helpful if pupils go to them with a problem	71	64	37
Totals	**n = 610**	**n = 577**	**n = 444**

Table 7.4 Teachers (ii): Please read the statements below about teachers and mark a bubble in each row to show whether you think this applies to: most of your teachers/many of your teachers/only a few of your teachers/hardly any of your teachers

	Most/many teachers (%)		
	Denmark	*England*	*France*
I believe teachers:			
1 Make pupils feel they aren't good enough in their work	24	25	58
2 Are a good example for their pupils	52	57	53
3 Are interested in pupils' opinions	68	61	42
4 Treat all pupils equally	50	53	48
5 Are more interested in pupils who can do well	43	48	57
6 Show what they really think and feel	30	43	29
7 Are interested in building friendly relationships with their pupils	71	45	49
8 Are respected by pupils	54	52	47
9 Make pupils feel they can be successful	72	67	59
10 Like and enjoy their job	69	61	65
11 Provide good guidance about how you can improve your work	72	74	58
12 Trust pupils	63	48	35
13 Do not listen to pupils	27	23	30
14 Try to make pupils get on well as a group	80	77	52
15 Spend too much time with pupils who need extra help	36	32	18
Totals	n = 610	n = 577	n = 444

their teachers as having trust in pupils. However, they did not feel that their teachers placed emphasis on making pupils want to work hard.

French responses once again emphasized a relatively difficult experience of school life. In the French pupils' view they had fewer teachers who built up their confidence and self-esteem or who were helpful with pupils' problems or worries. Fewer French teachers were interested in their pupils as people or in their opinions, fewer encouraged pupils to say what they thought in class or were willing to have a laugh with pupils. Nor were most French teachers seen as concerned with helping pupils to get on well as a group. Once again the findings reflect a national educational emphasis on the academic and cognitive functions of the educational system in France. In keeping with the more homogeneous grouping of French pupils and the existence of specialist professionals such as educational psychologists and counsellors, French teachers were less likely to be seen as spending too much time with pupils who need extra help.

However, the responses suggest that the French pupils were not particularly satisfied with the way in which teachers carried out their academic role. They saw themselves as having fewer teachers who provided good guidance about how you can improve your work, or who made them want to work hard. In contrast, in our previous study of primary pupils in England and France it was here in the academic and cognitive side of education that the strengths of French teaching seemed to emerge. At primary level, our sample of 800 French pupils saw their schools and teachers in a very positive light, emphasizing that their teacher was useful and helpful to them and was there to make them work hard (Osborn *et al.* 1998). Although the two samples of French children at primary and secondary level were different, both were from schools selected to be as representative as possible of a socio-economic, ethnic and geographical spread. Any conclusions drawn from this comparison must be tentative, but this certainly suggests that there may be a particularly strong fall in positive perceptions of schooling between the primary and secondary phases of schooling which should be of some concern to French educationalists. This fall does not appear to be connected to a greater prevalence of anti-school peer pressure. There is evidence from the current study that French pupils at secondary level experience less of this pressure from their peers than pupils in other countries. For example, French pupils were more likely to see doing good work as making them popular with their friends (27 percent) compared with 13 percent of English and 11 percent of Danish pupils.

In keeping with the English emphasis on affective education the English pupils were most likely to have teachers who encouraged pupils to say what they think in class and who were interested in pupils as people. Teachers in England were also seen as the most likely to show pupils 'what they really think and feel'. Interestingly English teachers also emerged as the most likely to make pupils want to work hard and to provide good guidance on how pupils could improve their work. In spite of all this English pupils apparently had more teachers who did not enjoy their job! This resonates with recent studies of teachers across Europe, which suggested that teachers in England perceived themselves as more stressed and disaffected than teachers in many other countries.

The findings suggest that within each country social inequality and gender issues may be mediated differently within the three education systems so that the impact of these factors on the way in which pupil views of themselves are structured may vary. These issues are discussed in detail in Chapter 9.

Key factors in pupil responses

When a factor analysis was carried out on some of the key attitude questions in the questionnaire the findings above were reflected even more strongly. In relation to pupils feelings about their own school life (Q.10, Appendix 1), English pupils' responses were grouped into only two factors, representing a 'pro-school' and an 'anti-school stance', whereas both Danish and French pupils' responses included a third factor, which we have called 'adult life orientation', suggesting that they saw a specific link between school and their future life as adults. However, these factors accounted for only 38 percent of the variance in England, whereas the three factors accounted for 52 percent in France and 53 percent in Denmark.

In relation to school in general (Q.10, Appendix 1), French pupils' responses displayed a more compartmentalized view of school life than did the English and Danish ones. French pupils were either 'instrumentalist' in their response to school (grouping together the instrumental function of school life such as getting a job and qualifications) or socially orientated (seeing school as helping you to understand other people's feelings, learning to cooperate, sort out your life or meet up with friends). English pupils were 'holistics', reflecting a more holistic and extended view of school life, grouping together both the instrumental and the social functions of school rather than separating them. Another factor reflecting a 'personal developmental' function of school also emerged for English pupils (seeing school as making you aware of your own strengths and weaknesses, helping you to understand feelings, learn to cooperate and to become mature). Danish responses also grouped in a more holistic and extended way like the English. Two other factors emerged for the French responses: a slightly blurred 'personal development' factor which included 'learning to obey rules', as well as 'becoming mature', 'learning to express your ideas and understand your strengths and weaknesses', and a 'negative orientation' to school factor, seeing school 'as a place where it is difficult to succeed' and 'boring'. This 'negativity' also emerged as a third factor in England. These factors accounted for 52 percent of the variance in France, 48 percent in England and 44 percent in Denmark.

In responses to two other questions about learning (Q.13, Appendix 1 and Q.19, Appendix 1), similar groupings emerged. French responses demonstrated an 'instrumental and lifelong learning' element, where the importance of 'going on learning in the future' was grouped with the importance of 'getting a good job', 'doing well', 'getting into a good class' and 'getting good marks'. English responses showed the importance of a 'personal fulfilment and personal relationship' element to learning, linking together 'liking' and 'being liked by the teacher', 'being known well by the teacher', 'being popular with friends', 'being happy at home' and 'happy at school', and 'liking to go on learning' and 'being interested in the subject'. Danish responses grouped together 'intrinsic interest' ('interested in subject', 'going on learning', 'enjoying subjects you are good at', 'doing well with subjects you are interested in'). Another important factor for the Danish students was the importance of being 'group collaborators' ('working with others', 'presenting results to others', 'learning a lot from discussions'). In all three countries the factors which emerged accounted for between 46 percent and 52 percent of the variance.

Strong similarities emerged between the three countries in relation to assessment (Q.27, Appendix 1). For all three, four clear factors emerged which grouped together responses relating to:

1 'the demotivating aspects of assessment' (for example, in France these were 'not caring about marks or grades', 'feeling like not trying any more after a bad marks', 'feeling that more guidance was needed about work')
2 'concern with the social and personal problems of assessment' (in France this group of responses included 'being embarrassed by wrong work' 'or when work is praised', 'worrying about getting work back' and 'not always agreeing with the mark')
3 'the positive role of formative assessment' (in France, 'seeing comments on your work as helping you to improve', 'working harder after a bad mark', 'getting feedback on how to get good marks')
4 'positive orientation to assessment' ('liking to get work back from teachers', 'liking to know one's marks', 'liking to know how well you are doing').

There was some internal variation in the groupings in the three countries, but broadly the same factors emerged in each, accounting for between 50 percent and 52 percent of the variance in each country. Not surprisingly, cluster analysis showed that lower achieving pupils were most likely to have emphasized the demotivating aspects of assessment, while higher achieving pupils were more likely to highlight the positive aspects of assessment.

One other question about home life, school life, friends and teachers (Q.30), showed important similarities and differences in the factors that emerged. In all three countries, a 'peer group pressure' factor emerged as an issue, grouping together responses such as 'sometimes feeling left out at school', 'friends sometimes making fun of me', 'classmates acceptance not being easy to get', 'doing well makes life difficult with your friends'.

A 'home/school separation' factor emerged in all three countries also, although perhaps the grouped responses reflected this more strongly in France than in the other two countries. (French responses which grouped together to form this factor were 'friends opinion is more important than teacher's', 'I am not myself at school', 'I am different in and out of school', 'I have different friends in and out of school', 'home and school are separate'. In England and Denmark, this factor included some of the same dimensions but fewer of them.)

Similarly, 'Fitting in with school life' emerged as an important factor for all three, reflecting a perception that a good deal of effort was required of pupils to fit in with teachers and with school life. However, an 'anti-school group sub-culture' factor and an 'alienation from school' factor emerged strongly for England and Denmark but not for France. (Anti-school group culture items were 'I don't care what teachers think', 'my friends like to fool around', 'my friends' opinions are more important than the teachers'). These factors accounted for between 46 percent and 50 percent of the variance in the three countries.

Concerns of European pupils

Thus the study found clear evidence of difference between the three countries in pupils' views of their learning, but also many common concerns. In both the questionnaires and the individual and group interviews certain universal issues which suggest enduring features of the teaching/learning situation emerged. This section draws upon the open-ended questionnaire responses and the individual and group pupil interviews in order to illuminate understanding of the relationship between social and cultural influences and cultural practices, and to explore how these might affect pupil behaviour and ultimately pupil learning. Using the pupils' own voices as far as possible, the key concerns of the pupils are considered under three headings: The teacher–pupil relationship; social identity; and pupils' perception of learning.

The teacher–pupil relationship

There were notable differences between pupils in the three countries in how they perceived the teacher–pupil relationship. Pupils in France expressed a strong perception of distance between teacher and pupil. There was a strong difference in status relating to a concept of adult (and particularly teachers as the fount of all knowledge) superiority and pupil inferiority. Adults were '*grands*' (teachers were particularly '*grands*' as their role was to form children), children and pupils were '*petits*': '*Des êtres incomplets, encore naturels, parfois dangereux, et qu'il convient de dresser*' ('Incomplete beings, sometimes natural, sometimes dangerous, who need training') (Dubet and Martuccelli 1996: 31). French pupils were very aware of their perceived inferiority:

> *Un prof c'est plus grand que nous, il nous apprend des trucs.* (Teachers are bigger (more important) than us, they teach us things.)

French pupils thought that teachers used their perceived superior status to maintain their distance from pupils:

> *Les professeurs, ils méprisent les élèves. Nous on est des enfants et ils ne considèrent pas vraiment ce qu'on dit. Ils disent que ça nous concerne pas.* (Teachers look down on pupils. We're children and they don't pay much attention to what we say. They say it's got nothing to do with us.)

Pupils used terms like '*esclaves*' (slaves), and '*robots*' (robots), to describe their role in relation to teachers. There was also a distance between French teacher and pupil in terms of time and social class. Both high and low achieving pupils from middle class and working class backgrounds of French and ethnic minority parentage thought that many teachers had not changed with the times and did not understand the needs of the new generation. They felt that teachers were out of touch with their lives:

> *Un professeur qui est dans les cinquante ans, c'est plus son temps. Lui quand il était jeune, les élèves ils étaient comme ça . . . mais évidemment c'est plus comme ça, ça a complètement changé'.* (A teacher who's in his fifties is out of step. When he was young children were like that . . . but obviously it's not like that anymore.)
>
> (High achieving girl from Paris)

> *C'est pas le même environment que quand eux ils ont grandi. Eux quand ils ont grandi on leur a toujours dit . . . mais nous on est livré à nous même, c'est dehors qu'on apprend. Il faut comprendre que nous on est jeune, on est d'une autre génération. Il faut qu'ils se renseignent sur ce qui se passe. Ils nous voient pas quand on est dehors ce qu'on subit.* (It's not the same world as when they grew up. When they were little they were always told what to do, but we bring ourselves up, we learn outside school. They have to understand that we're young and that we're from a different generation. They need to find out what's happening now.)
>
> (Low achieving boy in a Paris school who described himself as 'half Arab')

The distance between French teacher and pupil was traditional and institutionalized. English pupils were less conscious of the difference between teacher and pupil status. In some cases they acknowledged that there was an imbalance of power:

> Some teachers think they are higher than you.

and there was some awareness of time and social distance:

> They're still back in the seventies

> They have to realise there's drink and drugs . . . they don't want to believe that's going on, but it is.

But it was not an issue which overtly preoccupied them. Instead in most cases English pupils were more concerned with negotiating their own individual status with their teachers. Arguably this type of individual relationship held by pupil and teacher in England is likely to have a greater impact on the pupil's academic performance. The strength of individualization and differentiation in the English context of education made the teacher–pupil relationship more open to negotiation.

Danish pupils, like English pupils, referred to, but did not dwell on, the time distance between teacher and pupils. They were concerned that their teachers be relatively young and up to date. As one pupil expressed it they wanted 'modern teachers, fairly young teachers who have modern views on teaching and learning'. However, like English pupils, they were more concerned with their personal relationships with teachers which were independent of institutionalized norms. Relationships between teachers and pupils were again open to negotiation, and negotiation itself was institutionalized.

The concept of a teacher as a friend was particularly difficult for French pupils to comprehend. English pupils had less difficulty with the idea but were reluctant to identify teachers as 'friends' in any real sense: 'They're just teachers', 'Not someone you would go out with at weekends', 'When you're in trouble they can't forgive you; they've got to punish you'.

Danish pupils, although held back, in this respect like English and French pupils, by the concern that teachers should not be too friendly in case this led to interference with their private lives, did acknowledge in some cases that teachers could almost be friends: 'Not a real friend, but someone who knows something about you . . . with whom you feel good'.

An important 'constant' for pupils from all three countries which prevented them from regarding teachers as real friends and confiding in them, was their concern about their teachers' personal and professional ability to keep confidences.

Another significant 'constant' for English, French and Danish pupils was that there should be mutual respect between teachers and pupils before learning could take place. In talking about their teachers both quantitatively (responding to fixed response statements in the questionnaire) and qualitatively (responding to open-ended questions in the questionnaires and in individual interviews) English, French and Danish pupils all emphasized the same four qualities as of paramount importance. All children thought it most important to have teachers who respect their pupils, teachers who explain things well, teachers who give interesting lessons and teachers who are firm but above all fair.

A strong sense came from all the children's interviews that some teachers are far more prepared than others to spend time explaining things that have not been understood. However, it was particularly noticeable in France that children had strong concerns about teachers who were unwilling to give proper explanations. These were allied with the importance of teachers having 'respect' for pupils, which it was felt was often lacking. Florence, at a *collège* in a disadvantaged outer suburb of Paris, talked of the three things she disliked about school:

> The attitude of people, their behaviour. Pupils who don't respect teachers. Teachers who don't respect pupils. For example, at the end of the exercise, when we haven't understood. They don't explain properly what we have to do. There are some teachers who explain well, but there are others who, who don't really explain well.

Daniel, in the same school where most of the pupils were of ethnic minority, mainly North African origin, used similar concepts, 'There are teachers who respect us and there are those who don't respect us.' Those teachers with whom he was particularly out of sympathy were:

> Those [teachers] who are only interested in those who get good marks. Those [pupils] who don't get good marks, they just say that they only have to listen in class.

A Danish pupil, Mette, from Province school in the west of Denmark, also talked of some teachers who 'are better at explaining than others'. However, she felt that there were a significant number of teachers where, 'They try to kind of explain to everyone. If you don't understand it immediately then they explain it again, so . . .' If you got a wrong answer in class then 'the teacher will try to explain it and ask you to try again or something or maybe they'll pick someone else'. She felt that a good way of learning was:

> by getting it explained and getting some problems we can sit and work out while the teacher goes round, and then if you can't manage something, you get it explained again and then. But also – there are a lot of ways, like with a report or something – there are many possible ways of presenting it.

In the English context respect was not automatic for either party. Teachers could earn their pupils' respect by a combination of listening to pupils and giving them a voice. Pupils were more likely to gain respect from their teachers if they had a positive work attitude. English pupils in particular seemed to be caught by contradictory pressures: the need to negotiate a good working relationship with their teacher by earning their respect through their positive work orientation at the same time as the need to not be too positive towards their work for fear of losing their peers' support.

Social identity and class solidarity

An important cultural difference in how English, Danish and French pupils responded to their teachers and their schools' demands was in relation to the presence or absence of a sense of solidarity within the class. In the English context of classes with changing pupil composition, due to the relative use of banding, setting and streaming in the three schools, there was little evidence of classroom solidarity or even of solidarity with the school as a whole. Internal classroom social relationships were more pertinent to English pupils' sense of social identity. However, there were similarities between France and Denmark in the pupils' attitude to solidarity and commonality. In the Danish cultural context of consensus and where the school practice is for pupils to remain in the same class for key subjects over many years, pupils had a strong sense of commonality in their class, 'because that's where you spend most of your time'. The class was a collective unit: 'The class holds us together not the school'.

In the French cultural context of universalism and republicanism and where the school practice is for pupils to remain in the same class for nearly all subjects on a yearly basis, pupils seemed to use classroom solidarity as a positive strategy for mutual support:

> *La classe c'est un ensemble. C'est à nous de les aider, nous sommes un groupe.* (The class is a group. It's up to us to help them, we make up a group.)
>
> *Il faut se tenir la main pour que ça marche. Il faut se tenir à l'écoute, il faut s'entre aider.* (We've got to stand together to make things work. You've got to be ready to listen, you've got to help each other.)

Teachers were aware of pupil solidarity:

> *La classe c'est un groupe, c'est tout un groupe, ils font un bloc.* (The class is a group, one group, they're one entity.)

Occasionally solidarity seemed to be a contrived rather than reflecting reality:

> *Il n'y a pas de groupes [dans la classe], il n'y a qu'un seul groupe* (There aren't any separate groups we're all one group)

which suggests that French pupils were responding to the relatively harsh learning environment of the French context by presenting a face of solidarity; in accordance with the French saying, 'L'union fait la force' ('There's strength in unity'). Perhaps the strategy of solidarity and the pupils' exploitation of the institutional distance between French teacher and pupil enabled French pupils to protect themselves from entering into more individual relationships with teachers, which in the face of relatively high negative teacher assessment, might have had negative consequences on pupils' 'real' identities.

A concern which emerged more strongly for English pupils than for the other groups was the importance of having a secure and well developed social life in school. For Ann, a pupil in an inner city comprehensive, friendships originated, were developed and sustained by talk, chat and 'having a laugh'. Humour and having a laugh were an important aspect of lessons. While it was OK to work, it was not acceptable to simply keep one's head down and get on with one's work. The maintenance of her social relationships through 'humour' often took priority over work even lesson time:

> The main thing is to just have a laugh. Not just get on with work and not communicate with any body because we don't like that. It's all right to get on with work but not to not talk or not have a laugh.

She talked disparagingly of Jon, the class 'boffin':

> Jon the gnome. He's the class boffin. He's just the smartest in the class and he gets everything right. He's in all the top groups and he's just – agh! He's just clever. He just gets everything right and he's just good at everything. The only wrong thing with him is his handwriting. He doesn't chat or have a laugh. He just gets on with it.

Similarly, she particularly valued teachers who were able to have a laugh but at the same time get the children to work. Her assessment of and reaction to her teachers was subtle and sophisticated. One of her most liked teachers was Mrs Baxter. She recognized that:

> Mrs Baxter would like Jon because he's always trying his best, to the best of his ability. But Mrs Baxter's like, relaxed; likes a laugh and that. But she's serious, though. She'll make sure everyone works to the best of their ability.

In spite of other reservations about Mrs Baxter's criticisms of her, she still liked Mrs Baxter because 'she's just funny. She makes me laugh'.

In Ann's interview, and in the remarks of many other English secondary pupils, there were echoes of the findings of our earlier QUEST study carried out by three of the research team. In that comparison of pupils in the upper years of primary school in England and France we found that in England there was more evidence of the influence of peer group pressure in the classroom which made it not acceptable to pupils to be too successful in school. This led pupils not to want to be seen as a 'goodie', a 'keener' or a 'boffin' in class (Osborn *et al.* 1998). We argued that pupils' attitudes to school related to non-official criteria such as obtaining social approval and popularity with peers.

Measor and Woods (1984) and Pollard (1985) describe an 'informal' pupil culture in England which differs from the formal one and where the teacher's positive values of hard work and effort are translated by pupils into a negative one of being a 'boff', a 'goodie-goodie' or a 'keener'. In France, however, peer culture seemed to be less influential. Pupils adopted a strategic response to school which, at least superficially, resulted in an acceptance of school values. In part this may be a result of the separation of the person and the system, of personal and academic competences in French education (Dubet *et al.* 1996; Cousin 1998). Thus, in France, at both primary and secondary level, there is a strong distinction between '*la vie scolaire*' (the social domain) and '*l'instruction ou la pédagogie*' (the learning domain), with a different structure in place particularly within the secondary school to develop each. The English system ideologically does not make this strong distinction between learning and the social domain, conceptualizing learning in wider terms as embracing the 'whole child' rather than being restricted to teacher instruction in the classroom. This means that pupils are controlled with a stronger hidden message that, how one behaves, not only in the classroom, in the school and even outside school, affects learning. According to this view learning and behaviour are less easily separated, whereas in the French model they are seen as distinct. Thus, for example, in England an emphasis on strict rules connected with uniform or dress is perceived as linked to better exam results and the emphasis on a code of behaviour and discipline which extends even to outside the school gates. Possibly this stronger control over the 'whole person' in English education is related in a symbiotic way to the stronger influence of peer group pressure which we found in both our studies of primary and secondary schooling.

Attitudes to learning

Pupils in England, France and Denmark were in considerable agreement over what constituted effective teaching and learning. The first requirement was that pupils should be active: 'doing something' (French pupil), '*si on faisait que parler et copier sur le cahier personne apprendrait*' ('If all that happened was [the teacher] talking and us copying it down no-one would learn anything'), 'mixing the dry reading stuff with a film and the like . . . makes you feel more engaged' (English pupil). Pupils from the three countries all decried teacher monologues and copying. The second requirement for effective learning was that learning had to be interesting. 'Interesting' was defined in the three countries as a lesson which had an element of 'fun' or humour: '*Monsieur Giroud est rigolo tandis que Madame Bonnard . . . elle raconte, elle raconte, elle dicte, elle dicte*' ('Mr Giroud is funny whereas Mrs Bonnard goes on and on and on, she endlessly dictates'). '*C'est endormant, c'est toujours "ha hein ha hein ha hein ha hein". On dirait qu'ils rabâchent toujours les mêmes choses, c'est sur le même ton, toujours monotone*' ('It puts you to sleep, it's always blaa blaa blaa. They always seem to go over the same things, with the same monotonous tone of voice'). 'He goes on and on . . . reads it out' (English pupil).

Pupils in all three countries appreciated teachers who, 'have a laugh', 'can make a joke', 'liven it up'. In the event of the teacher not being able to fulfil these conditions it was pupils who provided the interest. As a French girl explained: '*Dans le cours il y a toujours quelqu'un là pour mettre de l'ambiance*' ('There's always someone in the lesson who'll make it interesting') and that role was generally occupied by a boy. Pupils from the three countries also thought that they learnt more when teachers brought in themes from contemporary life.

Danish pupils differed from English and French pupils in that they felt they had a considerable degree of choice in the content and organization of their lessons and that this helped their learning. For example, Danish pupils reported having a say in the history issues they wanted to work on, the form a biology report was to take, or whether pupils wanted to work in groups or as a class. In a German class a pupil reported, 'It's almost up to us to decide what to do'. Two Danish pupils summarized their degree of choice: 'To my mind we have a say in learning in this school', 'We can choose to say if we want or not . . . if we don't want, the teacher can't do anything.'

Effective teaching and learning in Denmark implied a certain amount of pupil choice. A Danish pupil explained: 'There is no reason for the teacher just to go on in one particular way'. French pupils differed from English and Danish pupils in their criticism of how their teachers differentiated between low ('*mauvais élèves*') and high achieving pupils ('*bons élèves*') in the same class. French pupils of all levels of achievement thought that many of their teachers neglected lower achieving pupils with negative consequences for their learning:

> *Les professeurs ils s'occupent que des élèves qui travaillent, mais les élèves qui travaillent pas ils les abandonnent.* (Teachers only relate to hard-working pupils, they give up on those that don't work.)
>
> (Low achieving girl in a Paris school)

> *Les professeurs ils mettent les mauvais élèves à part. Ils n'essayent pas tous. Il y en a qui les laissent à part. J'avais une prof de français et franchement elle mettait ceux qui ne travallaient pas au fond de la classe et elle les laissait dormir, elle ne faisait pas d'efforts.* (Teachers put the weak pupils to one side. They don't all try to help them. They leave them out. I had a teacher of French who quite honestly put those that didn't work at the back of the class and she let them go to sleep. She made no effort.)
>
> (High achieving girl from Bordeaux)

This common criticism of French teachers is another example of French pupils' expression of solidarity.

Conclusion

Overall many of the findings presented here suggest that pupils' perceptions, filtered as they are through the mediation of teachers and the particular interpretations which pupils bring to school with them, do nevertheless resonate fairly closely with the particular emphases of the goals of the national systems and therefore continue to reflect significant differences in the way in which pupils experience school. Thus the Danish emphasis on collaboration and consensus and the concern with education for citizenship and democracy as well as with the academic goals of education emerged strongly in the pupils' responses. Danish pupils were broadly the most positive towards schooling, learning and teachers. They saw school as helping them to fit into a group situation rather than emphasizing the development of the individual. They did not in general feel that their teachers placed a great deal of emphasis on making them work hard. They were less likely than the other groups to want to leave school as soon as they could or to see school as getting in the way of their lives.

In some respects the English children, like those we studied previously at primary level, were still the least enthusiastic about school. They enjoyed school and lessons the least and were the most likely to want to leave school as soon as they could and to feel that school got in the way of their lives. However, there were a number of positive elements of teaching for this group who emphasized their teachers' concern with pupils expressing their own ideas and with pupils as people. Encouragingly, they also felt that they had good feedback from teachers about their work and felt that teachers made them work hard. The English pupils' responses reflected the emphasis at national level on the affective dimension of education as well as the cognitive, and the stress on individualization and differentiation. In terms of the dimension shown in Table 7.1, the English findings did suggest that the dual concerns at national level with both the whole child and the child as student were equally reflected in their school experiences.

In France with its emphasis on universalism and republicanism and on all children being treated equally, and with its separation of academic and social/personal development goals, children nevertheless had strong concerns about teachers who do not respect pupils and who do not explain things properly. The French secondary pupils in our sample did not show much evidence of having experienced an affective or social and personal dimension to their school experience. Neither did they feel that they were getting the guidance they needed to improve or an emphasis on hard work from teachers. There is some suggestion from these findings of a lowering of teacher expectations at secondary level and a drop in pupil motivation.

Although there was continuing evidence from these results of the influence of national context on pupil perceptions of schooling, there was also a clear suggestion of the globalization of many concerns. All pupils shared a certain number of similar priorities for teaching and a similar concern with the economic function of education and its link to the job market.

Constants and contexts in pupil experience

Part of the value of cross-cultural research is the extent to which it is able to identify both constants and contexts in educational experience (Broadfoot and Osborn 1988). Cross-cultural comparisons of pupil experience identify pupil responses to learning which are more universal to the situation of 'being a secondary school pupil' from those which may be more culturally specific. As we have attempted to show, pupils in England, Denmark and France have to engage with school contexts and teacher mediations which relate to cultural, philosophical, political and historical differences between the three countries. These, in turn are mediated by pupil concerns and perceptions of schooling and learning and will ultimately affect behaviour and learning outcomes. Identifying these universals and specifics or 'constants' and 'contexts' enable us to consider the extent to which children's experience of secondary phase schooling in different European countries is becoming more similar or moving towards convergence. Some of the findings relating to universals and specifics or constants and contexts in pupil experience cross-culturally, are summarized below.

'Constants' in pupil concerns included the following:

- The importance of the economic function of education and its link to the job market;
- The importance of teacher 'respect' for pupils and of pupil–pupil 'respect';
- That learning should be active and teaching should be interesting;
- That lessons should have an element of 'fun' or humour;
- Concern about the impact of assessment; and

- Gender differences in perceptions of schooling in all three countries (see Chapter 9).

'Contexts' included the following:

- Student responses related closely to the goals of the national education systems;
- National variations in how positive pupil perceptions were towards teaching, learning, and schooling;
- National variations in the influence of socio-economic differences (see Chapter 9);
- Differences in the degree of distance seen as desirable in the teacher–pupil relationship;
- Differences in the degree of separation between home and school;
- Differences in orientation to learning;
- Absence or presence of a sense of solidarity among students within the class; and
- Differences in social identity and differentiation.

Thus, in terms of pupils' own perceptions about effective learning there was striking unanimity about the definition of an 'interesting' lesson and a 'good' teacher, despite the national and institutional differences in pupils' school contexts. What still needs to be explored more fully is the relation between pupils' contrasting national, social and cultural responses to the school context and actual pupil learning. Does the French pupil response of solidarity help to motivate pupils, particularly lower achieving pupils? Does the English pupil response of complex social interactions and negotiation of group identity divert and de-focus English pupils from a learning objective? Does the Danish pupil response of downplaying academic objectives in favour of social relationship objectives have a negative effect on pupil learning? Chapter 8 takes up some of these themes through in-depth profiles of particular pupils in the three countries. Chapter 9 considers some of the issues in relation to socio-economic and ethnic differences and in relation to the crucial stage of 'pupil choice' in upper-secondary and further education.

What is clear, however, is that, in spite of the many pressures towards greater homogenization of educational systems, the national culture and educational traditions of the three European countries under study continue to lead to significant differences in the way in which pupils define their relationship to school. Overall this chapter emphasizes the importance of understanding how pupil attitudes to teaching, learning and schooling are situated within a wider cultural context.

8 Constructing identities

Introduction

The previous chapter looked at identifiable trends in the ways that the large sample of students thought and felt about school. In this chapter we focus on individuals from this group who were researched in greater depth. We consider how the nexus of factors which are embedded in national and local cultures and expressed in policy, school organization and structures, in teacher–student interactions, in the attitudes and values encountered from peers, homes and communities – how all these factors combined to create the stage on which these individuals engaged in the work of constructing their identities. Through a number of case studies we consider how the students in these countries engaged in the process of identity construction with the aim of adding to our understanding of how individual personality, cultural influences and school practices interact to influence pupils' behaviour and learning. In particular we look at the consequences of these processes for individuals and the degree of congruence or tension between the notion of an individual's identity as a 'learner' and as a 'person'.

Contextual factors

The differences between the three systems, highlighted by our outsider/insider approach were, we argued, rooted in the specific cultural and historical environments of the three countries. What was most remarked on in England was the range of activities related to building a whole school ethos and positive reputation and to expressing this publicly in ways which would establish a clear identity for each school in its locality. Combined with this was the enduring value many teachers attached to nurturing 'the whole child' and responding to individual needs. In France, in contrast, outsiders were struck by relatively low levels of concern about school identity. Instead, the social unit that emerged as important was the class, in association with an emphasis on the pupil in relation to the curriculum subject and strong pedagogic framing. In our Danish schools what was most noticeable was the strength of the outward focus in identification with the community, especially with parents; with this went a strong value-base in consensus and in the pupil developing socially within the class group.

Similarly, as we have shown, there were differences in the deployment and activity of teachers and headteachers, in school organization and in approaches to the academic and the affective in the curriculum. All these, as we will see, play a part in the identity story which this chapter unfolds, and it is useful to identify at the outset some of the factors which feature in this narrative. In connection with school organization we should note the different ways in which pupils were located in class groups. In Denmark we found longitudinal continuity in class groups and in the person of the *klasselærer*. Classes were comprised of pupils of mixed achievement levels. In France there was subject continuity but classes were heterogeneous with students of different achievement levels; there was no setting and almost no individual curriculum options. In England pupils experienced banding, and setting across subjects, and an increasing range of choices within and beyond the national curriculum, although the extent of this varied from school to school. As a result the composition of the classes in which English pupils worked was rarely the same from lesson to lesson. Related to the concept of a 'class' in the three countries was the approach of each to the affective domain. In Denmark this was completely integrated in the curriculum. The *klasselærer* who remained with the class and taught a number of subjects had the responsibility of ensuring that students were socially comfortable and secure in the class unit, that they learned to operate as a member of this social unit, to collaborate and cooperate. In France there was complete division and structural separation; the non-academic aspects of education (*la vie scolaire* – conceptualized as distinct from intellectual learning and instruction) was dealt with by a different group of staff with little or no overlap between the two functions. In England, although roles were separately defined, they were carried out by subject teachers and conceived as mutually reinforcing in the quest of social integration and, increasingly foregrounded, academic attainment (see Table 6.1).

One outcome of the different approaches to pupil organization in classes and to the affective domain was the notion of 'distance' perceived by students between themselves and their teachers and, related to this, their perception of school as a location where notions of the individual as 'a person' and as 'a pupil' became salient. As we will see later in this chapter, the positioning of our case study students with regard to these ideas, became significant.

What do we mean by identity?

Identity is manifest in the range of choices individuals make in the process of presenting themselves to others and seeking social definition; it is what we do, how we behave. Identity construction is situated in specific national and local contexts where interacting factors (such as power and status) produce dominant, contested or alternative representations through which we seek to participate as social actors. Part of any individual's self-concept derives from the value and emotional significance associated with membership of such socially defined group (or groups) (Tajfel and Forgas 1981; Tajfel 1982).

A theory of social representations or social identity allows us, then, to consider individuals as constructed in terms of the groups of which they are members (Moscovici 1981, 1984; Duveen and Lloyd 1993). In this study our focus is on the range of social representations of what it is to be 'a learner/pupil'. We are interested in the idea that schools and classrooms produce social identities which are 'available' to individual students. Criteria at national level for what constitutes 'a good citizen' or 'a good learner/pupil' are articulated locally by schools and teachers and thus ideal identities are available for emulation. However, the students in our study were all adolescent – a moment when social identity as a gendered individual and as a 'social' person becomes highly significant. How does the identity the individual chooses to project as a learner form part of this stage of development? If school is a main arena where identities are reconstructed, we are interested in the degree of agency which different pupils exhibit in conforming to or contesting officially sanctioned group behaviour/representations. If the very presence of 'ideal' identities makes available an 'other' in relation to which alternative identities can be elaborated, which students seek membership of these groups? This study enabled us to assess to what extent available identities were similar or different in the three countries. We also considered how the different cultures observed in the schools and classrooms in this study affected the ways in which individuals negotiated their developing identities as adolescents and learners and how this cultural patterning helped to determine their personal and learning priorities.

The school and classroom are the immediate context for learner identity but pupil choices on how this is articulated are influenced by additional factors of ethnicity, economic and social status, home and peer culture, the values, beliefs and attitudes of significant others. In a postmodern context pupils' identities as learners are constructed from the often contradictory worlds they experience and using whatever (often unequal) resources they have available to them. Their view of the usefulness of the school to them in achieving their final goals, the degree to which they share the dominant values of the school, their academic skills and cultural capital, their take on youth culture: all these factors, as much as the behaviour and discourse of teachers, the values, systems and structures of school, are evident in our case studies. In our discussion of the young people in our study we use the terms 'learner identity' and 'social identity'; accepting that all identities are socially constructed, we are making a distinction here between the individual's sense of themselves as a learner in relation to the educational system and as a person in relation to their peer group.

Case studies

The cases presented here are based on data from questionnaires, interviews with students, alone and in focus groups with others they had chosen. We also drew on evidence from teacher interviews and classroom observations. The core of the chapter is concerned with 12 individuals, two high and two low achieving pupils from each of six schools (two in each country). The pairs of schools are contrasted by location, and by socio-economic and ethnic composition.

France

Pierre and Simone: high achievers, France

Pierre was a high-achieving boy at Cathédrale, an academically orientated and socially advantaged school in Bordeaux. Pierre's view of himself as a successful pupil was strong. There was an exact match between how Pierre's teachers viewed him and his own self-assessment; they agreed on '*tres bon*'. From the perspective of his *professeur principal* Pierre was well-behaved, popular, something of a leader, '*un garçon qui est très gentil, qui a beaucoup de tact et qui est très mûr*' ('a boy who is very kind, very tactful, very mature') and who had a good relationship with his teachers, making jokes with them and getting involved with extra-curricular activity. His peer group in school, pupils in a class specially selected to do Latin, were equally positively perceived: '*Ils sont même brillants . . . Ils sont sérieux, c'est prèsqu'une classe modèle*' ('They are brilliant. They are conscientious, it's almost a model class'). Pierre acknowledged that he was not one to mess about in class, that he was strongly self-motivated, wanted to achieve and realized that school was important for his career prospects. However, he was not sure if he liked school; he found many of his lessons boring and thought the best parts of his life were not those he spent there. He was in fact very critical of his school and his teachers. Teachers, as seen by Pierre and his friends, discriminated between good and poor students; they were not interested in students who did not achieve; they failed to distinguish between those who were lazy and those

Pierre and Simone: high achievers, France – continued

who made an effort but got nowhere, and they were more lenient with high achievers. Pierre's group characterized most of their teachers' attitude as: '*Je vais de 9H a 4H, je recycle mon cour, je dis "Bonjour", "Au revoir", et c'est tout*' ('I go from 9H to 4H, I re-cycle my classes, I say "hello", "goodbye" and that's all'). Pierre himself saw teachers as too dominant in class; and again, in a group interview, there was a chorus of unanimous agreement about this view: '*On a le droit de rien dire*', '*C'est moi qui commande*', '*C'est – Tais-toi.*' ('We haven't got the right to say anything', 'It is me who is in charge', 'It's be quiet.') They disliked being treated as children who had nothing of interest to say. This approach did not facilitate the self-direction, debate and discussion which Pierre and his friends felt was their preferred way of learning. However, in spite of all this, Pierre recognized the value of a pragmatic conformity. His goals, and the school's for him, were sufficiently congruent to induce in Pierre an instrumentality and an accommodation which would produce the marks he needed to get where he wanted to go. He was also aware that this exposed him, as a good student, to being rejected by weaker students but this did not bother him. He was secure within his own 'élite' group and his own values which were entirely congruent with those of his home and family. '*Les voyoux ils disent qu'un mauvais entourage c'est les intellectuels, les intellectuels disent qu'un mauvais entourage c'est eux. Souvent on est rejeté parce qu'ils sont jaloux.*' ('The wastrels say that the intellectuals are a bad crowd, the intellectuals say it's them [the wastrels] who are the bad crowd. Often you are rejected because they are jealous.')

In the very different socio-economic context of Montand school in the Paris suburbs, Simone, another high achiever, echoed Pierre's views. She also assessed herself as '*très bonne*' ('very good') and was seen by her teachers as '*élève sérieuse*', '*excellente élève*', '*de très bons resultats . . . elle a un très bon niveau*' ('conscientious pupil', 'excellent pupil', 'very good results . . . she has a high achievement level'). However, she too was not enthusiastic about school and saw it, equally instrumentally, as the pathway to qualifications and a career in medicine. Like Pierre she was in a group of friends who shared her aspirations. The group's view of teachers was strikingly similar to those of the boys at Cathédrale: they saw teachers as having little respect for pupils and their views; they thought they discriminated between pupils on the basis of their marks and gave more attention to hardworking and high achieving students. The general view was that teachers were only interested in getting pupils through exams. Simone also felt that her teachers relied too much on appearances, jumped to conclusions and were too ready to attribute poor assessments to the bad influence of friends. She rarely enjoyed any of her lessons and thought that the dominant teaching/learning style – heavily teacher-controlled and textbook based – was not her preferred way of working. She felt she worked best on her own, when she had a

Pierre and Simone: high achievers, France – continued

greater degree of choice, and when the lessons were interesting, which she and her friends construed as more lively, less monotonous in delivery and with a good '*ambiance*'. Strategically, however, she decided to conform.

Pierre and Simone accommodated strategically to their reading of the school's view of what it is to be a 'good pupil'. The available identity they assumed was as hardworking, compliant, achieving pupils in teacher-dominated classes. Both accepted less satisfying learning experiences as the price of achieving long-term goals which they perceived would follow from conformity to their teachers' ideal. With these two young students we encounter most sharply a distinction between the identities of 'pupil' and 'learner'. Both were able to articulate alternative models of learner behaviour associated with independence, autonomy, intrinsic interest and pupil interaction but in the school context they saw no opportunity to enact or develop these.

Socially both Pierre and Simone were part of a homogeneous group within the class. Members of this group shared a view of learning and sustained each other in enduring the more negative consequences of their choices. They looked to life outside school as the source of strongest satisfaction. Pierre had a different group of friends outside school which, for him, made the total separation of learner and social identities very possible. Outside school Simone went to music lessons, played and practised her violin, was a member of the local group of a national organization for girls, and looked after her dog. She was not allowed out alone after school but she was in total agreement with her parents about this, and repeated her mother's words: '*Si on voit après ce qui se passe dans la rue . . .*' ('If you could see what goes on in the street later'.) She thought that other parents gave their children too much freedom whereas hers had taught her a work ethic and she was grateful; they wanted her to have the opportunities they had not had and she was determined to repay them for their support.

Sylvie and Fayaz: low achievers, France

In the same two schools were two low achievers whose response to being at school was very different. Both were seen as problem pupils by their teachers. At Cathédrale, Sylvie was hostile to her teachers, blaming them for her 'redoublement', or having to repeat the year, which she saw as a stigma and as a sign of discrimination between good and poor pupils. Her view of teachers was remarkably consistent with that of Pierre and his group. Teachers, Sylvie told us, were only interested in their own subjects and made her feel a failure; they paid attention only to those pupils who were successful and did not spend enough time with pupils who had problems; most didn't listen, some were narrow-minded or

Sylvie and Fayaz: low achievers, France – continued

frightening; they didn't explain well and wouldn't repeat things if you didn't understand; they labelled pupils and did not look beyond the surface. Sylvie was worried about her marks and the prospect of public humiliation. She accepted the school's view and assessed herself as '*pas très bonne*' for school work. Her response to her failure as a learner was to focus on a sphere in which she was acceptable, the social sphere of her friends. Her group, she said, did not think it was important to do well at school and liked to mess around in class. They were aware of their negative reputation and used the characteristics attributed to them as the basis for a strong group identity outside school: '*On nous dit qu'on s'interésse beaucoup à autre chose, aux garcons, au physique, qu'on vient au collège pas pour travailler mais pour se faire remarquer . . . La meilleure expérience c'est entre nous, entre copains.*' ('They tell us that we are too interested in other things, in boys, in appearance, that we come to school not to work but to get noticed . . . The best experiences are between us, between our friends.') Sylvie positioned herself in interview in opposition to higher achieving students whom she saw as teachers' pets and who showed off about how good they were. Although she claimed to be motivated by the idea of getting a good job and attributed her lack of success to the fact that she made little effort with her work, she would not contemplate (or could not risk) buying into the system. In this context it would be difficult socially for Sylvie if she exhibited any interest in learning or started to get good marks.

At Montand Fayaz, as seen by his teachers, was lazy, lacked motivation, would make no effort. He was assessed as '*en perdition complète*', '*Nul*', '*Élève particulierement pénible.*' ('completely lost', 'nothing', 'a particularly weak pupil.') However, he was also described as 'quite intelligent.' Fayaz was not aware of this more positive view of his potential as a learner. As he saw it '*Si je suis nul, que je fais des efforts ou pas, je serais toujours nul.*' ('If I am nothing, if I make an effort or not I shall always be nothing'.) Like Sylvie his strategic response to a negative assessment was to differentiate himself more strongly from a system which appeared to him to be unable to accommodate him. His view of teachers echoed those of the other French pupils we have considered so far but (unlike Pierre and Simone) he was not willing or able to ignore their perceived deficiencies for instrumental ends. The idea of teachers as out of touch, uninterested in pupils as people, unwilling to listen was most strongly expressed by Fayaz. In interview he spoke of the distance between teachers and pupils and his sense of the inequality and injustice, of being constantly put in the wrong. Here, in contrast to Simone, a black student who made no reference to her ethnicity, he specifically pointed to cultural and ethnic difference. '*Ils nous voient pas quand on est déhors, ce qu'on subit, moi je suis moitié arabe, moitié français.*' ('They don't see us outside, what we experience, I'm half Arab, half French.') For Fayaz it was

Sylvie and Fayaz: low achievers, France – continued

his identification with his peer group that offered satisfaction and security. They conformed in school only when strategically necessary. Outside school they played football, watched films, wore clothes that gave them an identity with the estate where they lived and were 'cool'. Fayaz sang with a group in a club but he did not tell his music teacher about this. The strength of this social identity (and the weakness of a positive identity as a learner in the face of it) is shown in this assertion from the group interview: *'On se sent en securité quand on a des copains. Ça fait une force dans la morale.'* ('There is a sense of security when you have friends. That's a big boost.')

In France, then, we have looked at four pupils who all shared a similar view of teachers but who had very different responses to this and very different attainment. Pierre and Simone presented themselves as conformist and instrumental; prepared to put success as a 'pupil' above enjoyment as a 'person'. Sylvie and Fayaz could not or would not conform to the dominant school model of the pupil; their identities were constructed outside this ideal model and were strongly associated with membership of a peer group.

England

Daniel and Emma: high achievers, England

Like the French pupils, the English quartet came from contrasting schools: one a Catholic school, St Theresa's, which had a good reputation for discipline and for above average attainment; the other, Westway, was located in an area of social disadvantage with an ethnically mixed population and a mission to raise achievement. Daniel, at St Theresa's, was a high achiever with a belief in hard work and a view of himself as very good at school work. The school reflected this: 'Very well motivated, very able, well organized, creative. Gets a buzz out of using his skills and mind. Always engaged.' In contrast to Pierre and Simone, Daniel thought that he generally enjoyed school and liked his teachers. Although he felt he had little say in how he learned and was not sure if school was a place where he could express his own ideas, he felt that most teachers listened to him, didn't make him feel a failure and understood about pupils' problems and worries. He and his friends in a group interview distinguished 'good' teachers (who are approachable and have a laugh, who make you want to learn and help you to learn) from 'bad' teachers ('If they are too strict, you don't get on with them and you don't want to learn and the lesson is boring'). The quality of their relationship with the teacher was important to them, and firmly intertwined with their assessment of teacher effectiveness for them as learners. However, they also saw

Daniel and Emma: high achievers, England – continued

teachers as giving help more readily to those who tried hard even if they did not succeed; teachers, they felt, were reluctant to help the undeserving. 'Teachers prefer those who are working hard. If they don't do well teachers ignore them and they do even worse and they behave badly.' Daniel and his friends were happy to conform, in general, to school norms and expectations for work and behaviour. Although the school saw Daniel and his group as high achievers, they described themselves as 'in the middle, normal, hardworking but not keeners'. They defined a 'keener' as someone who 'always works hard, sucks up, always helps teacher, does homework on time, stays in at break, works too hard.' This version of a school ideal was an identity they sought to distance themselves from; they wanted to be 'normal'. To be seen as 'a keener' was to jeopardize your position with your peers. In Year 9 Daniel was more aware of the necessity for strategic action in relation to a learning identity than he had been in his first year in the school. In Year 7 he told us, 'Sometimes they call me one [keener]. I don't care, I take it as a joke. I say something back like, "At least I can get it right." ' By Year 9 he was less concerned with asserting his learning achievements than in dealing with the 'popular/hard group' he was exposed to in his 'mixed ability' classes who might bully or ridicule a keener. He was part of a well established sociable, sporty group and he skilfully used these advantages to avoid being labelled as 'working too hard' without in fact compromising his work ethic or his achievement. Their in-group solidarity was reinforced by a view of the 'hard group' as losers: 'If they don't realise soon they will just be bums. They need a good talking to.' 'They laugh at us now but in ten years we will be well-off and the hard work will have been worth it. People will look back and say, "Why couldn't I have done better." '

The case of Emma, at Westway, provides another contrast with France – and with Daniel. A high achiever, Emma was most concerned with constructing an identity as a learner in opposition to her view of the school ideal. As she left primary school she was insisting, 'If she gave me some work I would get on with it but I would be talking all the time, I'm not a goody-goody . . . sucking up to teachers and – you know – that sort of person.' In Year 7 she identified the ideal pupil as 'Smart, clever – doesn't always need the teacher's help. Not a bully. Someone they can rely on' and described herself as different: 'I'm not that smart. You can't always rely on me. I won't always be good. If people annoy me I just lash out.' Her friendships at school were stormy and fraught with much falling out and even violence. In Year 8 she constructed herself as 'clever but lazy . . . I like having a laugh and a chat. I can be a little bit bullysome . . . as long as my friends like me, nothing else matters.' A teacher commented: 'I suspect Emma is just looking for some sort of happiness in school with her friends, and being accepted rather than looking for achievement and success . . . at the moment.' Her

Daniel and Emma: high achievers, England – continued

teachers in general were very aware that Emma was coasting, was not fulfilling her potential, could do better if she pushed herself, reacted badly to what she perceived as excessive authority, could be loud and uncouth. However, they continued to support, encourage and challenge her. Emma was aware of this ('They're always going on about how I'm smart and could do better than this and things like that') and saw it not as nagging but as a signal that they cared about her. She named four teachers who she thought were interested in her as a person.

Emma and her friends were well aware of the interaction between an individual's behaviour as a learner and their social status with their peer group. In particular they identified a specific gender dimension to this. In Year 9 Emma explained that, as a girl, she would not entirely compromise her social identity if she started to work hard. 'If I started doing my work you lot [her friends] wouldn't mind. If Wayne started doing work they'd all start teasing him – he doesn't get on in case the other boys start teasing him . . . for boys there's an image to keep up about not working hard.' In the context of this London school it was more difficult for boys to take the line of Daniel and his friends. As Emma's group saw it, the negotiation of social identity (in particular being attractive to girls) required boys to make people laugh, mess around or confront teachers. The only strategy open to boys who were high achievers, if they wanted to avoid being seen as 'stuck-up nerds' and teased for having no social life, was to be funny in class.

As she approached the end of Key Stage 3 there were signs that for Emma her identity as a learner was becoming more involved with and dependent on grades and standardized assessment. 'I'm not doing as well as I could but I'm doing OK. I will try harder when it comes to GCSEs. I know I will.' In Maths with a teacher who, she felt, understood her, she became very grade conscious. 'If I get a bad mark I go into a sulk. I got level 7 not level 8 and I'd asked Mr L what I had to do and I did everything, so I was angry.' Her teacher allowed her to take the test again to prove to herself that she could get the level, and she did. Emma wanted to achieve; her long-term goals were as congruent with the school's as Pierre's in France and Daniel's. What is different is that Emma had resisted a conventional learner identity as hardworking, cooperative, conformist in favour of constructing herself as individualistic and 'difficult'; a great deal of her energy went into her mercurial relationships with her friends. She was conscious that at some time in the future she would adapt her behaviour and attitude as a learner. For the moment her sense of herself as someone who was going to achieve was sustained by her perception of her teachers as interested in her, by their extreme patience with her and their optimism that she would do what was necessary as a learner to succeed in the system.

Tracey and Melanie: low achievers, England

Westway's attention, as a school, to the connections between pupils' social and learner identity can also be seen in the case of a low achiever. 'Tracey looked miserable and unhappy most of the time. She didn't seem to feel she had any friends in her tutor group. She asked if she could change so we moved her where she wanted to go. She's done very well, fitted in, seems happier and is a better attender. The work's still not brilliant but she's better than she was.' Interviewed after the change of group, Tracey told us she liked her school and the teachers. 'It's fun. They help you – and you find new friends here.' The association between having friends and feeling good about learning was important for Tracey. As learners Tracey and her friends subscribed to the view that effort is important. They said, 'We sometimes chat but we do the work'. They were rarely on report for bad behaviour. At the same time they were clear about the processes by which they saw that social identity was secured. They thought it was important to 'look nice, wear the right labels – top brands, especially trainers – not cheap stuff.'

However, Tracey and her group did not have a strong sense of themselves as successful learners and they were vulnerable to adverse teacher comment. Some teachers, they reported, compared their work with others. 'They say "You're stupid. Do you want to leave school as a loser?" ' When this happened they did not work harder or seek assistance, they lost confidence; the view of teachers as people who 'help you' faded. 'If you're not confident about the work you can't get it better.' 'Teachers only care if you're good or not. If you're bad they don't care what you do.' As they spoke of their problems with learning Tracey and her friends associated this with a distance between some teachers and their pupils and a lack of understanding of young people today. 'In the old days pupils just showed respect – now pupils answer back – they only work if they feel respected and well-treated. Some teachers don't speak our language, understand our world. The teachers want us to be what they want us to be. "Don't talk. Be quiet. Get on with your work" – even if you don't know what to do. And if you get work wrong teachers have a bad idea of you.'

This account echoes something of our French students' experience. But there are differences. Tracey, like Daniel at St Theresa's, distinguished between 'some teachers' and others; this is not a general characterization as it was for Pierre and the others. Similarly Tracey's use of 'our' and 'us' as she talked about teachers is indeed a reflection of the distance she felt and of the separation she wanted to make between herself as a member of her peer group and the school. However, the solidarity Tracey invoked was not related to her class group but to a larger, more generalized and vague school-wide population. In fact her class-based social group was small and on the margins. To feel secure in a group was very important to Tracey, enough to prompt her to action in getting her tutor group changed. Friends, though, appeared to be needed to insulate her from the

Tracey and Melanie: low achievers, England – continued

more risky aspects of learning rather than to develop a more positive and active learner identity. Tracey's view was that teachers must be minimally appeased, you had to 'do what they say' and try to stay out of trouble. Overall she had a very weak and poorly developed sense of herself as a learner.

Melanie, at St Theresa's, was more aware of herself as a learner: she thought that it was important to go to school, ultimately, to secure a good job. However, she found it difficult to make learning a priority for herself. She was a happy, sociable pupil popular with boys and girls and with a secure background of a loving extended family. In Year 8 her teachers remarked on her lively sense of humour, her maturity, her fairness and reluctance to gossip. They also mentioned 'her hormones' in connection with a growing flirtatiousness. Her academic attainment was low to average. Melanie thought she could improve her work if she listened more and told us she was constantly being told not to chat. To do this, though, would have run counter to her preferred style of learning which was to work in a group of friends on individual work while engaging in a mix of work related and social talk and having one to one contact with the teacher as she needed. The reciprocity she felt she had with her friends in work situations, emerged from and was cemented by the social bond: 'Some knows more things about something than I do, and I knows more things than them, so we like helps each other out.' She was, however, quite dependent and preferred the security of being told precisely what to do by her teacher or another pupil. Melanie's sense of herself as a funny, rather scatty but very likeable girl who was good company was not confined to school; she insisted that she was the same at home. Her social group was very stable and close-knit – her three closest friends had been with her in primary school and she saw them after school and at weekends to go shopping, visit the cinema or play tennis. 'We just tells each other everything – they're all funny and we has a laugh'.

School for Melanie provided an extension for her customary style of social interaction. 'Some people like, just gets on and does it. That's where I doodles about getting everything ready and all that . . . most of the clever people and all that, they don't chat.' She also made it clear that she was ambivalent about making learning a priority. 'Well sometimes, when I know I'm doing it wrong, but I just can't be bothered to ask, I just does it how I think it is.' Asking and revealing a lack of understanding also carried social risks for Melanie: 'You feels, like, embarrassed asking because, like, it's all silent and then everyone listens to what you are saying when you put your hand up.' Her friends were all average or low average achievers; there was little sense in the group of challenge or competition – rather a mutually reinforcing satisfaction about being 'in the middle' and out of trouble. In order to maintain this happy situation and continue to enjoy school as a place for a laugh and a chat Melanie was quite strategic in her dealings with her

Tracey and Melanie: low achievers, England – continued

teachers. She thought they liked 'clever pupils who work hard or those who get on with them'. As she was unlikely to do what was necessary to become one of the former she worked hard on being one of the latter. 'You always got to be nice to her . . . and sometimes, if you knows a question, you've got to put your hand up and when you walk past them, smile at them and all that [so they don't] think I'm horrible or nothing.' Melanie's social identity was maintained consistently and elaborated by her in relation to learning.

In these English schools and classrooms we see that Daniel, Emma, Tracey and Melanie talked as much (or more) about their social relationships with their teachers and their peers as they did about their learning. In addition the construction of themselves as learners was closely involved with these relationships. As she described it, Melanie's success in making herself 'likeable' as a person in her teachers' eyes allowed her to maintain a consistency between her social behaviour and her behaviour as a learner. This consistency enabled her to survive happily, if not flourish academically. Though less flamboyant, Tracey, similarly was concerned to keep her teachers 'happy'. She used the system to achieve a minimal degree of social integration, while managing to maintain a very restricted sense of herself as a learner. Daniel, aware of the social dangers of exhibiting 'ideal pupil' attributes, sought actively, with his friends, to construct an acceptable 'in the middle' identity while privately maintaining very clear long-term learning goals. Emma, confident in the knowledge that her teachers shared her own belief in her ultimate success and supported by their interest and tolerance, was able to project herself as non-conforming, even deviant.

Denmark

Torben and Mette: high achievers, Denmark

In Denmark, again, we look at four pupils in two contrasting schools – the North school in an affluent community and the Periphery school in a socially disadvantaged estate on the edge of Copenhagen. Torben, at the North school, was a member of a small family; his parents both worked in medicine and his father was chair of the school board. He wanted to achieve good grades because it would help him to get a good job eventually. From his responses in interview it is clear that a strong identity as a learner and achiever was in some conflict with his understanding of the importance his teacher placed on class solidarity. In his class there was no value in being the best at something, but individually he wanted to achieve his potential; he resolved this tension with a creative justification. 'It's not important to me . . . to do better than the others –

Torben and Mette: high achievers, Denmark – continued

I've no ambitions to be the best . . . At the moment one of the reasons I put so much effort into being the best is that I probably am the best. I'm good at academic subjects and . . . when the others get a better grade than me in something or other they're pleased and proud of themselves and all that.' Like his English and French counterparts Torben had had to negotiate his way round academic success. He had been at the receiving end of some unpleasant teasing. His teacher commented: 'He's talented . . . kind of precocious, rather sensible but I think he's become a lot more – um – likeable than he was. He was a bit high and mighty. He was teased a fair bit earlier . . . but it's disappeared now.'

Torben's teacher was working hard to break up what she perceived as 'cliques' in the class. The pupils we interviewed described these groups and where they saw themselves fitting in; but, in the face of their teacher's values of social equality, many felt ambivalent about these groups in school. The basis of group membership, in fact, was located outside school and not associated with behaviour or attitudes to learning. Torben spoke of 'the ones who go to all the cool parties and drink the most'. Girls in the class perceived divisions based on what parents allowed them to do (or not do) in the evenings; these also were mainly concerned with going out and drinking. Torben's response to being teased because of his intellectual leanings and his lack of 'cool' was to become part of another social 'clique' which spent a great deal of time out of school on war games: 'Warhammer really takes up a lot of my time.' Membership of this group gave Torben a secure social identity; with these friends it did not matter that he liked to 'read an awful lot' and was 'not an outdoor type'. He told us he was 'quite happy at the moment' but as a learner he wished that his teachers could be 'a little more critical. If you sit there saying that you're not very good at things, they say, "Yes you are", that kind of thing. Maybe they could be a little better at that.' This desire for critical evaluation of his work is one indicator that Torben was able to maintain a strong sense of himself as a learner and academic achiever while dissembling strategically in class in order to be perceived as 'more likeable'.

At the Periphery school, Mette shared some of the same characteristics as Emma and was classed by the school as a very high achiever. She described herself as 'kind of independent . . . someone who stands by their opinion . . . I like the fact that people are different and that they have different opinions to mine.' She valued her friends because 'they don't back off if I have a different opinion. They can't be so easily manipulated, maybe I do that sometimes with people.' In class, however, she could be stubborn and impatient of others. Mette saw her class as 'quite unified' but the members as dispersed to different groups after school. However, when she and her friends decided who to work with on a collaborative project they employed a definite strategy: 'It's mostly the people on

Torben and Mette: high achievers, Denmark – continued

your own level. You don't go and choose someone if he's going to find it dead difficult if you're good yourself . . . it's like a tacit working plan and it just runs smoothly.' Mette was very secure and confident in her social identity. Mette's friendship group identified two separate groups of girls in class. They thought their group was very different from the other: 'it's kind of like we aren't at the same place at the same time and . . . there's a tendency to talk behind people's backs sometimes.' In identifying the difference the girls were also signalling their social superiority and power. Class observations showed Mette and her friends talking, giggling, passing notes, withholding participation, being rude to the teacher, and teasing another girl pupil quite cruelly. However, unlike Emma, Mette had no hesitation in identifying herself as an 'ideal pupil' which she saw as one who was 'interested'. She felt she had a slightly strained relationship with one of her teachers 'at the moment' but in general she was sure that she had the school's support and approval. She was strategically aware that she should not be 'hot-tempered, rude and unfriendly' because 'the teachers wouldn't want to help me then.' As a learner she was interested in her teachers' assessments of her work, both formative and summative, and in how this corresponded to her self-assessments: 'Sometimes the teachers forget to tell me what I can do to improve things . . . and then there are some when I don't think I've done particularly good work – they say I've done very good work. I can be a bit surprised about that.' Mette had a strong sense of herself as an independent learner with a number of strategies to support this. Because of her secure and dominant social identity, she had no need, when she chose to show it, to disguise her interest in school work or achievement.

Though presenting very different social identities, Torben and Mette were both conscious of themselves as academic high achievers. As learners, both would like to be in a context where their teachers did more to show them how they could improve their work. In an education system which largely was still resisting grades, this feeling contrasts sharply with the response to adverse assessment experienced by Per and his friends at Periphery school.

Per and Jesper: low achievers, Denmark

Per did not see himself as good at anything and he claimed that he couldn't be bothered to put in any effort when others were better than him. His only pleasure in school was 'the breaks and good classmates'. His attitude to learning was to work with his two friends so that they could do everything for him. At one time his group had successfully constructed an identity as 'trouble-makers, answering

Per and Jesper: low achievers, Denmark – continued

back and calling the teachers names'; but he had to confess, sadly, that this dominance had been eclipsed by pupils in a parallel class who had been even more outrageous. Per and his two friends, one as abnormally tall as he was small, 'have fun together' and out of school (where they were mildly bullied, which they accepted as 'normal') he had a very varied social life. In school he found any learning which was not active and writing-free unacceptable. If there was too much noise and chaos in class he walked out; an action that was condoned because he suffered from headaches. Similarly if he could not do his homework his mother wrote a note to explain. As a learner Per had a range of avoidance strategies available to him although sometimes he got told off and his teachers contacted his home about missing work. His chosen social identity was constructed partly in response to his failure as a learner and to his need to avoid facing this.

Jesper, in Torben's class in the North school, was also, in his teacher's words 'academically weak'. For him, the best thing about school was 'friends'. At one point in his interview he mentioned many friends and talked of feeling part of both of the two boys' groups in the class. One of these groups consisted of the popular boys who set the agenda in class and who went to parties and socialized with the girls. This was the group everyone wanted to be in. The other boys' group was the Warhammer group to which Torben belonged. Jesper's teacher saw him as immature and not well placed in the class: 'He ought to be in the 7th grade . . . It's a pity the parents haven't listened to us . . . they won't move him . . . He isn't happy. He hasn't got many resources to draw on.' He characterized himself as 'not very talkative in school' but as someone who liked to have fun and wanted something to be happening all the time with other people: 'I can't do anything alone.' However, when he talked in more detail about the popular boys' group of which he claimed to feel a part he said they were 'quite nice' but they call some people 'weird' and 'babies'; 'they don't say very much and you don't talk with them very much'. Jesper was also aware of the importance of wearing the 'right' clothes and seemed to feel pressurized in this respect. Out of school he said he watched TV with friends (never family) and listened to music; he also went to the youth club.

Overall, Jesper appeared to belong nowhere with any certainty. He seemed in search of a social identity and the lack of this made it difficult for him to focus on learning. He could not achieve, like Torben, and as a result found constructing a positive learner identity challenging. His view of himself was that he learned best when the teacher taught them all together or when he worked alone, not in a group. Again suggesting that he found it difficult to fit into a group. He was, though, an active seeker and not without a strategy. He told us he would like to become a member of the Pupil Council and was well informed about the

Per and Jesper: low achievers, Denmark – continued

qualifications needed. He seemed to feel that achieving this position would provide him with an identity and status in class; he thought that in class lessons the council members had a lot of influence, particularly with their class teacher.

In Per and Jesper, as with the rest of the 12 cases, we can see the complex interaction of personality, social identity and learner identity. Some key aspects of the twelve pupils' experience are summarized in Tables 8.1, 8.2 and 8.3 on pages 164–9.

In the outcomes what similarities and differences can we identify that can be accounted for by the educational systems in the three countries?

Typologies

Educational research has produced a number of typologies of classroom behaviour and learning style. In England we have 'goodies, jokers and gangs' (Pollard 1985) 'attention seekers, hard grinders, easy riders/intermittent workers' (Galton *et al.* 1980), 'knife-edgers' (Measor and Woods 1984). All these deal variously with the degree to which learners challenge, reject, conform to or negotiate with teachers and systems. Pollard and Filer (1996) suggest that effective learners are produced when their strategies and presentation of identities are, or become, well adapted to the working consensus, social understandings and power relations that obtain in the learning context. We have suggested that the three national cultures produce subtly different contexts for learning. It follows that typologies of behaviour should not fit neatly in every country. In addition the processes a system requires for a pupil to be 'well adapted' will be different.

Our colleague in this study, Olivier Cousin (2002), has produced a typology of pupil behaviour based on data collected from first year secondary students in three French schools with a large proportion of pupils from ethnic minorities. He looked at the way in which social and learner identity are juxtaposed and proposed four types:

- *'bon élève'* – the average pupil, conforms to group norms, espouses notions of solidarity, learner and social identity exist side by side;
- *'intello'* – pejorative connotations applied by other pupils; perceived as individualistic, unsociable, identifies with the school, ambivalent about pupil solidarity, learner identity dominates;
- *'frimeur'* – rebel, disruptive, social identity dominates;
- *'frontalier'* – strategist, separates school and learner identity and moves between the two as appropriate.

Table 8.1 Aspects in the creation of identity: France, Cathédrale

	Perspectives on classroom learning	*Perspectives on peer group*	*Out of school contexts*	*Summary*
Pierre, Cathédrale	Sense of self as high achiever, positively perceived by teachers. Has reservations about pedagogy and teacher attitudes. Frequently bored by lessons; thinks that teachers positively discriminate in their approach to pupils like him. Ambitious to gain appropriate qualifications. Adopts strategic instrumental acceptance of ideal pupil identity offered by school to achieve within system.	Generally popular and respected. Not bothered that girls and boys don't mix much in school. Member of an élite class which enjoys strong teacher approval. Friendship group resents being infantilized by teachers; but members conform to achieve academic goals. Group status provides security for identity of 'intellectual' in opposition to lower achieving, non-conforming groups.	Looks to friends in school for solidarity, support and light relief. However, not dependent on them for social identity and has different friends out of school. Mother, a widow with a profession, is a parent representative at school. He has an older sister.	Conforms to the school's concept of learner and manages tensions between this and his own ideal. Supported by co-learners who are similarly strategic and instrumental. Free to see himself as an intellectual. Social and cultural capital contribute to his confidence, independence and security; school provides no opportunities for developing self-directed learner identity.
Sylvie, Cathédrale	Accepts school's assessment of her as low achiever. Feels a failure. Hostile to teachers who are seen as out of touch with pupils, unfair, unhelpful and uninterested in her. Afraid of public humiliation that feels goes with failure in class. Wants to achieve but says she makes no effort. The style of teaching does not suit her.	Like-minded friends offer a refuge. Identity in her group is constructed in opposition to dominant school values; negative reputation a source of strength. Think teachers treat them like children, deny them a voice. Interests are non-academic. Friendship seen as most positive aspect of school.	Lives with mother, father and two sisters. Says her parents want her to do well but cannot help her with her school work. Says her friends are her main support group. When her family moved a little further away, Sylvie refused to change schools.	In school, has very positive social identity which is secured in opposition to the 'low achiever' label offered by the school and school expectations of learner behaviour. Friends are very significant in school. There is very little room for manoeuvre.

Simone, Montand	Aware that is perceived positively as high achieving pupil by teachers. Sees herself as serious, reserved and well organized. Believes in efficacy of effort. Dislikes the strongly teacher controlled pedagogy – no independence or choice – but is motivated by assessment and gaining qualifications. Doesn't enjoy school – resents teachers who do not know pupils and who blame underachievement on the bad influence of friends.	Is member of like-minded group who share her view that their social and economic aspirations are dependent on gaining qualifications. They adopt a strategic conformity to school ideals. Accepting of values and work ethic of their parents. Feel indebted to parents for their support; feel advantaged by the opportunities available to their generation.	Close stable family. Ethnic minority. Relative economic disadvantage. Belief that moral and relational stability in a family is more important than the financial situation. Parents strict; rules not resisted by Simone. Parents support her career ambitions. Cultural activity occupies out of school time: plays viola, member of an organized girls' group, has a pet.	Strong congruence in values between home and peer group. Family and friends share aspirations for the younger generation's success in the dominant culture. School assessment confirms sense of self as an achiever; sense of self as a learner developed independently; school endured as a route to qualifications.
Fayaz, Montand	Accepts school's assessment of self as academically hopeless – unaware that some teachers suggest he is 'quite intelligent'. Rejects strategy of 'effort' as useless. Feels strongly distanced from the school system. Opts out. Sense of inequality and injustice. School a waste of time; teachers out of touch.	In a group whose members also reject school values and norms. Seen as a problem because of their disruptive behaviour in class. This friendship, for Fayaz, provides a refuge from boredom in school.	Lives with mother and step-father who are concerned about him. Resents step-father's interference. Cultural dissonance with messages from natural father returned to North Africa. Out of school activity the source of a strong social identity. Learning here seen as unrelated to school learning.	Fayaz experiences conflict in his sense of available identities as a learner. School gives him a sense of failure and helplessness; he rejects it and its ideals, assuming the identity of a disruptive pupil as a response to boredom. Out of school he develops a very strong and positive identity, completely separated from school.

Table 8.2 Aspects in the creation of identity: England, St Theresa's

	Perspectives on classroom learning	*Perspectives on peer group*	*Out of school contexts*	*Summary*
Daniel, St Theresa's	A high achiever, but says he is 'in the middle'. Strong belief in hard work and effort. Resents time teachers spend with demanding and disruptive pupils. Thinks teacher–pupil relationships affect how teachers teach. Prefers teachers to be relaxed and informal. Thinks learning should be enjoyable and active. Likes and respects most teachers. Sees them as supportive and caring. Relates this to the fact that he works hard and conforms.	In a small group of like minded friends. They identify sub-groups as 'keeners', 'the "hard" group' seen as 'losers' and 'the normal, in the middle group' – like them. Daniel avoids the negative behaviour accorded to 'keeners' by successful participation in sport. Daniel and his friends want learning to be enjoyable and assert long-term goals, achievable by success in school.	Member of a small close-knit family. Older brother at the same school. Extended family close by. Both parents in low paid manual work. They think it is important that Daniel does well at school, attend parents' evenings and reward his success. Daniel does not want to move far away from family and neighbourhood. He plays football outside school as well as in.	Daniel experiences no conflict between personal, home and school attitudes and values. Manages this congruence and secures a positive social identity at school, with the help of his friendship group and his sporting achievements. Aware of the workings of peer group and teacher–pupil relationships. He sees himself as 'a good pupil'.
Melanie, St Theresa's	Accepts that she could do better. Knows what she should do to achieve more. Not strongly motivated to change approach to work or classroom behaviour. Likes to chat; seeks to avoid embarrassment by not asking or answering questions; depends on her friends for help, dislikes working individually. She does not see herself as an ideal 'clever' pupil but thinks that, making sure teachers like her, will facilitate her dependence on them too.	Classroom is a context for social activity as well as learning. Member of a long established, close-knit group. Social identities and behaviours of group members are clear, consistent and mutually reinforced in and out of school. General avoidance of challenge, 'over achievement' or competition in learning. Strategic avoidance of 'trouble' by a minimally acceptable level of conformity to teachers' and school's demands.	The youngest and the only daughter in a close-knit family. Two brothers, at the same school, protective of her. Both parents work, her father in a managerial role. No particular concern about her academic attainment. Family and friends provide Melanie with a context for elaborating her identity as a popular, sociable girl. Melanie aspires to a good time, followed by marriage and children and living near her parents.	Melanie accedes that attainment at school is useful, but is more concerned to secure a congenial atmosphere and minimal demands for learning tasks and activity. School provides an extended location for her social life and the confirmation of her social identity. She manages strategically to maintain a high degree of dependence on teachers and friends and to avoid learning challenge.

Emma, Westway	A high achiever, aware of her academic potential, Emma constructs her identity as a learner in opposition to the 'ideal'. Asserts her unconventionality, refuses to conform. Effort and achievement vary with her mood. Likes to have a laugh. Feels secure in her teachers' confidence that she will achieve, and supported by their concern for her in spite of her attitude and behaviour.	School is a place to meet your friends. Emma's relationships are frequently stormy; she likes to dominate. Very conscious of the interaction between behaviour as a learner and social status within the peer group. Sees a gender dimension – for boys, working hard in class and achieving endangers positive social identity; girls can do this and still be popular.	Emma lives in a two bedroom council flat with her mother and older brother who is frequently in trouble. Her mother works full-time as a secretary. She is encouraging and supportive, aware of what's happening in school. Emma socializes mainly with school friends, boys and girls.	Emma wants, ultimately, to achieve and feels she will do this. At present prefers to construct herself as a non-conforming individualist. Frequently in trouble and finding it difficult to sustain friendships, but she doesn't feel excluded from school and learning. She has tolerant friends, a supportive parent and she is clear that her teachers have faith that her academic potential will be realized.
Tracey, Westway	A low achiever. Concerned to be in a group which will insulate her from risk and exposure. Dislikes having her work adversely compared with others and feeling that she is failing. Aims to escape teacher attention, make minimal effort and chat with friends. Sees some teachers as remote and unhelpful.	Tracey is shy and not confident. Her small group is socially on the margins. They observe and comment on their more popular peers. Aware of various sub-groups and the connection between social status and learning. Generally keep a low profile and avoid attention.	Tracey lives in a two bedroom council flat with her five sisters, mother and father and a dog. Tracey is the middle child. Other family members, including her oldest sister who has two children, live on the estate. Her father is long-term unemployed.	Tracey has a very weak sense of herself as a learner. Concerned to keep her teachers 'happy' and minimally appeased. Sees the locus of control in relation to learning as outside herself; has no strategy or inclination to change this. Main goal in school, to feel secure in a small mutually protective social group.

Table 8.3 Aspects in the creation of identity: Denmark, North School

	Perspectives on classroom learning	*Perspectives on peer group*	*Out of school contexts*	*Summary*
Torben, North school	A strong sense of himself as a high achiever. Would like to be challenged more. Thinks he does best at subjects he likes best. Likes intensive individual work and collaborative projects. Feels some tension between his individual achievements and the ideal of class solidarity pursued by the teacher. Understands strategic requirement to be likeable and not 'precocious' if he is to avoid teasing. Sees home/school meetings, rather than classroom feedback, as the best source of advice on school work.	Has a small group of friends, united by an interest in war games which they pursue in and out of school. Sees this group as supportive but not exclusive. Identifies sub-groups in class based on out of school socializing and interests. Thinks there is a degree of competitiveness in class but in general they all *get al*.ong. Teachers work hard to avoid cliques developing.	Lives with both parents and his younger brother. Parents have professional posts in medical area. Father is chairman of school board. Strong identification with school. Torben gets help and support with school work. Same friends in and out of school with shared interests. Spends a lot of time on war gaming and reading.	Strong links between home and school. Torben has consciously reflected on social operations. Has moderated the expression of his enthusiasm for learning and his awareness of his own high level of attainment so that he 'fits in' with the class. Sees the need to avoid creating cliques. Finds support from his family and friends. Would like more challenge but thinks he fits the teacher's notion of the ideal pupil – interested and well behaved.
Jesper, North school	Assessed as 'academically weak'. His discourse about the classroom which stresses 'friends' and social groups rather than learning, may be a response to this. He talks of having fun and liking things to be happening. He thinks he learns best when the teacher teaches the whole class or when he works on his own, suggesting he has problems working in groups.	Sees two clear groups in the class – social partygoers and intellectuals. Says he feels part of both but appears to belong in neither and is teased. His teacher sees him as immature and wrongly placed in this class. Says he sometimes feels left out but thinks that becoming a member of the Pupil Council will give him status and influence with peers and teacher.	An only child. Mother is training in social work; father is a technician. His leisure time is rarely spent with his family. He likes watching TV, listening to music, going to the youth club where he plays indoor football.	Jesper is having difficulty finding a place in his class and feeling that he has a positive social identity. This, combined with low attainment, seems to be making it hard for him to construct a positive identity as a learner.

Mette, Periphery school	A strong sense of herself as a high achiever, an independent learner and an 'ideal pupil'. Enjoys being challenged. Engineers groups so that she works with others 'on the same level'. Manages relationships with teachers to secure their support. Interested in teachers' assessment, wants more feedback.	A leading member of a socially dominant group. Sense of separation, social superiority and power in relation to other groups evident in classroom behaviour. Thinks the class is 'quite unified' but strongly aware of after school groupings. Thinks the Pupil Council is a waste of time.	Lives with her divorced mother, step-father and younger sister. Mother is a systems analyst, step-father is in catering. She gets lots of help and support from home. Feels close to her family. Allowed a lot of freedom to organize her time. Has a loyal group of friends who have 'good fun' together. Aspires to a 'challenging job'.	Mette is reflective, independent and with a strong sense of herself as a learner and as an achiever. Her sense of being in control is reinforced by her social group and by her family context.
Per, Periphery school	A low achiever. Sees himself as useless. Disinclined to effort, which is seen as not effective, except in subjects he likes and are not 'boring'. Classroom identity is as a trouble-maker. Has a range of avoidance strategies – some agreed by the teacher.	Per is physically small. Frequently teased. Has few friends, also trouble-makers – the main source of their identities in school. Thinks the breaks and his friends are the only good things about school, which is a waste of space.	Lives with his divorced mother, step-father and two younger siblings. Both parents are in skilled manual work. Per has a job after school. He has a computer, his own TV and does gymnastics. His mother is quite strict. She helps with schoolwork when she can.	Per's life out of school provides him with a stronger and more positive identity than the school context. In school, which he says he dislikes, his chosen social identity as a trouble-maker is constructed in response to his failure as a learner and acceptable classmate.

What is striking is the degree to which Cousin's categories deal with the notion of pupil solidarity in the classroom. As we have seen in Chapter 6 the notion of *'l'union fait la force'* which is evident in French classrooms is barely discernible in the English schools. With an organizational system where pupils were frequently mixed for different subjects they emphasized their differentiated social groups rather than their solidarity as a class. The French pupils' attitude, we argue, is an expression of French cultural values, school organization and a response to the perceived huge distance between pupils and teachers in the French system.

The English pupils, in all three schools, produced, unprompted, their own typology for us. It appears at first glance to echo Cousin's categories. However, when we offered some of the types to pupil focus groups in the other countries, French and Danish pupils had (different) difficulties in applying these meanings neatly to their situation. We want to argue too that English pupils' sensitivity to identities and the ability to generate types was itself a product of the cultural context, national and local, of the schools they inhabited.

The constructs produced by the English pupils contained aspects of both learner identity and social identity. In broad terms one type consisted of very hardworking, interested, generally high achieving pupils who were well behaved and conformist (referred to, as we have already seen by Daniel and others, variously as 'boffins' or 'keeners'), the second group were 'in between', did some work and some messing about, but generally tried hard. The third group were people who had a bad attitude to work, didn't work hard, were badly behaved, which could include smoking, drinking, bullying and constantly being in trouble. The flavour of this typology is conveyed by one version of it from Westway school in London:

> There's boffins – really brainy, always quiet, always answer the question, always do their work. They know what they're doing; they push hard with their work . . . Don't talk when they are working, never stop to enjoy themselves, put their heads down in their books even when everyone else is laughing. Some other people talk and mess about in lessons but they still do their work as well. Then there's people who smoke, drink, bully, get on report for being late and bad behaviour

This neat three-part typology is further complicated, however, by the distinction made to accommodate pupils who 'mess about' but are positively perceived by their peers because they make people laugh: '*bad* boys – they're popular, like to joke'. And by one further addition: the charismatic student who can get away with anything: 'There's Jason, it wouldn't matter what he did; he could come to school in a bathing hat and the next week everyone would want to have one.'

What we have here, in a very crude form, is a statement of a number of identities that were available to the English pupil sample. As might be expected the exact description of these groups was dependent on who was doing the describing and their claimed relationship to this particular sub-set. The flavour of the speaker's own positioning is evident in the example above and evidences the characteristic preference for a position 'in the middle'. For all the pupils in the English sample the epithet of 'boffin' or 'keener' (Cousin's '*intello*') was not particularly complimentary, though, for some, not always unwelcome. For average and low achievers it was a way of categorizing 'the other' as something undesirable and became entwined with social conformity to school rules, uniform and a certain degree of social exclusion as these quotations from pupils at St Theresa's illustrate:

> Everything perfect – not just work. The right school uniform – not hipsters, not thick soles or jewellery . . . no make-up.

> Top of the class, always do the work, set their pencil cases out tidily . . . they probably have a good time in their little group.

The English system, then, produced a range of available identities which our pupils operated with some subtlety in the three schools. The construction of identity as a learner for most English pupils was inextricably bound up with the construction of social identity. The assumption of particular attitudes, behaviour in class, approaches to learning were markers of membership of groups which secured a social identity. Salient factors in this process in England were cultural assumptions about assessment, the affective domain and social relationships in school; all of which operated differently in Denmark and France.

Assessment, the affective domain, teacher–pupil relationships

In the case of the 12 students we have discussed, the assessment culture of the three national systems had an influence on their identity construction. For high achievers this manifested itself in different ways. In England the foregrounding of assessment as 'high stakes' for institutions and individuals made more public ranking of students a salient feature. This combined with the conventional English mistrust of the intellectual and dislike of the over-striver made an identity as 'boffin' or 'keener' difficult for high achievers and in particular for boys. In France, where pupils are also regularly graded, although, Cousin's category of '*intello*' was also pejorative and there was some reluctance among pupils to be thus perceived, the concept was in no way as strongly marked. In interview, both Pierre and Simone referred unself-consciously (and not ironically) to themselves and their friends as 'les intellectuels'. They were not unhappy with this label and even identified with it. In Denmark assessment is low key, the social and the academic are intertwined inextricably and there is a powerful focus on consensus. In this context Torben appeared reluctant to adopt, publicly, an achievement focused identity as a learner, not only because this would cause problems with some of his peers but also that this differentiation ran counter to the values pursued by his teacher in the classroom. In France, in contrast, Pierre received the whole-hearted reinforcement and approval of the system. In England, Emma was supported because of her perceived academic potential.

The relative use of grades in assessment also played a part. In general, across all three countries, the high achievers wanted to be shown how they could improve. They were very much for assessment but their view of what this involved was culturally shaped. In France, Pierre and Simone welcomed getting marks and especially comments, even though it could be painful if they were bad, as it showed them how to improve and motivated them to work harder. Pierre found the French system of error analysis helpful in identifying where he needed to concentrate his learning. Mette, in Denmark, was against tests and grades which she thought were 'a strange kind of assessment' and made her nervous. She wanted more focused and more stringent feedback from her teachers and implied that they were too easily pleased with what she produced.

For low achievers the story was equally varied. At the Periphery school in Denmark, Per and his friends were not in any way as resilient as Mette. 'A bad grade makes you . . . feel just like giving up – like dropping everything.' They needed positive reinforcement to keep them going. Jesper, at the North school, had an equally poorly developed sense of himself as a successful learner. Although Per and Jesper's behaviour in school was problematic they did not construct themselves as rebels, nor were they perceived as such by their teachers. In Denmark, social identities are accommodated as a focus for development and so there was much less for them to rebel against. School was an acceptable location for Jesper and Per's search for a social identity. In France social identity was constructed in part outside the school context and also as a protection against it. The rebels, Fayaz and Sylvie, could find no place for their social identity within the system and so constructed themselves in opposition to it.

Here we can see how the nature of teacher–pupil relationships and cultural assumptions about the affective domain in learning, in combination with the assessment culture, played a part in creating a range of available identities and a context within which these operated. Overall we can identify some of the major differences observable in the three countries.

In France pupils in the study were unanimous in expressing the tensions they felt between their sense of themselves as people and learners and the strength of the system in constructing them. Their sense of an unequal power relationship and a positioning of themselves as immature was most powerfully signified by the convention that teachers used '*tu*' in addressing pupils while pupils were required to use '*vous*' to teachers. In addition the strongly signalled separation between the social and the academic meant that the system produced a limited range of available identities: pupils had little choice or room for manoeuvre. This in a way made it simpler for them, but there were costs. The high achievers got focus and security but in the main were driven by instrumentality: they adopted a strategic school produced identity in order to succeed because that is what the system required. This was often in conflict with their own articulation of what it is to be a learner, which they suppressed or left undeveloped. The low achievers had little choice but to be anti-school because the system allowed them no room for negotiation within it. Losses and gains for our students were more clearly marked in France.

The distance between teachers and pupils was much less strongly felt in England. The schools' concern for both the cognitive and the affective dimensions of learning offered room for more negotiation and more hurdles to surmount. The range of factors which were interacting in the English pupils' construction of themselves as learner/pupils and as people affected, in different ways, their academic achievement. The assumption of particular attitudes, behaviour in class, approaches to learning were markers of membership of groups which secured a social identity. English pupils were able to identify very specific group characteristics and to allocate themselves and others to these categories with some subtlety. Membership of a group which secured social identity could support or hinder academic achievement; in particular negotiating academic attainment and social success posed more problems for boys than girls. Because of the focus on teacher–pupil relationships in learning, pupils had the possibility of adjusting the range and focus of their identities with individual teachers. This variety of choices placed huge demands on pupils' social skills.

Some English pupils gained in this more negotiable context. Emma, for example, was fortunate in being accommodated by her English school and could be contrasted with Sylvie who had little choice in France but to rebel. At the extreme there were some pupils – not included in our vignettes – who refused to accommodate in any way to school. However there were more like Melanie and Tracey about whom there are questions to be asked. Secure in their social groups they were enjoying school, attending fairly regularly and causing little trouble but there was less evidence that they felt a need to develop a learning identity that would facilitate achievement.

In Denmark, concern for the development of the whole child and with the affective dimension of education is very strong. This legitimated an emphasis which many Danish pupils placed on social, rather than academic identity – or perhaps more correctly made it more difficult to disentangle the two. Danish pupils were aware of the desirability of 'fitting in' and the value their teachers placed on cooperation and social conformity, in learning as well as in other areas of life. As adolescents with different out of school interests and experiences they, like their English counterparts, were inclined to differentiate themselves but felt the pressure to conform. Within the system 'difficult' pupils were accommodated; there was a sense that there was plenty of time and space for development. However, pupils like Torben felt ambivalent about exhibiting too great an enthusiasm for learning and for demonstrating their own excellence.

In summary we could say that in the three countries the development of social and pupil/learner identity for our students was different. In France the development of social identity was as far as possible excluded from academic learning: pupils' sense of themselves as learners and as people was assumed to develop separately. In England an individual's identity as a learner and as a person were developed in association with each other: school and classroom were identified as contexts for identity work of both kinds. In Denmark the development of learning identity was subservient to the development of social identity. In France a strongly articulated and approved 'pupil identity' and in Denmark an equally strongly articulated and approved 'social identity' offered models in relation to which individuals reacted with relative degrees of force. In England, although there was an idea of the ideal conformist pupil, there was more room for negotiation and thus more uncertainty and variety.

Conclusions

It is useful, finally, to consider whether these students are 'trapped' – for good or ill – in the identities they adopted for themselves. Hall (1990) suggests that identity is never inexorably fixed and that life stages and events are among a number of factors which are the basis for identity transformation. In addition the concept of 'a learning career' (Goffman 1971; Pollard and Filer 1999; Bloomer and Hodkinson 2000) provides evidence of changes in individuals' sense of themselves in a variety of domains. There is evidence in this study that some of the English pupils, who – at the end of our research period were the first to arrive at a significant moment in their school careers: the selection of their 14–16 curriculum – felt that review and reappraisal was appropriate. With this in mind we need to consider to what extent the contexts in which they operate will make it possible for them to engineer transformation should they so wish. Perceptions of both power relations and personal interest come into play in identity construction. We have already seen the way that identities legitimated by the dominant social representation of teachers, schools or peers have featured in the individual stories of our students in the form of acceptance, strategic compliance or uneasy tension. Similarly we have seen oppositional identities constructed out of exclusion and resistance. What are the conditions under which new identities are built, subjectivities redefined and transformation sought? What sort of shifts in overall structure are required to make room for this identity project? (Castells 1997). Moscovici (1981, 1984) refers to opposition or struggle between groups as 'a dialogue with an imaginary interlocutor'; MacLure (1993) suggests that identity claims can be seen as a form of argument – as devices for justifying, explaining and making sense. If construction is a matter of structure and agency then it is a question of whether a way can be found to enable the voices of pupils – their *argument* – to be more clearly heard in a real dialogue about learning. That they felt they had no voice or were not being properly listened to was a recurrent theme in all three countries. Official fora, such as school councils, for so-called democratic participation in Denmark and, to a lesser extent in England, were assessed as limited in their power, operation and usefulness.

We also have to return to the idea of the available resources that pupils draw on as they seek to inhabit, elaborate or construct these identities. As we have seen, factors such as national culture and institutional values are variable within the three systems. But we also need to consider variables such as the values and aspirations of individual families, socio-economic status, gender and the perception of the functional value of school to the individual. In the next chapter we look at the way in which some of the factors which we have identified as significant for learners operate as variables within each of the three countries.

9 Young learners: what makes a difference? The influence of socio-economic status, gender and ethnicity

Introduction

Part 3 of the book has been concerned with the way in which national policy discourse and the espoused 'aims' of education systems are eventually translated to, and mediated by, pupils through the filters of their own particular perceptions and values.

This chapter continues the focus on pupil perceptions and looks at the influence of intra-national differences within the three countries, particularly those deriving from differences in socio-economic status, gender and ethnicity. Here we consider the relative significance of such differences in influencing childrens' perceptions of schooling and their achievements compared with the influence of the inter-national differences which have been documented in earlier chapters. Thus the key question for this chapter is how do children construct an identity as a learner and as a pupil *within* different national contexts, in the light of crucial influences such as differences in social class, gender and ethnicity? To what extent are these differences mediated in different or similar ways by the different education systems of England, France and Denmark? What can we understand from this about the extent to which children's experience of secondary schooling is becoming more similar or moving towards convergence in the context of Europeanization, globalization, and the internationalization of adolescent/peer culture? Are new forms of inequality and exclusion emerging in the light of such influences? First we move to examine the education policy discourse of the three countries with regard to issues of disadvantage, educational opportunity and inequality and we briefly describe the context of the case study schools in areas of disadvantage, before turning to the perceptions of the young learners themselves.

Disadvantage and educational policy in England, France and Denmark

In addressing the issues of educational opportunity, social disadvantage and inequality, the education systems of England, France and Denmark have evolved very different approaches. In France where the educational system has developed constitutionally and where there is a strong tradition of republicanism, the origin of which may be traced back to the works of Condorcet, the policy rhetoric emphasizes the moral unacceptability of treating pupils differentially. In the discourse of government and indeed in individual teachers' discourse, the idea that all citizens should be seen to have equal rights under the law recurs repeatedly as a fundamental principle. Schools have consequently been expected to provide the same curriculum and pedagogy to all pupils regardless of who they are, where they live or even (within limits) their ability level (Holmes 1985; Sharpe 1992). Traditionally therefore the French education system has avoided differentiation and has, in principle, adopted a policy of equal entitlement for all pupils. Ideologically at least, there is great emphasis placed on the goals of equal opportunity. Emphasis on the 'public good' aspects of education is enforced by strong centralization and a pre-eminent role for the state in educational decision making and control. Thus equality is one of the principles of the French state and schools which did not appear to comply with equal opportunities would be seen as unlawful and un-French.

> *Toute forme de discrimination va à l'encontre du principe fondamental d'égalité entre les citoyens. Elle met aussi en danger la cohésion de l'ensemble de la societé, la solidité du pacte republicain et la portée même de la societé, la solidité du pacte republicain et la portée même de la notion de citoyenneté.* (All forms of discrimination are against the fundamental principle of equality between citizens. They endanger the cohesion of society as a whole, the solidity of the republican pact and even the capability of the society, the solidity of the republican pact and even the effectiveness of the notion of citizenship.)
>
> (www.premier.ministre.gouv.fr/p.cfm)

So far as pupils of different ethnicity are concerned, it would be considered unacceptable and indeed racist to aim policies within schools particularly at them, so positive discrimination in the schools is aimed at underachieving pupils in general. Incidents such as the banning of the wearing of the headscarf by Muslim girls in French schools can be seen within this context of the deliberate avoidance of difference and of differentiation and on the distancing of local religious and cultural community feelings (Raveaud 2003). The

Republican model relegates such influences to the private sphere and emphasizes integration and a shared high culture (Schnapper 1991).

In contrast, the English educational system emphasizes a multicultural model which rests on the recognition of diversity and respect for different cultures. Historically it has developed in a far more 'piecemeal' fashion, based on what is 'customary' rather than on constitutional principles (Archer 1984). Unlike France, where the Revolution and subsequent Napoleonic era had led to a formal national commitment to a unified system of provision, English education was strongly influenced in the past by voluntary agencies and the church, and by a tradition of diversity and individualism evolving from a variety of local initiatives. Religious education and concern with the personal and social development of children has always formed part of the remit of schools. Consequently a concern with the development of individual potential recurs as a theme both at the level of national policy discourse and in teachers' classrooms and staffroom discourse. Thus the system has enshrined the notion of differentiated teaching according to the perceived needs of children. In this view, greater equality within education cannot be achieved without understanding that children start school from rather different points and therefore require different teaching approaches.

Thus policies on equal opportunity are a government requirement for education in England where the aim is:

> To promote equality of opportunity in education and training and at work, including tackling social exclusion, deprivation and under-achievement – in particular, by combating discrimination by gender, age, race or disability.
>
> (World Data on Education, England (1998) INCA CD-ROM)

All the English schools in our sample had an individual school policy on equal opportunities and published school aims for pupils which often emphasized respect for diversity and understanding of other cultures.

In Denmark, as in France, there was a strong emphasis in the policy discourse on egalitarianism, that is on providing the same education for all regardless of differences in home background, socio-economic status, ethnicity and achievement. As in France, this was interpreted traditionally as emphasizing uniformity in order to ensure pupils' equal entitlement to education. The aims of the Danish *folkskole* emphasize the importance of contributing to pupils' understanding of other peoples' cultures and that 'the teaching of the school and its daily life must therefore build on intellectual freedom, equality and democracy'. Recent policy developments have laid increasing emphasis on differentiating the education each individual receives in order to give each individual the best possibility of developing according to their abilities. For example:

> To give the individual pupil the opportunity to develop as many of his/her talents as possible.
>
> (World Data on Education, Denmark (1998) INCA CD-ROM p. 1)

However, the Danish policy towards ethnic minority children in schools is still one of assimilation. The Danish schools in our sample interpreted this largely as requiring them to establish a basis for accepting and respecting the cultural circumstances of children.

As the preceding paragraphs suggest, there are different emphases in the policy rhetoric of the three countries. In reality, however, there is still a strong linkage between social origin, educational attainment and life chances in all three systems although there is some evidence that this may be less strong in Denmark, a society with less marked social class divisions. Thus schools are seen in the main to be simply reproducing the social conditions prevailing in the wider society (Halsey *et al.* 1980; Bourdieu and Passeron 1990; Charlot *et al.* 1992).

In England, concern about low standards and low teacher expectations in city schools has led to a range of recent government policy initiatives, such as the Excellence in Cities programme and the establishment, in 1998, of education action zones (EAZs), designed to raise standards of achievement in schools in socially disadvantaged areas. In France too there is concern that, despite strong educational expansion aimed at democratization, attainment remains strongly linked to pupils' social background with the children of manual workers still far less likely to reach the level of the '*Baccalauréat*' than the children of executives, professionals or service class members. Coincidentally, also in 1998, the French government relaunched its policy of zones d'education prioritaires (ZEPs), which, like the EAZs were designed to improve educational achievement in disadvantaged areas. This focus on positive discrimination represented a fundamental break with the republican tradition of French education and has created tremendous debate in French education about whether the increasing responsiveness to local needs which the ZEPs were designed to create, actually furthers social justice or reinforces a logic of separation and inequality (Hatcher 2001). There is other research evidence which suggests that, with policy changes such as the ZEPs and with increasing expansion in the education system, social inequalities appear to have shifted from access to lower-secondary school to access to upper-secondary but nevertheless remain strong (Duru-Bellat 1996; Duru-Bellat and van Zanten 1999).

Denmark appears to be a less divided society and school system in terms of social class differences but there have been dramatic changes more recently in the relatively homogeneous Danish population. Many of the schools now have a much higher proportion of ethnic minority children due to increased immigration. The response of Danish national culture has been put under scrutiny in the light of this changed school population, with differing religious and cultural norms and different demands on the educational system, and this response is still evolving. Racism is seen to be an issue by some Danish people but is denied by many others.

The case study schools in areas of disadvantage

Westway School in west London was described in the school prospectus as a 'mixed multi-ethnic comprehensive school'. Languages spoken by pupils included Bangladeshi, Urdu, Gujurati, Somali, Arabic, Hindi, Youraba, Swahili, Ibo, Twi and Caribbean creoles. English was an additional language for over 8 percent of the school's pupils (which is well above the national average). The school's socio-economic intake was from a disadvantaged population. Fifty percent of the school population received free school meals and 50 percent of pupils were defined as educationally and behaviourally disadvantaged.

Berbère school in the southern suburbs of Paris was also set in a disadvantaged urban area. In official statistics, the school population consisted of 84 percent French pupils and 16 percent 'foreign pupils'. However, these figures do not show the percentage of French pupils that were from ethnic minorities, or the percentage of foreign pupils that were not from ethnic minorities since the French view is that the concept of an ethnic minority is in itself discriminatory and unequal. Hence there are no statistics available on school populations or achievement levels according to ethnic minority status. Other school data throw more light on the school's pupil population: school statistics showed that 37 percent of pupils had repeated a year once in their school career, and 19 percent had repeated a year twice, indicators of a number of pupils in difficulties. Researcher observations noted a high proportion of pupils of African and Arab descent (probably close to 85 or 90 percent). Montand school, also located in the Parisian suburbs, drew upon a mixed population, many of whom were from working class families and also had a fairly high proportion of ethnic minority children.

City school in Copenhagen had an increasingly large intake of bilingual pupils. Close to 70 percent were from ethnic minority families with roots in over 30 different countries, in particular from Pakistan, the Arabic countries and Turkey. The school stood out as being the only school in the area which encompassed four language groups. Seven bi-cultural teachers were employed at the school. During the last ten years the school's catchment area had changed markedly. Moving from being a school for more or less socially stable Danish working class families, the school had experienced a change of circumstances in step with the influx of various ethnic groups. Increasingly Danish parents were moving their children to other schools with a higher proportion of Danish origin pupils. In the words of the headteacher, the school was therefore trying to re-structure its identity in order to maintain the intake of Danish origin pupils and to avoid 'dissatisfaction' and 'ignorance' on the part of the Danish parents. Periphery school in Denmark also drew upon socially disadvantaged families for its pupils. Most were living in a suburban municipal housing estate. However, relatively few were ethnic minority families.

School aims and school policies in the three countries

Since 1988, in England, responsibility for equal opportunities has moved from the local education authorities to the schools themselves. English schools are required to produce an individual school policy on equal opportunities for inspection by Ofsted (Office for Standards in Education). All three English schools had complied or were complying with this demand.

As part of their marketed image English schools also produce individual school aims. St Theresa's, a Catholic school serving a predominantly white working class area did not include a specific reference to multiculturalism or anti-racism in its school aims, which were,

> To be a community in which all are affirmed and encouraged to become self reliant, while having respect for others.

Both Lady Margaret School, which was situated in an affluent market town with few ethnic minority pupils, and Westway, had, in contrast, clear multicultural and equal opportunities statements in their school aims although there was no reference to anti-racism. For Lady Margaret School these were:

> To ensure that equal opportunities are available for every pupil to fulfill his or her potential, irrespective of physical or intellectual ability, gender or cultural background.
>
> The curriculum must be non-discriminatory. It must cater equally for boys and girls, in lesson content, in classroom organisation, in the promotion of positive images in the fields of race, gender and disability and in the avoidance of stereotypical attitudes.
>
> To encourage pupils to respect, value and benefit from the diversity of race, religion and culture in the world around them.
>
> To ensure that a positive appreciation of the contribution of other cultures to our society is gained through the Humanities, the Arts, Science and Mathematics.
>
> To understand the nature of and to respect other cultures in the world.

For Westway these were:

> We are a multi-faith school which celebrates diversity and promotes tolerance and mutual respect for each other's beliefs and values.

Westway had a policy of positive racial discrimination. The school was specifically targeting boys of Afro-Caribbean origin as a group in order to raise their achievement. The Westway African Caribbean Achievement Project had been set up, and action taken had included finding out the proportion of boys of Afro-Caribbean origin attending extra curricular activities and the running of a black mentoring scheme. Black pupils met up once a week with role models of successful black adults (volunteers), with the aim of taking pupils through three stages: 'identity', 'survival' and 'realization'. As the headteacher put it 'These kids need an identity, about who they are and what they can be'.

In France, where schools as individual units are given less importance, schools have to comply with national government requirements for equal opportunities which emphasize equality as a fundamental principle of the republican tradition:

> *Le système d'éducation repose en France sur les principes de la tradition républicaine: caractère du public du service de l'éducation, laïcité et égalité démocratique.* (The French education system rests on the principles of the republican tradition, the public service character of education, laicity and democratic equality.)
>
> (World Data on Education, France (1998) INCA CD-ROM)

Although their underachievement is recognized as a problem, French ethnic minority pupils, often referred to as 'les immigrés', are not defined as a distinct underachieving group, as this would be seen as racist and unrepublican. It is significant that official statistics are collected on nationality only, not on ethnic origin (Raveaud 2003), although as van Zanten (1997) points out, official permission has been given to do so. Positive discrimination in the schools was therefore aimed at underachieving pupils in general. Both Berbère and Montand schools were targeting underachievement by setting up special classes of only 15 pupils (*'classe d'aide et soutien'*) and were applying for the status of educational priority areas ('zone d'education prioritaire') in order to increase their resources.

In Denmark equal educational opportunities are provided for by the local municipalities and by the schools through differentiated teaching or support lessons. As in England, there is no repeating the year in Danish schools. The ethos of the City school was, according to the headteacher based on views of a multicultural community and a recognition of each other's languages, religious persuasions and attitudes. Each year the school arranged an 'international class teacher day' in which the focus was on the background of bilingual children. Parents brought maps, display boards and food from their home countries and talked about their own country. And each year there was an Arabic, Pakistani and Turkish evening, with a dialogue concerning upbringing and education. These debate evenings took place in the language of the parents, and were at the same time translated into Danish. On the one hand the school was trying to establish a basis for accepting and respecting the cultural circumstances of the pupils, but on the other hand there was a definite wish to socialize all pupils to be able to cope with and fit into Danish society.

Similar actions were taken at Periphery school, although not necessarily for ethnic minority children, to help socially and language deprived pupils in particular to learn to read and to gain self-confidence. 'First of all you have to teach the kids to read . . . kids who can't read become citizens with very little influence', the headteacher said. The pedagogical goals of the school project was that the pupils become able to cooperate, be responsible, be independent and be honest. From this brief description of the schools, differences in school policy in the three countries can be seen clearly – with a strong emphasis in France and a modified one in Denmark on assimilation and integration, and in England on multiculturalism and the recognition of difference.

Teacher perceptions of social equality issues

Teachers in all three countries felt that boys and girls received equal treatment in their schools. So far as equal opportunities for children of different social backgrounds was concerned, there was some evidence, similar to that in our earlier studies related to French and English primary teachers of a significant difference in the beliefs and values of teachers working in areas of disadvantage in England and France (Osborn *et al.* 1996). Teachers in France emphasized equal entitlement and a transmission-enlightenment model of education. They were concerned to treat all children in exactly the same way in order to achieve justice and educational results, and aimed to transmit the same academic body of knowledge to all pupils. In practice, however, some teachers did differentiate their teaching, particularly when working with pupils defined as having special needs. As van Zanten (2000) has shown, such teachers have adapted in various ways in order to deal with a professional situation where an uncritical following of republican principles is likely to make everyday life in the class untenable. In contrast, English teachers' discourse emphasized the needs of disadvantaged children as different from the mainstream and requiring a different response from schools. Danish teachers' discourse was closer to that of French teachers in respect of disadvantaged children. They believed strongly in the importance of giving all children access to the Danish and European cultural heritage of literature, art and history, although there was much more attempt to engage the interest and concerns of children than was often evident in France.

Few of the teachers in the study talked specifically about ethnic minorities or racism. French teachers, in line with French government policy, made little reference to ethnic minority pupils as a separate group. One science teacher at Berbère, however, did refer to what he saw as the problems of Muslim children's understanding of science. He argued that the 'superstition of their religion reinforced by local religious leaders', mitigated against the pupils' acceptance of the logic and rationality of science.

Only two teachers in England, both from Westway School, made specific reference to racial equality issues. The first, a teacher of English thought that racism was: 'Barely an issue . . . I haven't really encountered any racist attitudes.' The second, however, a black special educational needs teacher and counsellor, was critical of the school's policy of avoiding the issue of racism, 'It's there, but it's being contained, so it's being sort of held'. He felt that racism, like bullying, needed to be acknowledged and dealt with.

Ethnic minority pupils were often perceived as a 'problem' by Danish teachers from the City school. With the increase in the proportion of second generation pupils, still referred to as 'immigrants' (exacerbated by the loss of some white pupils transferring to other schools) the school and pupil behaviour were perceived to be changing. One teacher thought the high proportion of ethnic minority pupils was giving the school a bad reputation. Teachers experienced difficulties with parents, whose expectations were different. Unlike Danish parents, ethnic minority parents were seen by teachers as 'very passive', 'only interested in receiving information from the school and not actively participating in it'. Teachers also realized that ethnic minority parents were not happy about the lack of information about their children's assessment. The children were seen by teachers as posing problems too. This was particularly so in the case of Muslim boys. Their behaviour towards other pupils and teachers was seen as threatening. One teacher complained about verbal and physical violence, arguing that the pupil group which apparently had most difficulty in re-orienting itself to the Danish way of life was the group of Muslim children. Referring to some Muslim boys in 7th grade a teacher said 'they are idolised at home and are used to being able to do what they like'. The school attempted to make these children participate in various duties such as washing up, and found it difficult to achieve. The changes which had taken place as a consequence of the change of intake, one of the teachers argued, could be observed in a growing number of pupils, particularly those whose families were from Pakistan and Morocco, having ambitions of going to university to become lawyers and doctors. These ambitions were also noticeable in the pupils' answers to the questionnaires in this school area.

Muslim girls were also seen by some Danish teachers as 'problematic'. One teacher was sympathetic about the extent to which girls were caught between two cultures but at the same time this teacher had problems with Islam and what she perceived as its repressive attitude to girls. Muslim girls, she said, insisted on wearing head scarves at school. This particular teacher had tried to influence the girls not to do so on the grounds that it would go against them in the adult workplace. Danish teachers from the City school in general, felt strongly the clash in cultures between home and school environments and were outspoken about this. How were these national policy differences and teacher concerns received and mediated by pupils? The sections which follow examine findings from the questionnaire, individual and group interviews.

Issues of equality and inequality within the school: pupil perceptions

In the individual and group interviews we carried out with pupils there were several questions which dealt specifically with issues of equality and inequality. Individual pupils were asked 'Are some pupils treated differently from others?' In the group interviews pupils were shown quotations taken from the questionnaires completed by individual pupils. One of these quotes from a French pupil, directly addressed the issue of equality. She said 'The school must ensure equality for all and give the same opportunities to all.' There were also three prompting questions which were: 'Does the pupil's country of origin make a difference?', 'Does a pupil's home background make a difference?' and 'If there are differences made between pupils at school, what type of differences are they?'

Most English pupils, including ethnic minority pupils, argued that all pupils were treated equally in their school. Race was rarely expressed as an issue, even at the school with the highest ethnic minority population. As one pupil said: 'Everyone is treated equal. It's like our slogan *achieving for all* . . . the headmaster, he's always telling us. Prince Charles came into the school and told us about the black history project'.

The main equality issue for English pupils was gender. There was a widespread perception among boys that girls got preferential treatment. There was also concern about the extent to which pupils were differentiated on the basis of achievement with frequent discussion about how 'brainy people' received better treatment than others.

French pupils interpreted the question about equality as being about gender differences, ethnic differences, differences between high and low achieving pupils and those who worked and those who did not. Many pupils in the two most disadvantaged urban schools felt that their schools encouraged equality by giving greater help to weaker pupils and they were aware of antiracist policies in the schools: '*On a pas le droit de dire, "C'est les Noirs" ou "C'est l'Arabe" ou "C'est le Français"*.' ('We are not allowed to say "It's the Blacks" or "It's the Arab" or "It's the French guy" '). However, in both these schools, some groups of pupils complained about the racism of some individual teachers and often thought that these teachers used stereotypes: *'Ils nous mettent tous dans le meme tas. Par exemple, pour eux, un Noir, un Arabe, c'est la délinquance . . . les gens sont pas pareil. Il faut pas mélanger sa tête comme ça.'* ('They lump us all together. For example, for them a Black and Arab – they are seen as delinquents. People aren't the same. They shouldn't lump us together like that').

One pupil complained that:

> *L'année dernière mon professeur de technologie, il faisait toujours des différences entre les Noirs et tout ça; c'était toujours les Noirs, toujours les Noirs.* (Last year my technology teacher was always differentiating between Blacks and others and all that; it was always the 'Blacks', 'the Blacks'.)

and even pupils at the most affluent school, were aware of racism:

> *Il y a souvent des différences de nationalité entre professeurs et élèves . . . il y a toujours un peu de racisme dans les collèges.* (There are often race differences between the teachers and the pupils . . . there is always a bit of racism in the secondary schools.)

French pupils from all three schools were aware of their rights as French citizens. When one group at Cathédrale school, in an affluent area of southern France, was asked about equality at the school, a boy replied:

> *C'est obligé, ça c'est les droits, cest l'égalité des droits. Ça vient des droits de l'homme* (It's obligatory [that all pupils should be treated equally], it's the law, it's the equality of the law. It comes from the rights of man)

Cathédrale pupils agreed that the *'collège'* had to treat pupils equally, *'C'est ce qu'il est censé de faire'*, ('It's what they are supposed to do') but they added that in practice their school did nothing to help equality issues. There was some indication from pupil responses that French ethnic minority pupils had gained, not only in knowledge but also in confidence and identity from lessons in civic education.

In the group interviews, many pupils from Berbère school, in a suburban disadvantaged area of Paris, spontaneously brought up ethnic minority and equality issues in response to general pupil quotations and prompting questions. Pupils used the criterion of racism to judge teachers. A former teacher was disliked because, *'Elle n'aimait pas les Noirs'* ('She did not like Blacks'). Pupils had a positive attitude to the head of affective education, *'Les gens respectent M G . . . il a des amis de tous les pays'* ('People respect Monsieur G . . . he has friends from all countries').

When discussing the teacher–pupil relationship, pupils thought that half of pupils at the school did not respect teachers. Berbère pupils respected teachers who shared characteristics with pupils. These characteristics could be youthfulness, residence in the same area as pupils; *'Lui, il comprend mieux, il vient de la cité comme nous'* ('He understands better, he comes from the area like us'); or the same ethnicity:

> *Quand on a des gens pareil que nous . . . une personne 'Black', quand elle vient nous parler, à une autre personne 'Black', on a l'impression de se comprendre. Par exemple, les Noirs et les Arabes, nous on se considère comme plus des frères.* (When it is a person similar to us, a Black person, when she comes to speak to us, to another Black person, you get the impression that we understand each other. For example, the Blacks and the Arabs, we consider each other more like brothers.)

This raises a question about identity and the extent to which ethnic minority pupils in the three countries identify with other pupils and teachers with the same ethnicity. Berbère pupils made it clear that their definition of good teachers was:

> *Qu'ils ne fassent pas de différence entre nous.* (That they don't make any difference between us.)

> *Quand il y a pas de différence, quand il y a pas, par exemple, T'es Noir, t'es Arabe, t'es pas comme les autres.* (When there is no difference, when there is not, for example, 'You are Arab, you are not like the others.)

Cultural differences were also an issue for some ethnic minority pupils. One Muslim girl was offended by a history teacher's account of Roman belief systems, which she seemed to confuse with the teacher's own beliefs. She had confronted the teacher:

> *Mais Monsieur, je suis croyante, il n'y a qu'un Dieu sur terre.* (But sir, I am a believer, there is only God on earth.)

The girl was given a detention for her interruption. The teacher lost her respect. In this case a more multiculturally sensitive approach, could perhaps have avoided this breakdown in teacher–pupil relationships.

For many of these pupils then, the definition of a good teacher was one who did not differentiate according to race and a good school was one where there was no racism. The response from pupils suggested that although French policy discourse emphasized equality regardless of ethnic background these issues were played out rather differently at classroom level. In contrast few French thought that in school there was unequal treatment on grounds of sex or social origin.

The majority of Danish pupils felt that generally they were treated equally.

Few said that teachers discriminated in any way on the grounds of social origin or race. However, not all the pupils at the City school were totally convinced that they were treated equally. Some of the ethnic minority pupils felt particularly that they were not allowed to talk or to have a say in class. In one school pupils found that boys were treated more severely than girls, arguing that it might be because boys were more childish and girls were more absorbed in their school work. One pupil argued that 'It is impossible to make sure that some get equal opportunities in life, because you don't have similar ambitions'. Another felt that 'The pupils themselves make the differences – not the teachers'. Pupils saw the home background playing a role in school and the importance of having parents 'who support you – that you feel well in your family – where you treat each other well'. School areas were clearly reflected in the moral issues raised by the pupils. At the more affluent school in the west of Denmark a pupil said 'A good home brings you up well . . . that you are not impertinent to teachers'. A pupil in City school described the importance of having a home where 'the parents are not continuously quarrelling and there is no criminality around'.

As Chapter 8 suggested, all pupils were concerned with establishing a social identity, but for English pupils, social identity frequently dominated and determined learner identity and was defined by membership of three distinct groups within the classroom, those for whom working hard was important, those who managed to negotiate a balance between working and 'messing around' and those who were largely concerned with 'messing around' and gaining social popularity with their peers. This link between social and learner identity was particularly marked for young people in the inner London school drawing upon a disadvantaged and ethnically diverse area. These pupils had to devote considerable energy to maintaining a balance between social popularity and academic achievement.

There were also marked differences in the difficulties posed by this negotiation of a balance between social and academic identity for boys and girls in English schools. Boys were in a particularly difficult position as it was seen as more acceptable for girls to work hard than boys: 'For boys there is an image to keep up about not working hard'. The negotiation of social identity required boys to make people laugh, mess around or confront teachers. This quality was thought to be a particular asset for boys who wished to make themselves attractive to girls. A boy observed: 'Girls would say they liked a hard worker but they would really like one who had a laugh'. Boys with natural charisma could afford to be 'laid back'; others had to establish their credibility by: 'having a big mouth', 'being loud', 'being hard', 'doing the opposite of what the teachers tell you', and generally establishing an anti-work reputation.

Although in all three countries pupils distinguished groups of pupils who were hard working and high achieving from those who were not (see Chapter 8 for examples), there was less evidence in France and Denmark of this need to negotiate a balance between social and academic identity, or of boys needing to maintain a particular non-work image. In the inner city French schools particularly there was evidence that French pupils tended to play down the importance of learner and social differentiation. They tried again to convey the idea of unity. Lower achieving pupils stressed that '*intellos*' (high achieving pupils), whether boys or girls, were not discriminated against by the rest of the class. Pupils claimed that anyone could be friends with '*intellos*'. A boy explained, '*Ils sont avec nous*' ('They're with us').

In Denmark, both boys and girls were accepting of academic achievement but they appeared to be more preoccupied with social behaviour for both sexes: 'School is not just academic', 'You should behave well and be a good friend'. As one pupil put it: 'You are allowed to do well and be a bit of a "keener", but you also have to be nice towards others.'

In the Danish cultural context of a philosophy of 'consensus' and a school context of small classes, small schools and classes where pupils remained together for nine or ten years, maintaining good social relationships and behaving well were important survival skills as well as learning skills. For Danish pupils of both sexes, instead of academic achievement, it was personal interests, fashion (also important in England and France) and the degree of freedom allowed to pupils by their parents which seemed to dictate group composition.

Intra-national differences in perceptions of schooling: what makes a difference?

This section presents some key findings from the questionnaire data drawn from the 1800 pupils in all the study schools in the three countries. Here pupils completed both fixed response and open-ended questions about their attitudes to schooling, to their teachers and to learning. We were able to analyse these according to parental socio-economic status and to gender although not according to ethnicity. The findings as a whole suggested that within each education system, gender and socio-economic issues were mediated differently so that the impact of these on pupils' views of themselves as learners varied. There were gender differences in perceptions of schooling in all three countries, but the differences in perceptions of schooling between boys and girls were more marked in France than in the other two countries. In general, French boys were the least likely of all the groups to be positive about school.

In all three countries the girls in our sample were more positive about school and about teachers than the boys. Thus girls were less likely to see school as 'getting in the way of my life' (Table 9.1). However there were variations in the size of the 'gender' gap from one country to another. For example, Danish pupils were positive about their teachers regardless of gender (there were no significant differences between boys and girls), whereas in both

Table 9.1 Gender and attitudes to school: Here are some statements of what you might think about your school. Please show how much you agree or disagree by filling in the appropriate bubble

	Strongly agree / agree (%)					
	Denmark		*England*		*France*	
	Girl	*Boy*	*Girl*	*Boy*	*Girl*	*Boy*
1 On the whole I like my teachers	66.9	63.6	*71.3	66.7	*68.1	59.4
2 School gets in the way of my life	*18.1	25.3	*22.0	37.0	*26.3	35.1
3 I enjoy school	71.3	63.6	59.4	51.8	*66.8	44.7
4 I really enjoy most lessons	66.9	61.0	54.9	50.6	59.7	51.0
5 I want to do well at school	94.6	92.8	98.0	97.7	97.5	97.4
6 I feel as though I'm wasting my time at school	6.5	12.4	3.3	9.3	*7.3	18.2
7 The best part of my life is the time I spend in school	*7.9	13.0	15.0	19.3	*24.2	11.0
8 I'd like to leave school as soon as I can	13.6	18.9	21.1	24.7	14.0	20.8
9 School is the first step on the way to my career	*89.3	83.0	92.3	91.3	*87.8	83.2
10 School is boring	31.0	42.3	34.7	38.8	*18.8	36.7
Totals	**n=280**	**n=324**	**n=244**	**n=311**	**n=233**	**n=199**

Note: * = differences within each country which are statistically significant

England and France girls agreed significantly more often than boys that they liked their teachers.

Whereas the difference in the perspectives of boys and girls was statistically significant in all three countries, the gap was often smallest in Denmark and greatest in France, with England somewhere in the middle (see Figures 9.1 and 9.4). In Denmark and England, both boys and girls enjoyed school equally, whereas only 45 percent of French boys did so compared with 67 percent of French girls. French boys were also significantly more likely than girls to feel that they were wasting time at school, to feel bored by school and to disagree that 'the best part of my life is the time I spend in school'. Of the three countries England was the only one where there was no statistically significant gender gap in pupil views of the future. English boys and girls were equally likely to see school as the first step on the way to their career whereas in the other two countries girls were more likely than boys to see the career uses of school.

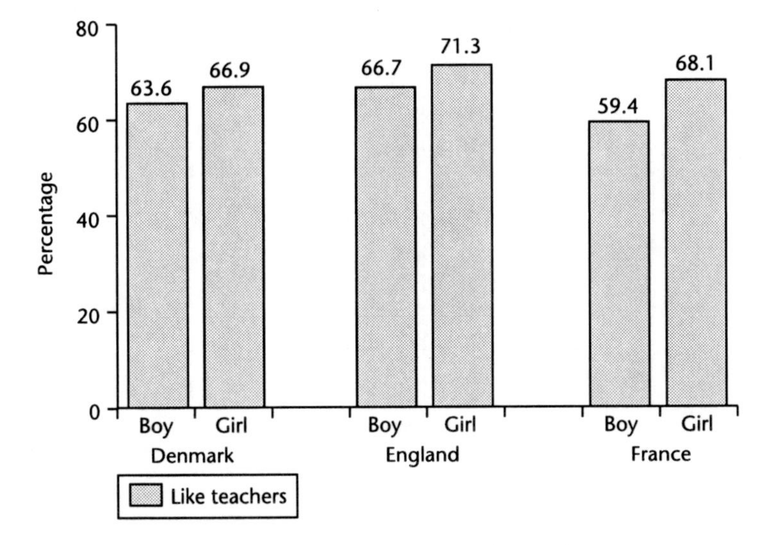

Figure 9.1 In general, I like my teachers (strongly agree/agree) (i)

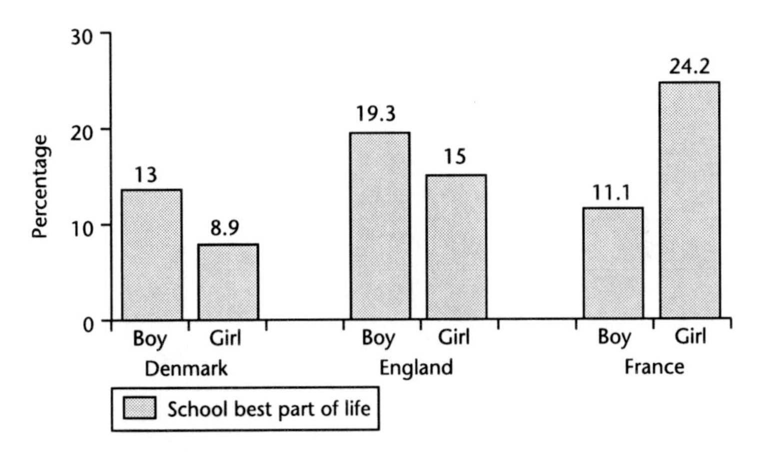

Figure 9.2 The best part of my life is the time I spend in school (strongly agree/agree) (ii)

In summary, for pupils of the age group, the much publicized 'gender' gap in England was not so striking as might have been expected, given the concern of English policymakers with boys underachievement and lack of motivation (Ofsted 1998). In fact the most significant gender differences occurred in France where the under-motivation of boys has only come to be seen as an issue relatively recently (*Le Monde de l'Education* 2003).

Socio-economic differences in perceptions of schooling were evident in all three countries, but were more significant in England and Denmark

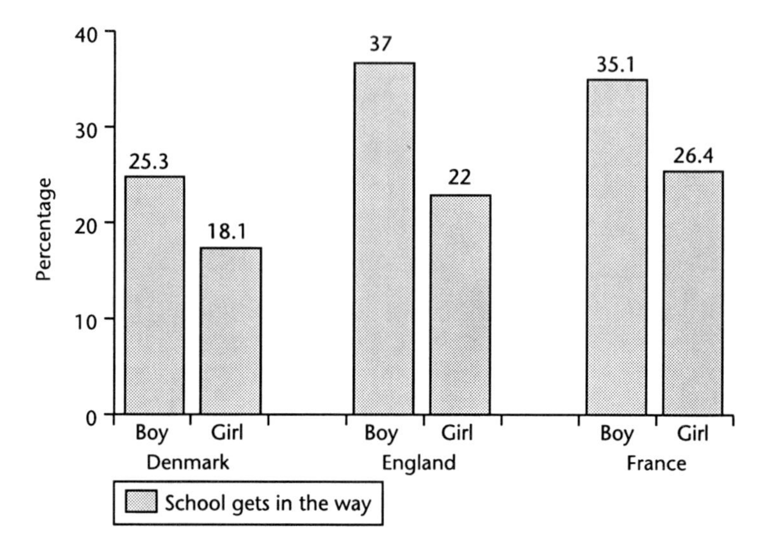

Figure 9.3 School gets in the way of my life (strongly agree/agree) (i)

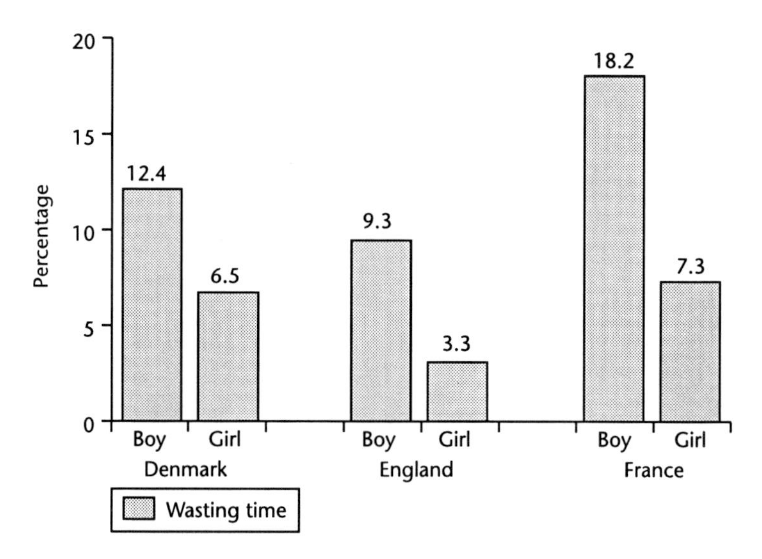

Figure 9.4 I feel as though I am wasting my time at school (strongly agree/agree) (i)

than in France, suggesting evidence of a 'long tail' of under-motivation of children from different social groups in these countries. In order to examine socio-economic differences in pupil perspectives, we divided pupils into three groups according to parental employment (either father's or mother's, whichever fell into the 'highest' category). Table 9.2 indicates how pupils

Table 9.2. Socio-economic status and attitudes to school: Here are some statements of what you might think about your school. Please show how much you agree or disagree by filling in the appropriate bubble

	Strongly agree / agree (%)								
	Denmark			*England*			*France*		
	P/M	*W/B-C*	*Unem.*	*P/M*	*W/B-C*	*Unem.*	*P/M*	*W/B-C*	*Unem.*
1 On the whole I like my teachers	*80.6	58.7	62.5	*71.1	74.2	68.6	*79.1	53.8	52.9
2 School gets in the way of my life	*13.2	23.5	29.5	*28.0	28.8	40.0	26.4	33.8	31.3
3 I enjoy school	*83.9	61.0	65.1	52.7	54.9	54.3	60.2	53.6	70.6
4 I really enjoy most lessons	72.3	60.1	67.2	47.6	54.6	51.4	52.6	55.3	62.5
5 I want to do well at school	95.5	92.8	95.3	98.4	98.1	91.4	97.6	97.2	100.0
6 I feel as though I'm wasting my time at school	*5.8	9.6	15.6	*2.7	5.1	17.1	10.4	14.3	18.8
7 The best part of my life is the time I spend in school	5.2	11.3	17.2	15.0	17.6	20.0	18.1	19.0	17.6
8 I'd like to leave school as soon as I can	8.4	18.8	20.6	18.7	23.0	34.3	22.7	25.0	8.8
9 School is the first step on the way to my career	85.9	86.0	85.9	93.0	92.1	91.4	87.9	83.9	94.1
Totals: n =	**155**	**293**	**64**	**108**	**125**	**16**	**172**	**208**	**17**

Note: * = differences which are statistically significant; P/M = Professional/Managerial; W/B-C = White/Blue Collar; Unem. = Unemployed

in each of these three categories responded to a series of statements about school, teachers and learning. On the whole, for each country, the pattern of difference is fairly consistent, with the children of professional/managerial parents the most positive. However, there were some exceptions to this and it is striking that in all three countries, pupils from all social groups were equally concerned to do well at school and to use school as a step to a future career.

In England and Denmark there were more statistically significant differences between social groups. The children of unemployed parents were the most likely to see school as a waste of time or as getting in the way of their lives. There were significant differences in enjoyment of school in Denmark with the children of professional/managerial parents far more positive than other social groups. Although in France this group more often liked their teachers than the children of white/blue collar or unemployed parents did, in general there were fewer significant differences in the perspectives of pupils from different social groups than was the case in the other countries (see Figures 9.4, 9.5, 9.6 and 9.7).

It is possible that the French emphasis on universalism and on a clear understanding of progress through the system, aimed at bringing all children to a common level of achievement, rather than on individualization and dif-

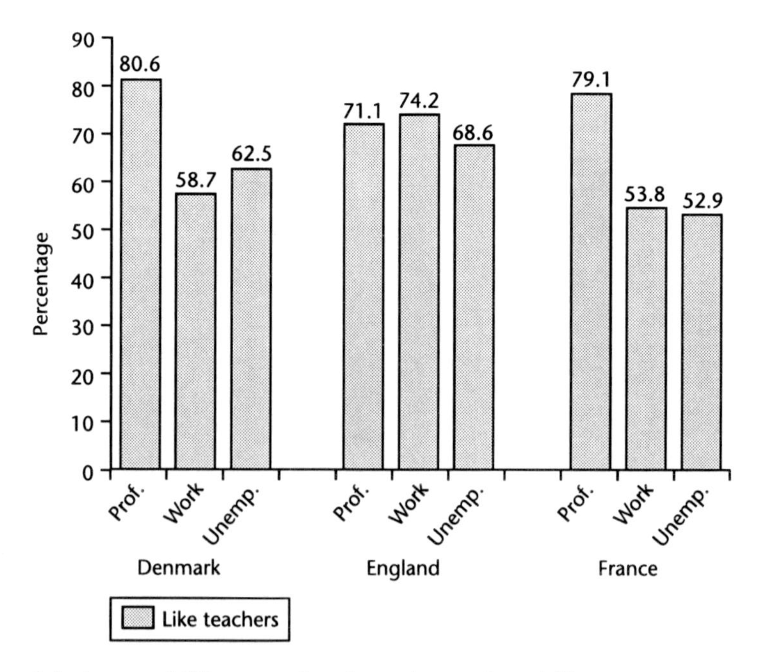

Figure 9.5 In general, I like my teachers (strongly agree/agree) (ii)

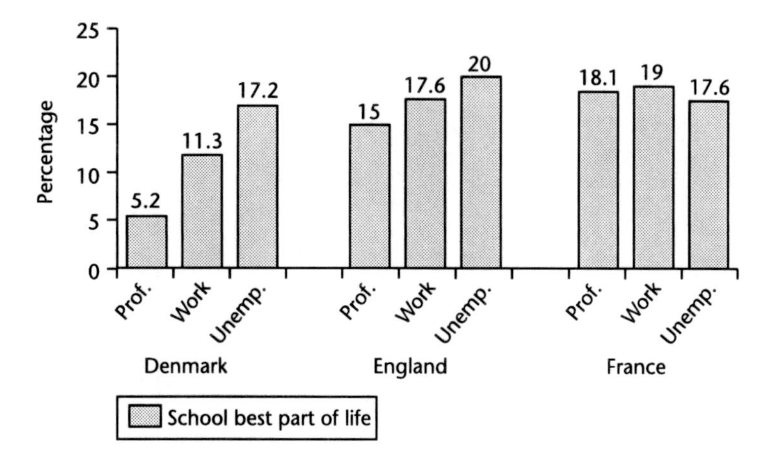

Figure 9.6 The best part of my life is the time I spend in school (strongly agree/agree) (ii)

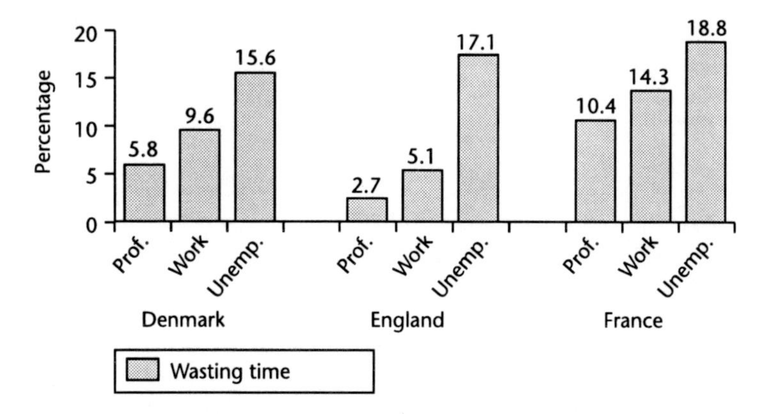

Figure 9.7 I feel as though I am wasting my time at school (strongly agree/agree) (ii)

ferentiation, may have contributed to the narrowing of the socio-economic gap in terms of pupil perceptions of learning. Unlike England where forms of selection (setting, banding, streaming or grouping for particular GCSE qualifications) begin relatively early in secondary education, the French system encourages all pupils to believe right up until the end of lower-secondary education that they can be successful and proceed to a '*seconde générale*' and a '*Bac général*' (the most prestigious route in upper-secondary education) by virtue of repeating the year and by other means. However, the equality gap widens at the point of movement into upper-secondary and our evidence on pupil 'choice' at this stage suggests that many of the more disadvantaged pupils,

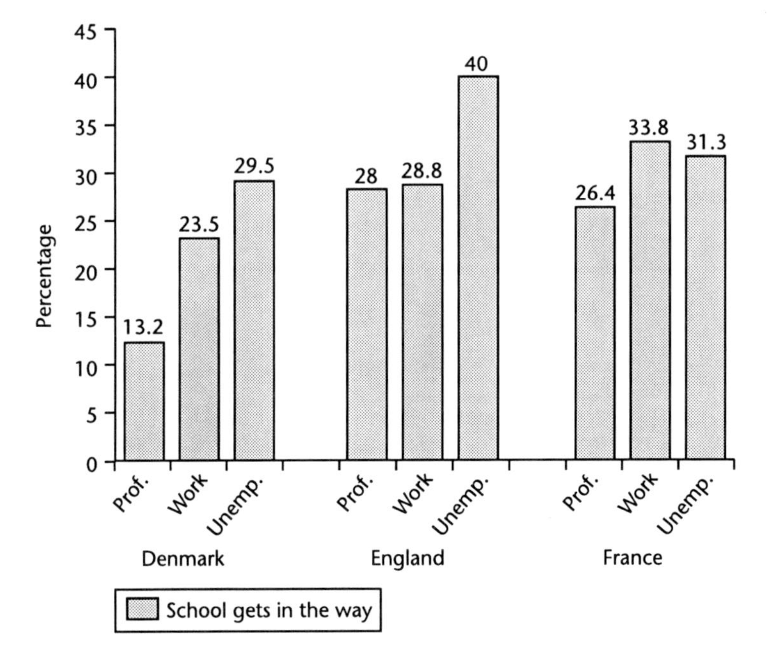

Figure 9.8 School gets in the way of my life (strongly agree/agree) (ii)

particularly the lower achieving individuals, were steered into vocational rather than academic routes for upper-secondary.

The evidence presented thus far suggests that the school systems in each country presented very different contexts within which young people of different social class, sex and ethnic groupings had to negotiate their identities as learners. In the section which follows we examine how this negotiation process worked for particular young people in each country. Did young people in disadvantaged circumstances have more in common with those in similar circumstances in other countries than they did with their counterparts from more affluent and advantaged backgrounds?

Profiles of young learners

In Chapter 8 we presented 12 case studies of young learners drawn from different social backgrounds. Here it is worth re-visiting some key issues from the studies of young learners drawn from the schools in more disadvantaged areas in the three countries: Westway in England, Montand and Berberè in France, and the City and Periphery schools in Denmark. Simone, a high achieving black student at Montand had learned to conform strategically to her reading of the school's view of what it is to be a 'good pupil'. She felt that the school made little concession to pupil interests or autonomy and she accepted less satisfying learning experiences as the price of achieving long-term goals. For Simone and her friends there was a sharp distinction between their social identities as adolescents and their identities as 'pupils'. This contrasted with the case of Fayaz, a lower achieving pupil at the same school who had given up a strategic stance in relation to school in favour of achieving satisfaction from his group of friends outside school. His identity was constructed in opposition to school norms.

In contrast, Westway, in England, also an urban disadvantaged school, had made an attempt to take on board the connections between a learner identity and a social or adolescent identity. This could be seen in the case of both Emma, a high achiever and Tracey, a low achiever. Both Emma and Tracey talked as much or more about their social relationships with their teachers and their peers as they did about their learning. In fact their view of themselves as learners was closely involved with those relationships. Emma, who wanted to achieve but who was concerned to avoid being seen as hard working and conformist to school norms, was sustained to some extent by her teachers' interest in her, and by their optimism about her ability to succeed. In contrast, Tracey had a very weak sense of herself as a learner and was concerned to simply keep her teachers 'happy' and minimally appeased.

In the Periphery school in Denmark, a socially disadvantaged estate on the edge of Copenhagen, Mette, a high achiever had a strong sense of herself as an independent learner and felt little need to disguise her interest in school work or achievement. She would have liked to have teachers who did more to show her how to improve her work. This contrasted with the avoidance strategies adopted by Per, a low achiever in the same school who had an adverse view of himself as a learner and avoided assessment whenever possible. In each of these six cases we can see the complex interaction of social context, personality, social identity and learner identity. What is striking is that the lower achieving disadvantaged pupils in the three systems had a considerable amount in common in the stance they had adopted in relation to school and in the alternative anti-school identities they had constructed for themselves.

Other profiles of young learners in the three countries also reflect the potential force of home in the construction of identity. In particular our data showed sharp contrasts in the amount of help pupils could expect from home. Most had parents who wanted them to succeed at school, but there were differences in the amount of social and cultural capital the parents themselves possessed and were able to pass on to their children. In France, Yann at Montand and Anaïs at Cathédrale provide a typical contrast. Yann was an 'average achieving' boy of Southeast Asian descent who lived with his father, older brother and younger sister in a council flat. His *professeur principal* (class teacher) did not mention to researchers that Yann came from a one parent family and the teacher had never met either of his parents. Yann's father was a technician who laid electrical cables, his mother, who lived elsewhere, was a receptionist. There were problems in his relationship with his father. According to his teacher:

> *Yann n'est pas très pris en compte, il est déconsidéré, il est laissé un peu se livrer a lui même. Il est nourri, logé mais pas plus.* (Yann is not much taken into account [at home]. He is not considered, he is more or less left to himself. He is fed and lodged but not much more.)

Yann was unclear about the role that his parents played in his education. He thought that they wanted him to do well, but when he received any help with school work it was from his brother rather than from either of his parents. Yann was seen as a potentially able underachiever by his teachers who blamed his behaviour in school and poor learning methods They did not think the peer group was a contributory factor. *'S'il ne travaille pas plus c'est de sa propre volonté. Il ne se laisse pas influencer par les autres'*. ('If he does not work it's down to him. He does not let himself be influenced by others.') No links were made by the teachers between his home background and his underachievement. Yann's description of himself more or less matched that of his teachers. *'Je suis un peu bruyant, assez intelligent mais si je veux je pourrais vraiment bien travailler'*. (I'm a bit noisy, intelligent enough but if I wanted to I could really work and get good results.)

In contrast, Anaïs at Cathédrale, was a high achieving girl who lived with her mother, a widow, and an older and younger brother in a privately owned detached house. Her teachers described her as 'serieuse' and 'autonome' in her work, not brilliant but 'très bonne'. Her mother, a primary school teacher, was also a parent representative at the school and, according to Anaïs, was well informed about what was going at school and was able to support her in her school work. Anaïs had private lessons in English at home and was also active in sport. According to her teachers, she was a girl who 'knows where she is going'. She wanted to do a *'Bac litéraire'* (literary Baccalauréat) and was prepared to do whatever was necessary to achieve this.

In Denmark, Sarina, at the City school and Malène, at the North school also had contrasting experiences in relation to the amount of help they could get from home and the amount of social and cultural capital available to them. Sarina's parents who came from Zanzibar had been in Denmark for 18–20 years and spoke Danish fluently. Both Arabic and Danish were spoken at home. Her mother, a home help, and her father, a machinist, felt unable to help her with school work at home because they saw it as too difficult for them. Sarina was sometimes able to get help with mathematics from her sister, but she felt that her parents thought that school was unimportant and did not know a lot about what went on at school. Sarina felt that some people were better at school work than others, partly because they were able to receive help from home, as well as 'having better brains'. She experienced difficulties with the difference between home and school culture, finding the rules and prohibitions at school very different from those at home. 'In school you're part of a crowd which sticks together. At home you're just the person you are'. She felt that many of the teachers did not listen to pupils, that they 'picked on one person' and that she herself was not taken seriously when she wanted to draw attention to things that were unfair.

Malène, who attended the North school in the west of Denmark, lived in a detached house with both parents, both of whom were engineers, and two brothers, one older and one younger. Malène described her parents as spending a lot of time in front of computers, but nevertheless she regularly received help with her homework 'when they had the energy'. She still felt that they should do it more often. She also had considerable help from her older brother who was very academically able. Malène was convinced that both parents thought it was important for her to do well at school. Malène described herself as a happy pupil 'mostly – I feel good about myself at any rate'. Her teacher described her as 'a very nice girl – she's good at her work, clever, gifted, meticulous. I can only think of good things to say about her.'

In England, Damian at Westway and Kate at Lady Margaret School also had very different experiences at home and at school. Damian was reported as having poor literacy skills and lacking self-control. The school target for him was to increase the words he could spell correctly and use, and to encourage him to take risks, to develop independence and to raise self-esteem. Damian lived with his mother, a 12-year-old sister and a new baby in a flat on a large west London council estate. Before she had the baby his mother worked part-time on a local industrial estate. His father, who had left home when Damian was 7, lived elsewhere on the estate. Damian never attended any school activities or clubs because after school he said that he needed to go straight home to help his mum with the new baby and tidy up. There was a history of domestic violence in the family and Damian was identified as on an 'at risk' register.

The school learning coordinator described Damian as 'struggling emotionally at present', although his teachers defined him as 'a bright boy'. Damian was aware that some of his friends were not a good influence, 'Most of my friends are always fighting or something – some work hard like Ben. I'm in Ben's French class. Joseph always wants me to sit next to him – he works but he's not a hard worker. Sometimes I say to Sir, don't sit me there'. Damian was aware of the social difficulties a boy could have if he was seen to work hard 'No one says anything to the girls, it's just that if a boy's a boffin, then they'll start getting called names and cussed and things like that.' In spite of this he still wanted to be able to work hard but had difficulties maintaining this:

'sometimes I can work hard, but sometimes I can't because of some of the people in my class'. He particularly disliked his maths tutor group, 'Just some of the people. Because they're like, because sometimes they get on my nerves because they throw things round the classroom'. Damian's mum sometimes helped him with his school work when she was able to. 'She just, she'll tell me what to do if she knows what I have to do . . . and she'll let me get on with it and just – and do it.' Since Damian was 'on report' at school (which involved getting a report 'signed every lesson, then get it signed before school, then go after school to get it signed, and then you can go home') his mother regularly had to look at this and talk about it with him. Damian was not happy at school and wanted to move elsewhere. In the future he wanted to be a professional footballer, but there was little evidence in his current home and school life that this was an achievable goal.

In contrast, Kate a high achieving pupil at Lady Margaret School, lived with both her parents and two brothers in a detached house in an affluent market town. Her father, who had a PhD, ran his own lighting design company. Her mother was a matron in a nursing home. Both parents had been to university. Kate saw them as very supportive of her school work. They rewarded her if she did well. They regularly attended parents' evenings and knew a lot about what was going on at her school. She was able to get help from her parents whenever she got stuck and her father would also find her books if she needed more information. She recognized that not everybody gets the same level of help at home, but she did not think that the amount of help people got at home affected how well they did at school. Kate had clear ideas about the future. She wanted to take A levels, then take a year out in China or Africa and then go on to college. Eventually she wanted to be married with children, be a partner in her own veterinary practice and live in a small country town somewhere.

In some of the utterances of English pupils at the end of Year 9 as they made decisions about their futures, the potential force of home in construction of identity was particularly evident. Joseph, a friend of Damian's at Westway, was beginning the process of negotiating between his position as a member of a very non-work orientated group who liked to mess about and have a laugh, and his awareness that something had to change if he was going to get where he, and his mother, wanted him to be. 'My mum says if I don't go to university like my brother she'll throw me out of the house. I'll have to start working harder, doing my work, reading books. Can't go out as much. I could work harder in another group. It will pay off in the future.'

Antony at St Theresa's who in Year 8 was 'one of the lads' and who boasted, 'I know when to do work and when not to do work' looked back at his former self as he faced Year 10. 'Those people, I don't hang around with them. They were the ones who brought down my grades – made me like really weird. They're life suckers, just suck all the life out of me. Now I'm with different people. I get on better. It's better for me in lessons. His new group were those he had previously categorized as 'keeners'. He said he was happier to be in trouble less and his mum and dad were pleased.

In contrast, Tracey, at Westway, continued to see the locus of control in relation to learning as outside herself. In making her choices for the 14–16 curriculum, Tracey showed little understanding of or interest in the systems and terminology involved. She had no sense of a progression that might lead to employment and chose geography rather than history because 'I didn't like the war; we was doing it for months and months.' Her parents had not come to school to discuss possibilities. She had mentioned it to her sister who was a year ahead of her but she couldn't remember what she had said. She'd like to be in a class with her friends: 'It's funnier; we have a laugh.'

We can see here, in all these profiles, a glimpse of the power of home and peers to interact in different ways with those of teachers and schools to affect learner identity. The variation in the degree of social and cultural capital which was available to these young people was equally marked in each country but the school and peer group culture in each country provided a very different context within which learner identity had to be negotiated.

Conclusions

First impressions suggest that the social differences discussed here played themselves out quite differently for young learners in the different national and social contexts. Gender differences and differences in social inequality were reflected in pupil perceptions in all three countries, but these were mediated differently within the three education systems. In the English schools, where the school culture was most characterized by fragmentation and differentiation between pupils, those in disadvantaged circumstances had to devote the most energy to maintaining a balance between a social and an academic identity. This was particularly marked for boys. This suggests that the much deplored and significant differences in English pupils' attitudes to achievement are far from inevitable since, in different ways, they are much less marked in the other two countries. In France, to be successful pupils often adopted a 'strategic' response to a school system which did little to take home experience, adolescent life or interest into account. Some of the most disadvantaged and lower achieving pupils, like Fayaz, simply rejected school as irrelevant. In Denmark to be successful pupils often had to 'play down' intellectual effort and achievement, even with their teachers, but most pupils did seem to enjoy school and to have a relatively happy experience of learning. A few of the most unsuccessful and lower achieving pupils, like Per, simply avoided learning situations as much as possible.

One clear conclusion is that the relative lack of adolescent disaffection with school, even among the more disadvantaged pupils and among boys in Denmark, and its high level in France, highlights the institutional and cultural, rather than biological, origins of this phenomenon. At the beginning of the chapter we posed a question about the significance of intra-national differences deriving from social class, gender and ethnicity compared with the influence of inter-national differences. Our conclusion on the basis of the data we have is a mixed one. For all these young people there were marked variations in the way the school system enabled them to deal with difference, whether it was social, ethnic or gender difference in negotiating a learner identity. On the whole it seemed to be the case that for higher achieving pupils who took on board, at least strategically, the learning values of the school, inter-national differences were still the most salient. However, our evidence also suggested that the experiences of these young learners in situations of the greatest social disadvantage had much in common. In particular the lower achieving pupils in each country, who lacked the necessary social and cultural capital and who had not developed the strategic identities necessary to enable them to negotiate and survive successfully in school, shared similar experiences. This suggests that those most marginalized and excluded within each system may share more in common than higher achieving and more privileged pupils who are more likely to reflect the differing priorities mediated to them through the school system.

PART 4

Conclusions: Culture, Context and Policy

10 Conclusions: culture, context and policy

Introduction

We started this book by referring to a possible crisis in contemporary schooling as a result of the rapidly changing needs and characteristics of twenty-first century society. It appears from other research studies that schools in many countries are finding it increasingly difficult to meet the range of expectations now being imposed on them by society, particularly given the influences to which they are exposed.

Thus the ENCOMPASS research project, which is the subject of this book, was designed to compare the schooling experiences of young adolescents concerning what it is to learn and to be a learner in three European countries – France, England and Denmark. In particular, the research was designed to explore how young people construct their identities as learners in the light of different national policy priorities, school structures and teacher practices. A central aim of the study was to trace the way in which different cultural dimensions affect pupils' learning, the relative importance in each country of, for example, gender, ethnicity, teacher–pupil relationships, home background, peer group and the socio-economic context in shaping a learner's career. It was hoped that this kind of detailed comparative study could contribute to identifying the key features of an effective socio-cultural climate for learning. We hoped to delineate those elements of a putative ideal model, which currently exist in different cultures. We also sought to establish the significance of the historical, national, cultural and institutional differences between the three countries for the changes currently confronting education.

In this book our goal has been 'to make the familiar strange' by using a comparative cultural approach. The 'neocomparative' approach we have adopted (Broadfoot 2000) is one that, unlike some other comparative education traditions, focuses upon the influence of culture on learning and uses a broadly socio-cultural theoretical framework. Our findings starkly demonstrate the unequivocally divergent aims and underpinning values of the three different education systems we have studied. At the same time they point to evidence of the impact of globalization and a tendency towards greater homogenization in the delivery of schooling as policymakers in each country strive to raise levels of achievement and increase systemic accountability. Thus a central theme of this book has been an exploration of the balance between the two competing influences of national context and globalization.

The book has offered what we hope is a series of unique comparative insights into the realities of pupils' experiences of their schools during early adolescence. Through documenting these experiences we hope to have illuminated key aspects of how educational systems actually operate. As set out in Chapter 1, the book has built consciously on previous theoretical and empirical comparative studies conducted by the authors which covered both younger pupils' (Broadfoot *et al.* 2000) and teachers' perspectives and responses to change (Broadfoot and Osborn 1992) in order to continue the process of teasing out the significance of cultural differences in educational provision.

As Chapter 2 described, we struggled to overcome our own in-built cultural assumptions by combining insider and outsider perspectives within a multinational research team representing all three of the countries under study. We also sought to use a judicious triangulation of research methods – an analysis of policy documents, questionnaires, teacher and pupil interviews, case studies and classroom observation – to provide a comprehensive picture of the values, understandings and institutional traditions that drive the participants within each of the three education systems. Chapter 2 also describes how the project sought to recognize the importance of 'intra-national' differences within a particular country in terms of social background, gender and ethnicity. We recognized that such key differences between students were also likely to be very influential on the development of an individual's 'learning career' (Bloomer and Hodkinson 2000a).

In this final chapter it is appropriate that we summarize some of the key findings from our study. Following the structure of the book itself, we deal firstly with differences at the level of the system itself in terms of the core social values that appear to inform each society and the ways in which these values have become embodied historically into their particular educational traditions. We also consider the context these established values and traditions provide for contemporary policymaking and the mediation of common international pressures.

Second we summarize the key similarities and differences that we reported in Chapter 5 concerning the day to day realities of school provision – in the organization of schools and in the content and processes of teaching and learning. Central here, as our earlier work has shown (Broadfoot and Osborn 1992), are the values and professional perspectives of teachers.

For the third and last element in our summary we return to what is arguably the heart of the study – the pupils themselves. In documenting similarities and differences in the values and perspectives of young people in England, France and Denmark and in the way in which they experience schooling, Part 2 of the book illuminated some of the issues which we believe are of critical importance in efforts to understand the influences that affect individual pupil's willingness and ability to engage with the process of education. The analysis teased out the variations that exist both between pupils from very different social backgrounds in the same national setting and between pupils from rather similar backgrounds in different national settings.

This last piece of the comparative jigsaw completed the picture of the 'constants' and the 'contexts' that inform the process of education in these three national settings. From these various elements we have been able to provide both an overview of the way in which modern education systems – at least in the European context – may be growing more similar in the light of globalization and Europeanization – and also an understanding of the more or less enduring influence of their different cultures which provide the distinctive context for education in each country and for each individual.

At the level of national policy discourse in the three countries, what are seen as the main aims of secondary schooling?

In Chapter 3 we distinguished the broad cultural traditions of the three education systems which are the subject of this study. We suggested that the English education system has grown out of a laissez-faire, liberal tradition which has been associated with voluntarism, local autonomy and differentiated provision. By contrast, education in France has been organized according to the republican ideal, which sees the state as having a duty to ensure a universal system, providing equal opportunities for all. Different again is Denmark, which, along with other Nordic countries, has a strong tradition of communitarianism which places less emphasis on professional autonomy and relies more on a powerful folk tradition of local democracy and social partnership. These different national cultural traditions are reflected in the organization and practices which characterize each of the three education systems. In particular they are reflected in the balance of emphasis placed on the two central roles of formal schooling systems which we identified in Chapter 1, namely the inculcation of knowledge and skills on the one hand (the 'cognitive' function) and on the other, the shaping of values and attitudes in preparation for the future role of citizen (the affective function). The different emphasis placed on 'affective' and 'cognitive' concerns within each education system is reflected both in the explicit and in the implicit *goals* of each system and also in the *approach* to educational processes as the next section shows.

How do schools mediate national policy discourses?

In Chapter 4 we linked the analysis of policy documents and related research on schools in the three countries to evidence from our own data concerning school ethos and practices. In Danish schools we found evidence of a strong concern with the development of the 'whole child' and with the affective dimension of education. We described how pastoral care is emphasized as part of the teacher's role, and the focus on participatory democracy and lessons in citizenship (Kryger and Reisby 1998). We highlighted the fact that children are encouraged to make decisions jointly with teachers about the direction of lessons as an illustration of the traditional emphasis on participatory democracy. Equally characteristic of Denmark's central concern with the whole child and the development of community is the practice of children remaining with the same class teacher throughout their school careers.

English schools share something of the same emphasis on the development of the future citizen and the needs of the whole child but this is balanced by an equally strong concern with more cognitive goals. While the existence of a national curriculum and national assessment emphasize academic objectives for pupils, structures such as the pastoral care system, the inclusion in the curriculum of personal and social education – now including health and spiritual dimensions as well as the new subject of citizenship – is clear evidence of an emphasis on behavioural and moral norms, on the child as 'person' (Best 1998). The wearing of school uniform, we suggested, provides a clear and almost unique manifestation of this concern.

In sharp contrast to both Denmark and England, the main focus of the school in France is on the child as 'pupil' and on cognitive rather than affective concerns. Academic objectives are emphasized as the school's main area of concern. A distinctive institutional ethos and associated behavioural norms are less important and concern with pastoral care is left to outside agencies (Audiger and Motta 1998; Cousin 1998). Evidence from the project suggests that these different national cultural traditions are the basis for differences in the structure of the three education systems. These, in turn, have given rise to three distinct models of the teacher's role that have an impact on the context in which the pupils experience learning.

How do teachers mediate these agenda to pupils?

In Chapter 5 we described how teachers mediate to pupils the national values that have helped to influence both their own professional training and the policy directives to which they are subject. We described, first, the English model of the subject specialist and group tutor that is characteristic of the 'secondary' stage of schooling after age 11. Subject specialists who teach classes of pupils throughout the age range are part of a 'department' or 'faculty' that gives them an identity which is distinct from that of teachers from other subject specialisms. Linked to this strong emphasis on academic priorities is the pronounced differentiation that characterizes many English schools with pupils spending many of their lessons grouped by ability. In addition many of the teachers had a pastoral responsibility as a group tutor for a particular class of pupils. However, our findings suggested that a highly prescriptive national curriculum coupled with an intense emphasis on raising standards has left many teachers unable to fulfil this role in practice and feeling stressed and overworked by the pressure to meet government targets and an intense inspection system.

By contrast, Danish teachers appeared to reflect the priorities of the education system as a whole by their clear emphasis on affective priorities and building the community. Most teachers within the Danish sample were 'class teachers' with academic and pastoral responsibility for a single group of some 18–20 pupils of mixed ability for the entire period of their compulsory schooling (from grade 1 to grade 9/10). Teacher's priorities were found to be the cohesion of the group and its ability to work together both academically and socially through building up close relationships in the classroom and with families.

France provided yet another different model – that of the autonomous subject specialist. As Chapter 5 reported, French teachers typically maintained a certain professional distance from pupils and their parents, their focus being clearly on inspiring pupils through their subject teaching and ensuring that as many pupils as possible achieved the necessary level to proceed at the end of the year. The clear demarcation between the teacher's professional role and that of the school's non-teaching staff in relation to the social and emotional needs of students was identified as one of the most characteristic features of the highly academic emphasis of French education.

In all three countries, however, there was clear evidence of pressures for change. In Denmark we reported a growing emphasis on competition within the system and a policy concern with national standards that has resulted in increasing curriculum specialization. Alongside this change of emphasis in the cognitive dimension of schooling – an apparent response to perceived international competition – we noted a change of emphasis in the affective traditions of Danish schooling as a result of the perceived need to find ways of responding effectively to the new challenge of integrating immigrants in the larger cities.

In France the traditional emphasis on central control, reason and didactic methods of instruction was found to be under pressure on two fronts. The first of these concerned the effects of policy initiatives aimed at introducing a measure of administrative devolution and school differentiation within the traditionally highly-centralized system. The second source of pressure for change was the needs of students with very different values and cultural backgrounds than was the case in the past. As a result, the traditional French conception of the teacher's restricted role was seen to be changing. At least some of the teachers in our sample were beginning to have a more extended conception of their role, which included an affective dimension and a concern with social and personal development.

In England the long established tension between the affective and the cognitive appeared to be increasingly acute as the 'quasi-market' between schools placed ever greater emphasis on school performance, accountability and raising standards and differentiation. The result was an apparent increase in instrumentalism on the part of both teachers and students. The increase in recent years of both top–down central control and bottom–up market pressures would appear to be making it difficult for teachers to pursue, in practice, their avowed concern for individual students' personal and social needs or the pedagogical approaches which start from these perceived needs.

Both the traditions which were typical of educational provision in the three systems and the effects of these growing tensions were detectable in the daily life of the classrooms we studied. As we document in Chapter 6, how classes are organized in terms of their membership; what they look like physically, the kinds of pedagogical, assessment and organizational practices that teachers use; the balance of power between teacher and pupil; and the quality of classroom relationships all manifest significant variations between the three countries. Even the familiar terms of 'class', 'classroom', 'pedagogy', pupil 'assessment' and 'learning' had very different significance in the three countries.

Thus it is clear that France, England and Denmark have very different educational traditions that reflect their particular confluence of historical events and cultural currents. Equally, it is clear that these differences centre on the two broad purposes of contemporary schooling that we have termed the cognitive and the affective – the inculcation of knowledge and skills on the one hand and values, attitudes and cultural norms on the other. The first part of the book traces the working through of these differences through various levels of the education system – from national policies and provision for the governance and accountability of the system to the institutional arrangements of individual schools, the organization and characteristics of classes, and teachers' perspectives and practices. Having established these contextual dimensions, we turn in the second part of the book to exploring how these differences impact upon the learners themselves.

What are the main influences on students' views of learning and on the development of their identity as a learner?

As has been suggested, France and Denmark share a commitment to the values of egalitarianism and collectivism. In Chapter 7 we document how these values underpinned the classroom interactions we observed in France and Denmark where the students often appeared to share a sense of solidarity and commonality with other students regardless of their social background and attainment level. Both teachers and students used a discourse which emphasized student solidarity. English teachers and students offered a significant contrast to this, showing little evidence of classroom solidarity. English students' identity as learners appeared rather to be dominated by issues surrounding the construction of their social identity. There was evidence to show that many English students typically perceived their class as divided into groups of three different types on the basis of academic attainment. English students' school experience appeared to be dominated by these academic and social groups, which tended to define their social identity. Thus for English students, the negotiation of a balance between social success with peers and the other, often conflicting agenda of success as a learner, appeared to be a central element in the creation of a learning identity. This was much less evident in the other two countries.

Both France and Denmark were also identified as having a more intellectual and knowledge-based approach to learning which was evident in teachers' and students' behaviour and interaction in the classroom. However, England and Denmark also shared values of individualism and experimentation in learning and these were evident in the typical pedagogical approach. These values underlay the relatively warmer and less distant teacher–student relationships in England and Denmark, where teacher control was often more flexible than in France. Both French teachers and students seemed to prefer to maintain a stronger social distance between them. For students this was seen as affording a protection against teacher control of the 'person' rather than of the 'student'.

Not surprisingly, as we saw in Chapters 7 and 8, students' experience of these different national classroom contexts contributed to the formation of their identities as learners, to their perceptions of schooling and learning, and ultimately to learning outcomes. Despite the influence of cultural filters that students brought into the process of schooling from their individual family backgrounds, students' perceptions nevertheless seemed to resonate fairly closely with the particular emphases of the goals of the national systems. Thus Chapter 7 described how the Danish emphasis on collaboration and consensus, and the concern with education for citizenship and democracy, as well as with the academic goals of education emerged strongly in the students' responses. Danish students were, in general, the most positive towards schooling, learning and teachers. They saw school as helping them to fit into a group situation rather than emphasizing the development of the individual. They did not feel that their teachers placed a great deal of emphasis on making them work hard. They were less likely than the other national groups to want to leave school as soon as they could or to see school as getting in the way of their lives.

By contrast, Chapter 7 documented how, in some respects at least, the English students, like those we studied previously at primary level, were the least enthusiastic about school. Among the three national samples they were the most likely to want to leave school as soon as they could and to feel that school got in the way of their lives. More positively, however, English students also valued the opportunity to express their own ideas that their teachers' afforded them, the feedback they received and the sense that teachers valued them as people. These responses echoed both the traditional concern within English education with the development of the whole person and the effects of current policies that embody a stress on individualization and differentiation. As might be expected, the French students in our sample showed little evidence of having experienced a social or personal dimension to their school experience. Nor did they feel that they were getting the guidance they needed from teachers to improve their work. Given that the policy discourse in France is one that emphasizes intellectualism, universalism and republicanism, and hence a lack of differentiation in teaching, the almost complete emphasis on cognitive goals and formal classroom control that the pupils reported was not unexpected. Chapter 8 showed, through detailed case studies of 12 young learners, the complex interplay of structure and agency, of school organization, teacher–student interaction and influences from peers, homes and communities within which identities are constructed. It suggested that in these countries, the emphasis and balances between the development of social identity and 'pupil identity' were different and reflected differences between the educational systems. In conclusion, the chapter showed that these identities were not fixed but shifting and fluid, with the possibility of change in relation to changing contexts.

What is the relative significance of intra-national differences in social class and gender and ethnicity as compared with inter-national differences?

The theme of constants and contexts in this research led us to consider whether the significant inter-national differences in learning context that we had identified were more or less salient than the differences which characterized students within a particular country. Although there are many potential dimensions of difference that might be examined in this respect such as religion and parental attitude, our study focused mainly on differences of gender, educational attainment, socio-economic background and ethnicity. Nevertheless, the juxtaposition of such intra- and inter-national comparisons is itself relatively novel and proved to be a powerful source of insight for the study as a whole.

As reported in Chapter 9, in addressing the issues of educational opportunity, social disadvantage and inequality, the education systems of England, France and Denmark have evolved very different approaches.

Consequently these issues are mediated differently within the three countries. Within each education system, gender and socio-economic background had variable significance and their impact on students' views of themselves as learners varied. There were gender differences in perceptions of schooling and learning in all three countries, but the differences in these perceptions of schooling and learning between boys and girls were more marked in France than in the other two countries. In general French boys were the least likely of all the groups to be positive about school. Whereas the difference in the perspectives of boys and girls was statistically significant in all three countries, the gap was often smallest in Denmark and greatest in France, with England somewhere in the middle.

The influence of socio-economic factors on students' attitudes to schooling was evident in all three countries. However, they were more significant in England and Denmark than in France, suggesting evidence of a 'long tail' of under-motivation of students from different social groups in these countries. Possibly the French emphasis on universalism and on a clear understanding of progress through the system, aimed at bringing all children to a common level of achievement, rather than on individualization and differentiation, may have contributed to the narrowing of the socio-economic gap in this respect. On the whole, however, the pattern of difference was fairly consistent for each country, with the children of professional/managerial parents most positive about school, teachers and learning, and the children of unemployed parents the least positive. But there were some exceptions to this. It was striking that in all three countries, students from all social groups were equally concerned to do well at school and to use school as a step to a future career.

Pupil perceptions of how ethnic differences were treated by the school also varied between the three countries and there were different concerns about teachers and issues of race and ethnicity. However, in spite of these overall differences, Chapter 9 documented how the experiences of young learners in situations of the greatest social disadvantage had much in common. It suggested that those most marginalized and excluded within each system might share more in common than higher achieving and more privileged pupils who are more likely to reflect the differing priorities mediated to them through the school system.

Constants and contexts in pupil experience

In the light of these overall quite significant national differences between students' classroom experiences in the three countries we studied, we are left with the question of how far young adolescents' experiences of schooling may be becoming more similar. Our cross-cultural comparison of student experience was also designed to identify student responses to formal educational provision that were more universal as well as those which were more culturally specific. While we have been able to report clear, culturally derived national differences in students' perspectives, we have also presented evidence of the universality of many of their concerns. Students in all three countries expected teachers to respect them and to be fair; to be able to explain things well; to make learning active and interesting; and to have a sense of humour. Indeed, there was striking unanimity among students about the definition of an 'interesting' lesson and a 'good' teacher, despite the national and institutional differences in school contexts. More generally, students also shared similar views about the economic function of education and its link to the job market.

What then is the significance of these similarities and differences? What still needs to be explored more fully is the relationship between students' contrasting national, social and cultural responses to the school context and learning itself. Does the French student's response of solidarity help to motivate them, particularly the lower achieving students? Does the English student's situation of complex social interactions and their concern with the negotiation of identity divert and de-focus them from learning? Does the Danish student's response of downplaying academic objectives in favour of social relationship objectives have a negative effect on learning? We return to these crucial questions later in this chapter. First, however, we summarize briefly the findings from another important element of our study. This concerned the relative significance of the differences between students *within* any one country – what we have termed the 'intra-national' differences.

Overview of findings

The insights which were produced by this combination of both across and within country comparisons is represented in Table 10.1. The table highlights the relationship between the informing ideology of a particular education system and the elements which we were able to identify to describe the characteristics of successive layers of activity within the education system. It summarizes some of the key findings from the study.

Among the most significant of the study's findings are that:

- French, English and Danish pupils could be located on a continuum representing respectively: the extent to which they were seen within the educational system as 'students' or as 'persons'; the degree of distance seen as desirable in the teacher–pupil relationship; the nature of the inter-pupil relationship and the balance of pupils' negative or positive feelings about school.
- The inherent ambiguity of adolescents' emerging identities within the school context was most marked in the English system with a

Table 10.1 Summary of research outcomes: The table below summarizes the relationship between national cultural educational goals, school and teacher organization, and pupil perceptions of learning and identity which are outlined in the preceding section

		Denmark	*England*	*France*
National policy discourse		Collaboration/ consensus	Differentiation Quasi-market	Universalism Equal entitlement
Teachers		Low distance Expressive	Medium distance Expressive Instrumental	High distance Instrumental
Pupil culture and attitudes to work and behaviour	*Peer groups*	Community within the class 'Organic' solidarity	Differentiation into sub-sets	Solidarity/lack of difference
	Gender	Low gender differences	High gender differences	High gender differences
	Socio-economic status	High differences between social groups	High differences between social groups	Low differences between social groups

culture characterized by the most fragmentation and differentiation in school.

- Gender differences and differences in social inequality were reflected in pupil perceptions of schooling and learning, but these were mediated differently within the three educational systems. For example, the often deplored and significant differences in English pupils' attitudes to achievement are far from inevitable since, in different ways, they are much less marked in the other countries studied.
- The relative absence of the problem of adolescent disaffection with school in Denmark and its high level in France highlights the institutional and cultural, rather than biological origins of this phenomenon.

By using a comparative perspective, the project has underlined the importance of problematizing what it is to learn as well as what it is to teach, in different countries. It has confirmed the hypotheses which were identified at the outset of the study, namely that:

- The policy priorities, institutional arrangements and classroom processes of a national education system are informed by and in turn help to reproduce the deep 'socio-cognitive' and cultural patterning of a particular nation state.

- Pupils' developing identities as adolescents and learners are negotiated according to this national cultural patterning which helps to determine both their personal and learning priorities, the balance between these and their expectations of their teachers and themselves as learners.
- Despite widespread and growing international forces encouraging convergence, these remain relatively superficial in their effect compared to the deep structure of pupil cultural patterning.
- Policymakers need to be sensitive to both the 'constants' and the 'contexts' in pupils' learning identities, as revealed by such comparative empirical studies, if they are to introduce policies which are to be successful in raising both achievement and the aspiration to learn.

Towards a new perspective on learning

The central lesson from our findings is the need for a social theory of learning which links the 'socio-historic' (national culture), the interpersonal (peer and sub-cultural groupings) and the 'intra-individual' (personal biography). As such, the project goes to the heart of the learning process. It challenges us to consider whether the kind of comparative study that we have reported here can form the foundation on which to build a new 'science' of education constructed on the basis of an understanding of the full range of social and psychological factors that influence learning. In the light of the new challenges facing all education systems that we identified earlier in this book, such a project is arguably pressing. Thus the final part of this chapter offers some more general observations concerning the implications of this study both for schooling today and in relation to the novel educational challenges of the future. To do so we deal with each of the three components identified above in turn as we seek to link issues of globalization, culture and individual learning.

The socio-historic: national culture and the implications of globalization

Schools as we know them today can be traced to a common origin:

> mass schooling . . . developed and spread as an increasingly familiar set of general ideological and organisational arrangements. Over historical time and through diverse processes, features of modern schooling into one normative institutional model (that) was increasingly linked to the ascendant nation-state (which was) itself fostered by a world political culture emerging from the conflicting dynamics of the

> world capitalist economy . . . Mass schooling becomes the central set of activities through which the reciprocal links between individuals and nation-states are forged.
>
> (Ramirez and Ventresca 1992, in Dale 2000: 430)

In seeking to unravel the role played by culture as part of the global shaping of education, Dale links this argument to that of Meyer *et al.* (1997) and their identification of the general features of western culture namely, rationality, progress, individualism and justice. As a result, suggests Dale, because dominant cultural forms, including the structure and boundaries of collective action, derive from a universalistic cultural ideology, they are relatively standardized across societies. There is hence only a loose relationship between organizational forms and the practical needs and goals relevant to local situations. In this sense, western organizational structures are to be seen as ritual enactments of broad-based cultural prescriptions rather than as rational responses to concrete problems. Dale identifies the two central bases of world culture as the state – the primary locus of social organization – and the individual – as the primary basis of social action, the ultimate source of value and the locus of social meaning. It is these two themes which we have termed 'structure' and 'agency' elsewhere in this book which are central to our analysis.

If Meyer's and others' 'Common World Educational Culture' (Dale 2000) analysis helps to explain the global similarity of education systems and indeed their remarkable resistance to change, it is also as much about the past and the *origin* of educational systems as it is about the present and the future. Today we face a qualitative change in the nature of national–supra-national relations as a result of globalization (Dale 1999). To the extent that international meta-narratives define the international agenda for educational debates, they represent the contemporary realization of globalization.

However, as the global discourse of education changes in response to new social, economic and political pressures, our analysis suggests that the effects of these changes are likely to be rehearsed in culturally specific ways within particular education systems. Since the process of globalization itself takes a variety of forms, so do the responses to it. In some cases it is possible to chart developments that are a direct response to external pressures – such as the Danish education system becoming more concerned with educational 'standards' as a result of international comparisons. Changes can also be the product of more explicitly orchestrated international initiatives such as governments seeking to harmonize qualifications between countries. Still other changes are not the result of specific policy decisions at all but proceed under their own momentum such as the impact of the borderless and apparently unstoppable development of information technology applications within education. Perhaps most important in this latter respect is the impact of international capitalism, commodification and consumerism, the influence of which increasingly transcends established norms and values whether these are national or regional cultural groupings. Thus, far from globalization increasing the homogeneity of policy and practice in education, its effects are likely to be relatively indirect and complex, the result of cultural mediations of its common messages.

In seeking to understand the socio-historical dimensions of learning we therefore need to be able to understand both the nature and origin of the common, international discourses and pressures that are impacting upon education at any given time and the nature and origin of the contextually specific discourses and structures that mediate these. As Bruner (1996: 13) points out 'Education is a major embodiment of a culture's way of life, not just a preparation for it'. 'It can be seen as the collective programming of the mind' (Hofstede 1991: 4). Culture is expressed at micro-interaction levels and in the underlying rules of communicative competence with national arrangements and priorities, the school, the class, the teacher and the pupil operating as successive axes of mediation for the underlying cultural discourse. Indeed the four central dimensions of culture may arguably be summarized as 'values', 'approaches', 'structures' and 'environments'. These dimensions are readily translatable into the elements that constitute an educational system.

It is culture then, as it embodies a community's values that ultimately defines the priorities of an education system. The structures and forms that deliver it may have had a broadly common origin as part of the then prevailing 'common world educational culture'. While the mechanisms for delivering education are arguably becoming increasingly similar – at least – superficially as a result of the impact of increasingly global educational discourses, its fundamental goals remain rooted in specific cultural traditions. It is not surprising then that the three education systems that we have described in this book are significantly different in their fundamental priorities. Between them they illustrate different balances between the three central purposes of education as we have defined them in this book – the inculcation of an existing body of knowledge, the building of social cohesion and the development of individual capacity and agency. Indeed, the variations between the three systems that we have described take us to the heart of the most enduring debates in educational philosophy. As has been suggested, much of the commonality between the three systems can be traced back to their common roots in the Enlightenment. Herein lies, in particular, the source of the domination of the preoccupation with imparting knowledge within the western European tradition. The liberal/humanistic tradition and the Enlightenment project more generally celebrates the need to train young minds in the Cartesian skills of rational analysis, critique and systematic enquiry as the basis for both quality of life and social progress. It is an educational philosophy that has its roots in the Platonic concept of the search for 'eternal' truths. The systems of educational assessment that evolved to express the success of the educational process are themselves dominated by these Cartesian values of rationality and individualism (Broadfoot *et al.* 1996). The French educational tradition arguably represents this philosophy in one of its most developed and successful forms.

Bernstein (1975) distinguishes between the 'instrumental discourse' relating to the transmission of skills and knowledge and the 'regulative' discourse, which is concerned with the principles of social order, relationships and identity. However, within this broad dichotomy, we have made a further distinction between the social integration function of schooling and its role in supporting individual development. The assumptions of the Cartesian educational tradition have long been challenged by protagonists of the other defining tradition of modern education – that of 'child-centred' education (Pollard *et al.* 1994). Central to this tradition are the 'progressive' educational ideas of John Dewey, whose philosophy emphasized learning through activity and experience, the value of the *process*, as much as of the *products* of learning and the capacity to cope with change through the development of the skills of enquiry, problem-solving and collaboration. Indeed, Glassman (2001) specifically argues that Dewey's original work was a reaction to the artificiality of much of what was being learned in school, its divorce from day to day life. 'Dewey combined the Hegelian idea that activity and thought were both part of a single experience with the pragmatist's notion that activity must be understood within the moment for its specific purposes and not as a means to an ideological end' (Glassman 2000: 4). Without an opportunity to come face to face with reality and its different views, Dewey argued, learners' capacity for agency becomes limited and they become slaves to their history and their habits.

Where opportunities for active learning are made available however, individuals are empowered to respond creatively to changing circumstances and so can help to build effective communities for the future. Or, as Bruner put it, 'Pedagogy, then is to help learners understand better, more powerfully; this is fostered through discussion and collaboration, the process of sharing knowledge in an unthreatening community' (Bruner 1996: 62).

Bruner contrasts this view of pedagogy with 'folk pedagogy' in which the emphasis is on the transmission of an existing corpus of knowledge to students whose task is to remember it and be able to apply it in future. As we have suggested it is this latter 'pedagogy' that has come to characterize the model of western schooling systems, which is now pervasive throughout the world. Rare indeed are sustained examples of attempts to realize Bruner's and Dewey's exhortations on any scale and still rarer are institutions where such approaches have survived over a long period. Despite the fact that the 'child-centred education' movement in England has historically been both influential and mainstream for significant periods, such as in English primary schools during the 1960s and 1970s, and even in France where many teachers have enthusiastically followed the 'progressive' educational ideas of the early twentieth century pedagogue, Freinet, it is clear from the analyses in this book that such movements have failed to achieve a fundamental change in national educational priorities.

Education in Denmark provides one of the clearest illustrations of Bernstein's regulative discourse in practice with its central emphasis on a collectivist agenda of social integration. As such, the Danish education system exemplifies the rationale of a different strand of educational philosophy – that of Vygotsky (1978). If Dewey's philosophy gives pre-eminence to the development of an individual thinker out of a social being, to the individual as an agent of social change, Vygotsky's ideas emphasize the importance of the social organization of the classroom and the larger social community from which its values derive. In Vygotsky's view it is the function of the group to mould the individual rather than the other way round. However, both scholars place a central emphasis on the importance of everyday activities and the social context and, hence, bring us closer to the key learning dimensions identified earlier.

The evidence from the ENCOMPASS project suggests that each of the countries studied represents one of these three traditions more or less powerfully in its education system – the Cartesian tradition in France; the child-centred educational tradition in England; and the communitarian tradition in Denmark. However, our evidence also suggests that each in its different way has become entrapped in its history and habits. The French system, emphasizing as it does the artificial detachment of classroom life from day to day reality, would appear to inhibit the growth of individual agency. The Danish system is perhaps excessively concerned with the integration of individuals into the community and so also, if in a different way, inhibits the scope for individual agency. By contrast, the English system appears to be increasingly in thrall to the mantra of standards and the tyranny of external indicators which provide a substitute for a more explicit ideology in a divided and pragmatic system. The result is an excessive emphasis on individuality, which appears to militate against social cohesion and motivation to learn. As Pepin and Haggarty (2001) report on the basis of another comparative study 'In Germany and France, teachers struggled with making their idealized traditions practical realities, whereas in England there appeared to be an uneasy alliance between the tradition of attending to the needs of the whole child and a climate of accountability'.

These fundamental differences in the conception of what education should be for and how it is best practised are arguably of greater pertinence today than ever before. As the relative certainties of the twentieth century give way to the uncertainties of the twenty-first and the acceptance of change as an enduring reality, the question of the relative merits of these different philosophies as the informing discourses of education becomes increasingly pertinent.

As each of these systems engages with the challenges of a new world order, it is clear that the impact of globalization is not the same in each case. However, it would appear to be the case that all three countries need to recognize the challenge to create greater scope for individual agency in a world where traditional value systems are breaking down and flexibility and change are the only certainties. Not only is it clear that young people are in many cases increasingly unwilling to accept the arbitrary imposition of institutional authority, they have also made it clear in this study that they learn best when there is scope for them to exercise initiative and they are provided with a significant measure of autonomy and respect as partners in the learning process.

We began this section by asserting the need to generate a social theory of learning if the diverse influences that affect any one student's learning are to be adequately understood and, hence, effectively responded to in the creation of learning settings fit for the contemporary world. We questioned whether it might be possible to identify a theory that would be valid despite cultural differences. In the course of this chapter we have sought to delineate the respective roles of 'constants' and 'contexts' in this respect. In exploring the socio-historical influences on learning we have argued that western models of educational provision have much in common, much, moreover, that militates against effective learning. We have also argued that the particular education systems that have grown up within this broad tradition have found different balances between the academic, social and personal priorities of education, differences that can be matched with some of the major informing philosophies of education in the twentieth century.

The implication of this part of our analysis is that none of the systems we have studied appears to be fulfilling the potential of what might be achieved if they were to take into account a research-based social theory of learning. Yet, we have argued, this is increasingly necessary if schools in all three countries – and by implication elsewhere – are to be able to cope effectively with the new educational and social challenges of the twenty-first century.

The interpersonal: the influence of peers and local cultural settings

The second element in the construction of a more comprehensive theory of learning was identified earlier as the interpersonal. If the ENCOMPASS project has a single clear message it is that learning is a social phenomenon. How teachers approach their professional task; the nature of the classrooms in which they operate; the curriculum goals they pursue and the nature of the social relationships that they construct with their pupils have all been shown to be social constructs. It follows that how individuals learn; whether they are motivated to engage with the learning opportunities presented at any given time; and how successful they are in making progress are all powerfully affected by the social and cultural context. To the extent that this is true it suggests that there is a need to redress the traditional emphasis in educational discourse on an *individual's* capacity for intellectual engagement and their effort to give much greater attention to the social dimensions of learning.

It also follows, as the findings of our study have clearly shown, that both cognitive and affective domains are important contributors to learning; indeed that they are probably inseparable in constituting an individual's learning dispositions (Dweck *et al.* 1995; Pollard and Filer 1996) if, as seems likely, personal qualities and relationships are crucial to effective learning. It would also appear to be the case that as so-called twenty-first century skills become increasingly important – problem solving, team work and target setting skills, for example, as well as more explicitly affective qualities such as emotional intelligence, the social aspects of learning are likely to increase in importance.

We have already seen in the summary with which we began this chapter that students in all three of the countries we studied agreed in their identification of a number of desirable features of the learning situation. These features were that teachers should create a climate of mutual respect and fairness; provide opportunities for active learning and for humour; they should make learning interesting; and explain things well. We may call these dimensions: relationships; opportunity to learn; and engagement. Significantly, other studies have confirmed that these dimensions are also perceived to be desirable by students in other cultures. A recent study of young adolescents in the United States, for example, identified four key factors of classroom environment which were perceived by students to be conducive to engagement and motivation. These were – a perception of the teacher as being supportive; opportunities to learn interactively and collaboratively; the creation of a climate of mutual respect and encouragement; and the down-playing of competition (Ryan and Patrick 2001: 456):

> when students believe they are encouraged to know, interact with and help classmates during lessons; when they view their classroom as one where students and their ideas are respected and not belittled; when students perceive their teachers as understanding and supportive; and when they feel their teacher does not publicly identify students relative performance.

Interestingly, there are indications that teachers too identify these dimensions as central for effective student engagement in learning. Hufton and Elliott document a number of international constants relating to teachers' beliefs about student motivation including the duration, depth and quality of teacher/student/parent relationship (relationships) and the extent and nature of the pedagogical deployment of assessment (type of assessment). As teachers rather than students it is not surprising perhaps that they also add to the list the availability and attractiveness of distracters from study; cultural and sub- and counter-cultural attitudes to and valuations of education (Hufton and Elliott 2000: 31). Further insights into what seem likely to be international constants of conducive learning settings are provided by Csikszentmihalyi *et al.* (1993) in their work on creative 'flow'. He argues that students that learn most effectively are those who are able to achieve a synergy between momentary involvement and long-term goals. This is most likely to be achieved in classrooms that are self-rewarding and in which the competitive pressures are kept to a minimum. Similar findings have been reported by Kaplan *et al.* (2002: 4) and Harlen and Deakin Crick (2003). These other international studies suggest a further three possible dimensions of positive learning environments that may be valid internationally: supportive assessment, lack of external distractors such as peer group pressure and the experience of 'flow'.

The extent to which any of these five dimensions of effective learning settings tend to be characteristic of schools in any particular education system is likely to be a reflection both of culturally derived assumptions about educational priorities and of established educational traditions as we discussed earlier in this chapter. Thus, for example, Elliott *et al.* (2001) suggest, that attempts to change English classrooms to foster more effective learning are unlikely to be successful in a policy climate of high stakes accountability and a cultural climate of anti-intellectualism, student complacency, inappropriate social influences and distractions and lack of parental support. Fostering more opportunities for effective learning is also likely to be difficult they argue, although for very different reasons, in countries such as France or Russia where there is the contrasting problem of teachers and students feeling ill at ease with informal learning situations which require thinking and collaboration and which are therefore devoid of traditional forms of control.

The culture of the home is clearly important in the way it shapes students' expectations and behaviour. Linn *et al.* (2000), for example, in their comparative study of US and Japanese classrooms argue that the activity-based methods typical of Japanese science classrooms, which are widely regarded as central to that country's high levels of achievement, are dependent on the inculcation at home of responsibility, helpfulness and the willingness, and capacity to express disagreement respectfully. They suggest therefore, that it is important to study educational attainment and the classroom processes that lead to it in the broader context of students' social and ethical development; yet few reform efforts in the US focus simultaneously on academic content, social development and character development' (Linn *et al.* 2000: 13). Such findings would suggest that the capacity to benefit from opportunities for active learning depend in part on students being prepared at home with the appropriate behaviours and attitudes, rather than, as happens in some societies, the assumption being made that learning is essentially the school's responsibility (Elliott *et al.* 2001).

However, it would also appear to be the case that despite such significant cultural differences in both educational priorities and practices, it is also possible to over-emphasize such cultural variations (Letendre *et al.* 2001) in the face of empirical data that reveal widespread similarities in the factors that students feel help them to learn. These views also seem to be confirmed by research evidence concerning teachers' beliefs. Thus, while recognizing the existence of a substantial body of evidence that confirms the ENCOMPASS finding that culturally derived differences in educational expectations and practices lead to significant variations in students' learning experiences, it would also seem appropriate to argue that there are meta-narratives about learning that are valid beyond the confines of particular cultures.

Moreover, given the definition of culture that we cited earlier in this chapter, it also seems reasonable to expect that such differences that do exist are more likely to be associated with the social functions of schooling, since it is in this latter regard that values are more overt, variable and culturally specific. If this is indeed the case it suggests that a learner's 'epistemic identity' is likely to be more constant than their social identity. Hence the existence of 'constants' relating to learning itself may be correspondingly more likely.

In sum then, it would seem, first, that it is reasonable to assume that there are 'constants' or 'universals' of the 'socio-cultural' dimension of learning, features that characterize productive learning environments that are valid cross-culturally. Second, it would seem to be the case that any particular culture will be likely to have a range of characteristics that are more or less supportive to the realization of such effective learning environments. Last, we would suggest that the process of identifying such features depends heavily on pursuing the kind of comparative study that is the subject of this book. We turn now to the third element that we identified earlier as a necessary component of a social theory of learning – a consideration of the individual themselves.

The intra-individual: influences in a 'learning career'

The notion of a learning career that develops during the course of an individual's life and is shaped by the myriad experiences encountered along the way, is a useful reminder that, as with societies and communities, individuals also develop an idiosyncratic pattern of beliefs, values and practices, of expectations and aspirations that characterize them. These represent an 'individual culture' that is the product of the interaction between their unique set of predispositions and their particular life history. Each individual mediates each new experience through the filter of their learning career, which in turn shapes their subsequent decisions and actions. The effect of both individual student dispositions and classroom factors need to be understood as part of complex cultural processes. Teacher–student relationships, for example, are constructed and continually negotiated within more or less strongly bounded and stable shared values. Students' learning careers, suggest Hodkinson and Bloomer (2000) are shaped by socially and culturally grounded experiences outside formal education, related to family, peer groups, home and employment, upon the often transforming dispositions to learning that make up young people's learning careers. In short, opportunities to learn are culture bound (Ireson 2001: 7).

Efforts to understand learning have taken many different routes. These have included studies of individual learning orientations, of cognitive functioning, of the social context of learning and of broader social factors. The concept of a learning career requires all these various dimensions to be brought together. As Hatcher (2001) argues, such a perspective requires full account to be taken of the role of both structure and agency in education. It needs to recognize the different ways in which knowledge, skill and meaning are created and transformed (Hatcher 2001: 589) through social practices. Such a concept recognizes the dialectic between the cultural habitus and institutional structures on the one hand, and the transformative power of individual action on the other. It conceives learning as an inseparable whole in which structure and agency are continually mutually reinforcing; in which action is shaped by 'the complexities of the relationships between positions and disposition, and between contexts, meanings, identity and learning' (Hatcher 2001: 593).

However, such an assertion highlights the fundamental question that this study has only begun to answer, namely: is it possible to delineate an ideal model of learning for the twenty-first century? Can studies such as ENCOMPASS disentangle the constants of effective learning sufficiently from the cultural context to make such a generalized model possible? Can they contribute insights for either policymakers or practitioners concerning how to promote a learning culture at the level of society, schools and individual classrooms? And if this is possible, what are the crucial components of an effective learning environment which are valid across a range of cultures?

Implications for policy and practice

Too much emphasis on the cultural context of education can create a culture of passivity. An over-emphasis on the isopomorphism of either individual classrooms or student learning careers precludes the possibility of delineating any generalized calls for action. This is not the message of the ENCOMPASS study. Although the influence of culture has been a constant theme in our analysis, so too has the issue of constants and the insights that comparative studies can provide, which are valid across individual cultures and systems. In this last chapter we have sought to draw out the nature of these constants based on our findings and related studies. The frame for this discussion has been the impact of globalization – a phenomenon that is presenting all contemporary societies in one way or another with new social, economic and political challenges. It is also uncovering tensions and limitations that have always been present in established systems of schooling; that are inherent in its conception. If there is indeed a looming crisis in schooling, as we suggested in Chapter 1, what guidance can the ENCOMPASS study provide? What can a comparative study of this kind say to policymakers and teachers faced with more or less fundamental, more or less similar, pressures for educational change?

The first and clearest message of this study is the need to pay attention to the evidence from numerous international studies about the factors that contribute positively to learning: to be willing to abandon familiar conceptions of teaching and learning and instead to recognize that the most effective learning appears to happen when students are active and involved with both peers and teacher; to recognize that student agency is crucial in sustaining motivation and 'flow' and that this depends directly on the quality of relationships both in the classroom and outside it; and to recognize that learning is strongly affected by social and emotional factors. Not only do such factors affect individual learning careers in crucial ways, they are also highly significant in creating a community culture, which helps or hinders the job of schools. If students are to be able to take advantage of opportunities for active learning in school, they need to be prepared at home with the appropriate attitudes and behaviours to make this possible.

However, the challenge is more fundamental than simply doing what we have historically done more effectively. We live in an age in which the traditional sources of 'ontological security' – trust, predictability and face to face associations – which are essential to the 'biographic project' (Giddens 1993) are being eroded. Yet 'in a world of manufactured uncertainty' schools have tended to resort to traditional approaches to curriculum and 'pedagogy' (Giddens 1993: 268), schools are increasingly caught up in modes of productivism, concentrating on producing human, at the expense of social, capital, and bracketing out the moral, equity and ethical issues that do not appear to fit. Yet as we now see through examples of systemic underachievement and alienation, youth suicide and outbreaks of violence, the repressed returns in unfortunate ways. As these examples indicate, it is not good enough that education is reduced to the barren lexicon of economics – with a little equity and welfare on the side. Education must move away from 'the false certainty of consensus that such language both suggests and seeks to effect. Education only flourishes in an environment that stimulates 'new ideas, dissident views, debates and critics in the context of mutual debate and trust' (Cox and Sanders

1994). Schools have a key role in building social as well as human capital, of developing 'trust and security, but at present they are not well placed to do so, being increasingly caught up in marketized and corporatized institutional management, and bureaucratized curricula, neither of which contributes to educational harmony. Indeed, both have a negative impact on schools' and systems' capacities to develop social capital and create the conditions for generative politics. Further, both encourage schools to adopt traditional authority relations with young people. In a post-traditional society, schools cannot assume that the building of trust, mutuality and productive risk-taking will happen automatically (Kenway and Baller 2000: 272).

This is a challenging and serious agenda for contemporary schooling. The ENCOMPASS project has shown that both within and between countries, schools start from different places in seeking to accommodate these new and very real pressures. However, if globalization means anything, it means that no system can afford to stand apart from change, to rest secure in the assumption that what has worked in the past will work in the future. Sooner or later the cracks that are now opening up in the fabric of education may force all countries into a radical reconsideration of their educational priorities, and towards a more morally and ethically sound policy discourse.

Our study provides clear lessons for education in the twenty-first century. It identifies culture in its various forms as the central theme of the educational project. First, there is the culture that defines the features of the national, local, institutional and classroom environment and informs the educational priorities that characterize them. Second, there is the culture of globalization, of change, insecurity and challenge. Last, but not least, there is the individual as the active creator of culture – mediating both global and local messages and contributing in turn to the development of communities at home, at school and in the peer group. Our evidence makes clear that individuals need to be empowered more and more to engage in this process in school. This is essential if they are to be equipped both to cope as individuals with the social, political and economic realities of the twenty-first century and to play their part in sustaining the fabric of the communities on which they will ultimately depend. A radical challenge calls for a radical vision. But then this is the raison d'être of comparative studies.

Appendices

Appendix 1

PUPIL QUESTIONNAIRE
SPRING/SUMMER 1998

Write the name of your school in this box:

Write the name of your tutor group in this box:

Write your name and date of birth in the following boxes:

NAME

DATE OF BIRTH

Please fill in one bubble like this: ●

Girl	Boy
○	○

We hope you enjoy answering these questions.
Your answers will help us. Thank you.

1 Where do you live?
Please mark one bubble.

I live in a	*Council*		*Private*	
	flat	○	flat	○
	terraced house	○	terraced house	○
	detached house	○	detached house	○
	other	○	*please explain:*____________	

2 Who do you live with?
Please mark all the bubbles that apply to you.

I live with my

mother	○
father	○
step-father	○
step-mother	○
grandparent	○
brother(s)	○
sister(s)	○
step-brother(s)	○
step-sister(s)	○
other	○

3 Brothers and sisters
Write the number in the boxes.

Number of brothers	☐
Number of sisters	☐
Number of step-brothers	☐
Number of step-sisters	☐

Please mark all the bubbles that apply to you

4 My mother works

at home	○
out of doors	○
in an office	○
in a factory	○
in a hospital	○
in a school	○
elsewhere	○
is not employed	○

5 My father works

at home	○
out of doors	○
in an office	○
in a factory	○
in a hospital	○
in a school	○
elsewhere	○
is not employed	○

6 My mother's job is ☐

7 My father's job is ☐

Please write in the boxes as exactly as you can (e.g. factory worker, nurse, office worker)

Imagine you were going to tell someone from another country about your school and about how it feels to be at your school. What good things and not so good things would you decide to talk about?

8 Three good things about my school are:

1 ______________________________

2 ______________________________

3 ______________________________

9 Three not so good things are:

1 ______________________________

2 ______________________________

3 ______________________________

My feelings about school

10 Here are some statements of what you might think about your school. Please show how much you agree or disagree by filling in the appropriate bubble.

Please mark one bubble in each row.

	Strongly agree	Agree	Disagree	Strongly disagree	Not sure
1 On the whole I like my teachers.	○	○	○	○	○
2 School gets in the way of my life.	○	○	○	○	○
3 I enjoy school.	○	○	○	○	○
4 I really enjoy most lessons.	○	○	○	○	○
5 I want to do well at school.	○	○	○	○	○
6 I feel as though I'm wasting my time at school.	○	○	○	○	○
7 The best part of my life is the time I spend in school.	○	○	○	○	○
8 I'd like to leave school as soon as I can.	○	○	○	○	○
9 School is the first step on the way to my career.	○	○	○	○	○

11 Here are some statements of what you might think of school in general. Please show how much you agree or disagree by filling in the appropriate bubble.

Please mark one bubble in each row.

	Strongly agree	Agree	Disagree	Strongly disagree	Not sure
1 School teaches you to understand other people's feelings.	○	○	○	○	○
2 An important thing about school is meeting up with your friends.	○	○	○	○	○

3 School helps you to sort out your life.	○	○	○	○	○
4 School helps you to become mature.	○	○	○	○	○
5 School is boring.	○	○	○	○	○
6 An important thing about school is learning to co-operate with others.	○	○	○	○	○
7 School is all about getting jobs when you leave.	○	○	○	○	○
8 An important thing about school is that it helps you to get qualifications.	○	○	○	○	○
9 An important thing about school is learning new things.	○	○	○	○	○
10 School makes you aware of your own strengths and weaknesses.	○	○	○	○	○
11 School is a place where you learn to obey rules.	○	○	○	○	○
12 School is a place where you can express your own ideas and opinions.	○	○	○	○	○
13 School is a place where it is difficult to succeed.	○	○	○	○	○

Thinking about you in school

12 How good do you think you are at the following things?

Please mark one bubble in each row.

	Very good	Good	OK	Not very good	Not sure
1 School work generally?	○	○	○	○	○
2 Sport?	○	○	○	○	○
3 Creative things such as art or music?	○	○	○	○	○
4 Making friends?	○	○	○	○	○
5 Making things with your hands?	○	○	○	○	○
6 Making trouble?	○	○	○	○	○
7 Taking responsibility in a group?	○	○	○	○	○
8 Helping other people?	○	○	○	○	○
9 Contributing to class discussions?	○	○	○	○	○
10 Being organised about your work?	○	○	○	○	○

13 When I want to do good work it's

Please mark one bubble in each row.

	Strongly agree	Agree	Disagree	Strongly disagree	Not sure
1 because otherwise I might get shouted at by the teachers.	○	○	○	○	○
2 because I like being praised.	○	○	○	○	○
3 because it's important to my parents.	○	○	○	○	○
4 because I want to be the best in the class.	○	○	○	○	○
5 because I want to get a good mark.	○	○	○	○	○
6 because my parents will give me a treat or some money.	○	○	○	○	○
7 because it's important to me to do well.	○	○	○	○	○
8 because it will help me to get a good job.	○	○	○	○	○
9 because I like my teacher.	○	○	○	○	○
10 because I am interested in the subject.	○	○	○	○	○
11 because it will make me popular with my friends.	○	○	○	○	○
12 because it will help me to get into the top set.	○	○	○	○	○
13 because I like to go on learning as long as I can.	○	○	○	○	○

Ability/effort

14 Do you agree or disagree with the sentences below?

Please mark one bubble in each row.

	Strongly agree	Agree	Disagree	Strongly disagree	Not sure
1 Anyone can do well at school if they work hard.	○	○	○	○	○
2 If the teachers give you a lot of help, you will do well at school work.	○	○	○	○	○
3 You are either good at school work or you aren't.	○	○	○	○	○
4 Sometimes you have to cheat to do well.	○	○	○	○	○

5 You only do well at school if you behave well.	○	○	○	○	○
6 To do well at school you have to be clever.	○	○	○	○	○
7 You do well at school if you listen to the teacher.	○	○	○	○	○
8 How well you do at school work depends on how much help you get at home.	○	○	○	○	○
9 You do better at school work if you have clever friends.	○	○	○	○	○

15 Do you agree or disagree with the sentences below?

Please mark one bubble in each row.

	Strongly agree	Agree	Disagree	Strongly disagree	Not sure
1 I always try my hardest.	○	○	○	○	○
2 I enjoy trying to do better than I did last time.	○	○	○	○	○
3 Trying to beat other pupils makes me work harder.	○	○	○	○	○
4 When other pupils are all doing better than me I don't bother making any effort.	○	○	○	○	○

16 SCHOOL SUBJECTS *Write in the boxes.*

1 Which subject do you like best at school?

2 Which subject do you like least at school?

3 What is the most important subject you do at school?

4 What is the least important subject you do at school?

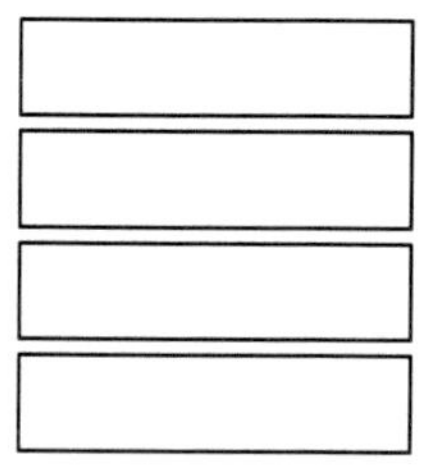

17 Here is a list of ways of working that might happen in your classes. Please fill in the appropriate bubble to show how frequently you work in this way.

Please mark one bubble in each row.

	Often	Sometimes	Never
1 We work in groups.	○	○	○
2 We work individually.	○	○	○
3 We work as a whole class.	○	○	○

4 We work by discussing with the teachers.	○	○	○
5 We make decisions together about what we do in class.	○	○	○

18 From which of the above ways of working do you think you learn most?

Write the number here ☐

eg. If you think "We work individually" is the most important, put number 2 in the box.

19 What do you think about how you learn?

Please mark one bubble in each row.

	Strongly agree	Agree	Disagree	Strongly disagree	Not sure
1 I learn better when I can choose to work in my own way.	○	○	○	○	○
2 You have to be happy at home before you can do well at school.	○	○	○	○	○
3 I learn better when I know it will be useful to me.	○	○	○	○	○
4 You have to be happy at school before you can do well.	○	○	○	○	○
5 I learn better from teachers who make the work interesting.	○	○	○	○	○
6 I learn a lot from textbooks.	○	○	○	○	○
7 I learn a lot from discussions in class.	○	○	○	○	○
8 I learn a lot from studying on my own.	○	○	○	○	○
9 You only enjoy the subjects you're good at.	○	○	○	○	○
10 You only do well at subjects that you're interested in.	○	○	○	○	○
11 If you want to do well at school you have to be in a class where everyone behaves.	○	○	○	○	○
12 I learn better when I have a clear idea of what I am hoping to achieve.	○	○	○	○	○
13 Being good at something doesn't mean that you enjoy it.	○	○	○	○	○
14 You learn more when you have different teachers for different subjects.	○	○	○	○	○

15 You learn better when there is no noise in class.	○	○	○	○	○
16 It is important to have a teacher who knows you well.	○	○	○	○	○
17 I learn better from teachers who like me.	○	○	○	○	○
18 I learn better when I have to present my results to someone other than my teachers.	○	○	○	○	○
19 I learn better when the teacher uses ideas and experiences I am familiar with from outside school.	○	○	○	○	○
20 I learn better when I work with others.	○	○	○	○	○

Teachers

20 Finish the sentence "To my mind a good teacher should . . ."

____
____
____
____
____

21 Please read the statements below about teachers and mark a bubble in each row to show whether you think this applies to: Most of your teachers/many of your teachers/only a few of your teachers/hardly any of your teachers

Please mark one bubble in each row.

I believe teachers	Most teachers	Many teachers	A few teachers	Hardly any teachers
1 are there to help pupils pass exams.	○	○	○	○
2 are there to help pupils learn.	○	○	○	○
3 aren't really interested in pupils as people.	○	○	○	○
4 make all the decisions about what happens in lessons.	○	○	○	○
5 give challenging work.	○	○	○	○
6 really want their pupils to do well.	○	○	○	○
7 live in a different world from their pupils.	○	○	○	○

8 encourage pupils to say what they think in class.	○	○	○	○
9 will have a laugh with pupils.	○	○	○	○
10 make pupils want to work hard.	○	○	○	○
11 are understanding about pupils' problems and worries.	○	○	○	○
12 give pupils a say in how they learn.	○	○	○	○
13 are only interested in their own subject.	○	○	○	○
14 will be helpful if pupils go to them with a problem.	○	○	○	○
15 make pupils feel they aren't good enough in their work.	○	○	○	○
16 are a good example for their pupils.	○	○	○	○
17 are interested in pupils' opinions.	○	○	○	○
18 treat all pupils equally.	○	○	○	○
19 are more interested in pupils who can do well.	○	○	○	○
20 show what they really think and feel.	○	○	○	○
21 are interested in building friendly relationships with their pupils.	○	○	○	○
22 are respected by pupils.	○	○	○	○
23 make pupils feel they can be successful.	○	○	○	○
24 like and enjoy their job.	○	○	○	○
25 provide good guidance about how you can improve your work.	○	○	○	○
26 trust pupils.	○	○	○	○
27 do not listen to pupils.	○	○	○	○
28 try to make pupils get on well as a group.	○	○	○	○
29 spend too much time with pupils who need extra help.	○	○	○	○

22 What are the three most important things that a teacher should do?
Mark the three *most important things below.*

1 Be strict. ○
2 Be fair. ○
3 Give pupils some say in what they do. ○
4 Make children work hard. ○
5 Explain things well. ○
6 Give extra help to pupils who find things difficult. ○
7 Make the work interesting. ○
8 Encourage pupils to ask questions. ○
9 Try to understand how pupils feel. ○

10 Provide helpful guidance to pupils on how to improve their work. ○
11 Be friendly. ○

23 Which of the three things above that you have chosen is the most important?

Write the number here ☐

eg. If you think "Be strict." is the most important, put number 1 in the box.

Learning at school

24 Here are several different ways in which you might be able to find out how well you are doing with your work.
Please fill in the bubble to show whether or not (Yes/No) you have personally experienced any of these.

Please mark one bubble in each row.

	Yes	No
1 Results in tests and exams.	○	○
2 The marks I get for my work.	○	○
3 Teachers' written comments.	○	○
4 Teachers regularly telling me how I am doing.	○	○
5 Teachers talking to me during lessons.	○	○
6 What my friends say.	○	○
7 How teachers treat me.	○	○
8 By comparing my work with others.	○	○
9 My parents tell me how well they think I am doing.	○	○
10 Conversations between parents, teachers and pupils.	○	○
11 I tell the teacher how well I believe I am doing.	○	○

25 Which three ways are most important to you in helping you make progress?

Write the numbers here ☐ ☐ ☐

eg. If you think "What my friends say" is one of the most important, put number 6 in a box.

26 How do you think that your teacher knows how well you are doing?
Mark all the things which apply.

1 Through tests and exams. ○
2 Marking the work I do in class. ○
3 Talking to me in class. ○

4 Marking my homework.	○	
5 Watching me in class.	○	
6 Through talking to other teachers.	○	
7 Through talking to my parents.	○	
8 Any other ways?	○	*Please describe them here.* ____________ ____________

27 What do you think about the marking of your work?

Please mark one bubble in each row.

	Strongly agree	Agree	Disagree	Strongly disagree	Not sure
1 I like knowing what marks or grade I've got.	○	○	○	○	○
2 I find it embarrassing when teachers point out that my work is wrong in front of the class.	○	○	○	○	○
3 Usually I like it when teachers give me back my work.	○	○	○	○	○
4 I like to know how well I'm doing in my work.	○	○	○	○	○
5 Sometimes I feel worried when the teachers give me back my work.	○	○	○	○	○
6 I don't always agree with the mark I get.	○	○	○	○	○
7 I find it embarrassing when teachers praise my work in front of the class.	○	○	○	○	○
8 I know what I have to do to get good marks.	○	○	○	○	○
9 When I get work back the comments show me what I have to do to improve.	○	○	○	○	○
10 I don't really care about marks or grades.	○	○	○	○	○
11 When I get a bad mark it makes me try harder in the future.	○	○	○	○	○
12 I don't get enough guidance on how to improve my work.	○	○	○	○	○
13 A bad mark makes me feel like not trying any more.	○	○	○	○	○

The ideal pupil?

28 If a new pupil joined your class, what sort of person do you think your teachers would like them to be?

____

____

____

____

29 How much do you think you are like the pupil you've just described?
Please mark one bubble.

1 Very much. ○
2 A little. ○
3 Not much. ○
4 Not at all. ○

Home, friends and school

30 What's it like being at school?

Please mark one bubble in each row.

	Strongly agree	Agree	Disagree	Strongly disagree	Not sure
1 I like to keep my home life and my school life separate.	○	○	○	○	○
2 To be popular with teachers you've got to fit in with them.	○	○	○	○	○
3 I can't really be myself at school.	○	○	○	○	○
4 To be popular with classmates you've got to fit in with them.	○	○	○	○	○
5 What my friends think about me is more important than what my teachers think of me.	○	○	○	○	○
6 I'm very different outside school from how I am at school.	○	○	○	○	○
7 I have different friends in school and outside school.	○	○	○	○	○
8 I don't care what my classmates think of me.	○	○	○	○	○
9 My friends make fun of me when I get things wrong.	○	○	○	○	○
10 Sometimes it's not easy to be accepted by your classmates.	○	○	○	○	○

11 I don't care what my teachers think of me.	○	○	○	○	○
12 My friends like to fool around in class.	○	○	○	○	○
13 If you do too well in class it makes life difficult with your friends.	○	○	○	○	○
14 My friends think it's important to do well at school.	○	○	○	○	○
15 I sometimes feel left out.	○	○	○	○	○
16 Boys and girls don't mix much in our class.	○	○	○	○	○

31 Who do you think has most influence on how you behave in school?
Mark one of the following.

1 Your headteacher ○
2 Your teachers ○
3 Your friends ○
4 Your parents ○
5 Myself. ○
6 Other ○ *Please specify.*

____

____

Parents

32 What part do adults at home play in your school-life?

Please mark one bubble in each row.

	Strongly agree	Agree	Disagree	Strongly disagree	Not sure
1 Teachers do not encourage them to be involved with school.	○	○	○	○	○
2 They don't want to interfere in what goes on at school.	○	○	○	○	○
3 They sometimes help me with my school-work.	○	○	○	○	○
4 They think school is a waste of time.	○	○	○	○	○
5 They think it's important to do well at school.	○	○	○	○	○
6 They can't help me because they are not in touch with what goes on in class.	○	○	○	○	○

7 They reward me if I do well at school.	○	○	○	○	○
8 They don't mind if I do well at school or not.	○	○	○	○	○
9 They know a lot about what goes on in school.	○	○	○	○	○
10 They ask the school about how I'm getting on.	○	○	○	○	○
11 They can't help me because the work is too difficult.	○	○	○	○	○
12 They turn up to parent teacher evenings.	○	○	○	○	○
13 They contact the school when I have problems.	○	○	○	○	○
14 They are involved in making decisions about class rules.	○	○	○	○	○

School rules

33 What do you think about discipline in *your* school?

Please mark one bubble in each row.

	Strongly agree	**Agree**	**Disagree**	**Strongly disagree**	**Not sure**
1 When I'm in the classroom I mostly do what teachers tell me to do.	○	○	○	○	○
2 When I'm in the school buildings or playground I mostly do what teachers tell me to do.	○	○	○	○	○
3 In this school the pupil representatives have real power.	○	○	○	○	○
4 In most of my lessons the pupils behave well.	○	○	○	○	○
5 This school should have stricter rules.	○	○	○	○	○
6 I don't think that all the teachers at this school agree with the school rules.	○	○	○	○	○
7 I don't think that my parents agree with all the school rules.	○	○	○	○	○
8 This school has too many rules and regulations.	○	○	○	○	○
9 The rules in this school are different from the rules at home.	○	○	○	○	○

34 What do you think about school rules generally?

Please mark one bubble in each row.

	Strongly agree	Agree	Disagree	Strongly disagree	Not sure
1 Schools should have rules about what pupils wear.	○	○	○	○	○
2 Schools should have a school uniform.	○	○	○	○	○
3 Schools should have rules about how pupils behave in the street.	○	○	○	○	○
4 Schools should have rules about how pupils behave in the playground.	○	○	○	○	○
5 Schools should involve pupils in making decisions about rules.	○	○	○	○	○
6 Schools should involve parents in making decisions about school rules.	○	○	○	○	○
7 Schools should be strict about the language pupils use.	○	○	○	○	○

35 What do you think about the rules in *your* school?

Mark one of the following.

1 This school is too strict.	○
2 This school is not strict enough.	○
3 This school is about right.	○

School identity

36 How do you feel about *this* school?

Please mark one bubble in each row.

	Strongly agree	Agree	Disagree	Strongly disagree	Not sure
1 I am glad I am at *this* school rather than some others I know about.	○	○	○	○	○
2 I feel that I belong to this school.	○	○	○	○	○
3 There is not much difference between being at this school than other schools I could have gone to.	○	○	○	○	○
4 People from this school are different from those who are at other schools.	○	○	○	○	○

5 It annoys me when people from outside criticise this school.	○	○	○	○	○
6 This school makes most pupils feel part of school life.	○	○	○	○	○
7 I am proud of being at this school.	○	○	○	○	○
8 I can't get out of school fast enough at the end of the day.	○	○	○	○	○
9 I like staying in school after school time.	○	○	○	○	○

37 What do you think makes a good school?

____

____

____

____

____

Thank you very much for answering these questions.

Appendix 2

PUPIL INTERVIEW SCHEDULE
Spring/Summer 1998

School ....
Pupil ....
Tutor group ....
Date of birth ....
M/F ....
Interviewer ....
Date ....
Tape No ....

1 **Introduction. General perception of school.**
(Establish rapport) Thanks for agreeing to talk to us (again). We would like to talk to you about/we are interested in your school/what it's like to be at school in this country. *(Explain comparative dimension if appropriate)* We would like you to tell us about the things you do/the things that happen in school. What it's like to be at this school.

1a Can you please tell me:
Three things you like about your school

Three things you dislike about your school

1b What do you think people outside think of this school?

1c What do your parents think of this school?

1d Are you pleased to be at this school? Would you rather be somewhere else? *(Probe for reasons)*

1e If there was one thing you could change about this school what would it be?

1f How long do you expect you will stay in this school? *(Probe for reasons)*

1g Where will you go/what will you do next? *(Probe for reasons)*

2 Pupil Culture

2a Who are your friends in this school? *(Ask for up to four names)*

Did you know them before you came to this school?

Have they been your friends for long?

How did you get to know them/come to be friends with them? *(Probe for: impact of school organisation on friendship; size and nature of friendship group)*

2b Can you tell me a bit about them? What are they like? What do you like about them? *(Probe for evidence of pro-school/anti-school/pro-work/anti-work attitudes; identification with sub-cultures)*

What sorts of things do you do with your friends? Do you see any of them outside school time? *(Probe for degree of overlap between school culture and out-of-school culture)*

2c What happens during the breaks/lunch hour in this school? *(Probe for examples; explore gender difference; boy/girl relationships (and same sex relationships?); assumptions about role of school in breaks)*

2d Tell me about the people who are most popular in your year? What are they like? What do they do? What is it about them that makes them popular? *(Probe for clarification of interviewee's construct of a popular pupil. Does this hold generally or can you be popular in different ways with different groups?)*

Does what people wear, and/or the things they have, and/or the things they like make any difference to how popular they are? *(Probe for impact of fashion/music/sport or any other manifestation of popular culture)*

2e Are you at all like the people you have told me about? Would you like to be? *(Probe for attitude to this group; perception of "match"; any action consciously taken to conform or to differentiate self)*

2f What would someone/a new pupil have to do to become popular with the pupils in this school?

2g What sorts of people have a hard time? are unpopular? are not liked? *(Probe to explore role of academic achievement/aspiration; SES i.e. relative affluence/access to material goods; conformity to school norms in behaviour; negotiation of identity; survival strategies) (Follow-up if possible)*

How do people treat them? How do they react when people treat them like that?

2h Tell me about the sorts of pupils the teachers in this school really like?

2i Do you think you are at all like that? Would you want to be like that? What do most pupils think of people like that?

In what ways do you think you are different?

2j Are you involved in any school activities or clubs? *(note detail)* Do you have any special responsibilities in your class or in school? *(note detail)*

Have you ever represented your school in a sporting or other activity? Does this affect the way you feel about the school? *(Probe for details of feeling) (NB ADJUST FOR NATIONAL VARIATIONS)*

3 School organization – pupil groups

3a Which tutor group are you in?

3b Do you have lessons with your tutor group? *(If no, record details)*

How do you think the school decided which class/set to put you in for different lessons?

3c How do you feel about the tutor group you are in? *(Probe for "fit" with the group; feelings about the ethos/atmosphere of the group; sense of belonging/identity)*

3d How do you feel about the classes/sets you are in for lessons? *(Probe for "fit" with the group; feelings about the ethos/atmosphere of the group; sense of being able/not able to work/learn successfully/effectively; differentiation; feelings about setting/mixed ability)*

4 Views of purposes of schooling/assemblies/pupil power

4a What do you think is important about the things you learn in school? How does it help you? (Why should you come to school? What do you learn here?) *(Probe for: personal enjoyment; personal meaning; match with interests; getting grades; getting a job; usefulness for adult life etc.)*

4b Do you have assemblies in this school? *(Probe for details of when these occur)*

4c Why do you think the school holds these assemblies?

4d What are your thoughts about assemblies? *(Probe for personal feelings; view of usefulness; general attitude of pupils)*

4e Do any pupils in this school have particular responsibilities and powers? For instance do you have prefects? head boy or head girl? pupil representatives on some kind of Council? *(Probe for detail of each example and any additional suggestions offered)*

4f How do pupils get to have these powers and responsibilities? For example are they elected? Appointed by the head? Chosen by the staff or pupils? *(Probe for detail of processes involved for the various roles mentioned)*

4g What do you think/feel about the powers and responsibilities these pupils have? What do you think about the way they exercise their powers and responsibilities? How does it affect you? Is it a good thing to have pupils in these roles and positions? *(Probe for views of the purposes; usefulness/effectiveness of these roles and positions. If there is a School Council – or similar body – ask for views on its operation: how democratic is it? what specifically has it achieved? how much power does it have?)*

4h Have you ever held any positions of power or responsibility in this school? Would you like to? (i.e. be a prefect? head boy/girl? member of school council?) *(Probe for idea of what sorts of pupils assume these roles; interviewee's sense of "match" with this; views on pupil power and responsibility)*

5 **Curriculum/assessment/attainment**

5a Which subjects do you like best? Can you explain why? *(Probe for impact of relationship with the teacher on these preferences)*

5b Are these the ones you are particularly good at? *(If "no" ask "Which subjects are you particularly good at?)*

5c What subjects do you like least? Why is that? *(Probe for impact of relationships with teacher)*

What are you like at those subjects – good? OK? not so good?

5d Is there anything you are not so good at?

5e Are there any subjects you think *the school* thinks are particularly important? *(If "yes" note detail and probe)* Can you explain why that is?

5f Are there things you would like to learn in school that the school doesn't teach? *(Probe for reasons)*

5g What do you think is the most *useful* thing you learn in school?

5h What sorts of things do you think you will need to/want to learn in the future *(Probe for reasons)*

5i How in general are you doing with your work? How clear an idea do you get at school of how you are getting on?

5j How do you know how good you are in different subjects? What exactly is it that gives you an idea of how you are getting on? *(Probe for awareness of systems, marking practices, teacher reaction/behaviour. Encourage specific examples)*

5k Do you understand/know what you have to do to produce a good piece of work? *(Probe for awareness of criteria; differences between subjects/teachers)*

How did you come to know that? *(Probe for processes by which interviewee came to have this understanding/knowledge e.g. explicitly/implicitly? From teachers/pupils/self?)*

5l Do you know how you could improve your work? Does the feedback you get from your teachers help you to improve?

Is there anything else/different that your teachers could do that would help you know how to improve?

5m Why do you think some people do better in their school work than others?

5n How do you feel about giving work in for marking? Getting your work back from your teacher?

5o What happens if you get something wrong in your work in class? Do really badly in something?

5p Can you tell me about a time recently when you did really badly with some work? *(Encourage detailed narrative recall – could be a piece of work that was marked; could be an incident in class)*

5q Can you tell me about a time recently when you did really well with some work? *(Encourage detailed narrative recall – could be a piece of work that was marked; could be an incident in class)*

5r Do you have tests or examinations? *(Probe for details of when, how these occur; perceptions of why they happen: formative/summative)*

5s What do you think about tests and examination? Do you like/dislike doing them? *(Probe for perception of their importance/fairness; degree of acceptance; degree of self-confidence in undertaking this form of assessment – narrative?)*

5t What happens at this school if you do really well in something? *(Probe for details of any "public" rewards/commendations)* What do you think about that?

Has that ever happened to you *(narrative?)* How did you feel?

6 Pedagogy/learning style

6a How do you think you learn best? *(Wait for first response. If necessary, prompt: on your own, in a small group, in a big group, with the teacher one-to-one, with a friend . . .?)*

6b Are there some things that your teachers ask you to do that you think help you to learn? *(If necessary to get started provide examples e.g.: reading text books; listening to the teacher telling the class; demonstrations; practical work; asking questions; doing tests etc.)*

6c Do you think you learn in different ways depending on what (which subject?) you are learning? *(Probe for examples of different ways of teaching. Are the differences because of the subject or because of the teacher?)*

6d What stops you learning? What makes it hard to learn?

6e Is there anything your teachers could do that would help you learn more? *(Probe for specific examples: e.g. more choice? better control? clearer explanations?)*

6f Would you work if your teachers didn't make you?

6g What are the good things/not so good things about working on your own? *(Probe for views on advantages and disadvantages of each; personal examples)*

6h What are the good things/not so good things about working with other people? *(Encourage narrative in the form of personal experiences of working in groups)*

6i What sorts of things do you think people need to know about and understand if they are going to work well with others? *(Encourage narrative in the form of personal experiences of working in groups.)*

6j Have you learned any of these things in school? Do you think people can learn/be taught how to work well together on things? *(Probe for what has been learned; whether school was active in the learning process)*

6k Do you think that homework helps you to learn? *(If "yes")* In what way does it help?

(If "no") Why do you think it isn't helpful? Why do you think the school gives you work to do at home?

6l Do you get any help with your school work from people at home? *(If "yes")* How do they help you?

(For "yes" "no", probe) Does that make a difference to you do you think? Do you think everyone gets the same amount of help at home?

6m Do you think the classroom should be a place for discussing other pupils' opinions and attitudes? For exchanging ideas and thoughts with other pupils? Can you say why you think that?

6n Does that happen in this school? How does it happen? *(Identify in which "subjects"/activities/forum this occurs)*

7 Perceptions of school culture

7a How do you get on with your teachers?

7b Tell me about the teachers that you particularly like?

7c Tell me about the teachers that you don't like so much?

7d Does it matter to you what your teachers think of you? *(Probe for reasons)*

7e What is it about you and what you do that is important to your teachers, do you think? What do they care about? *(Probe for: academic performance; personal development; pressure to conformity; support for individuality; creativity; self-respect; self-confidence/self-esteem; caring for others)*

7f What do you think people at home think about the teachers in this school?

7g What sorts of things get pupils into trouble in this school? *(Identify perception of school rules. norms, priorities)*

7h What do you think about that? *(Probe for sense of congruence with school values/priorities; is it "fair"?)*

7i Where (ie. in what places) do the school rules apply? For instance – in the classroom? in the corridors? in the playground? outside the school gates? in the shops? in town?

7j Are there different rules in different places? Do some teachers have their own rules?

7k Do all the teachers in this school behave/react in the same way when you do something the school doesn't allow?

7l What happens if you get into trouble?

7m How do you feel about this?

7n Are boys/girls treated any differently from girls/boys in this school do you think? *(ask for examples and personal view of this)*

Are any children treated differently? *(ask for details)*

7o If a new teacher came to this school what would they have to be like/to do to be popular with the pupils?

8 **Pastoral system/attention paid to pupil as a person**
(NB for 8a, 8b, 8c: Note all people/systems referred to. If no-one in school is mentioned ask "Is there anyone in school you would go to see/talk to?")

8a If you were having a problem with your work at this school who would you go to?

8b If you were having a problem with other pupils in this school who would you go to? *(ask for examples/details)*

8c If you were having a problem outside school who would you go to?

(Now move to ask for details of what action interviewee says would be taken for each case where school was mentioned in previous answers)

8d What would the school do about a problem you were having with work?

8e What would the school do about a problem with other pupils?

8f What would the school do about a problem you were having outside school?

(Now ask for details where school was mentioned in previous answers)

8g Have **you** ever been to see someone in school about a problem with work? *(Probe for specifics if possible, otherwise get a general sense of the nature of the problem)* What did the school do? Did it work?/Was it any help to you?

8h Have **you** ever been to see someone in school about a problem with other pupils? *(Probe for specifics if possible, otherwise get a general sense of the nature of the problem)* What did the school do? Did it work?/Was it any help to you?

8i Have you ever been to see someone in school about a problem outside school? *(Probe for specifics if possible, otherwise get a general sense of the nature of the problem)* What did the school do? Did it work?/Was it any help to you?

8j Do you think schools should get involved with pupils' personal or home problems?

8k In general, problems apart, who in school talks to you about your feelings and ideas? Who in school is interested in you as a person? *(Probe for teachers and other pupils)*

9 Adolescent/pupil identity

9a How would you describe yourself as a person? *(Wait for first response. If necessary prompt: easy-going? hard-working? lazy? etc.)*

Do you think you are different at home from what you are like in school? *(If "yes")* In what ways are you different? Can you explain why you are different?

9b What is the first thing you do when you get home from school each day?

9c What sorts of things do you do out of school? *(Probe for details of organised activity e.g. clubs, teams; additional lessons e.g. music etc.; as well as general activities – hanging out with friends, reading, cycling, shopping, watching TV/ videos. Note the impact – if any – of international/global influences e.g. music, and of available finance)*

9d What of all those do you like doing best? *(Probe for reasons)*

9e Do you watch much TV? What do you like to watch most? *(Probe for information about viewing preferences in relation to "international" and national/local "product". If appropriate extend this to cinema/video)*

9f Do you like to keep home life and school life separate? Or do you find that the two overlap?

9g Do you talk much about school with your family?

9h Do you talk much about school with your friends?

9i Does the school have any influence on what you do, how you behave outside school? *(Probe for reasons/examples; perception of whether the school tries to have an influence)*

9j How do you feel when the school tells your parents something about you e.g. how you are getting on with your work; or about your behaviour?

9k Do you think that school tries to help you to understand/deal with things that happen in life outside school? *(Prompt: e.g. with current affairs, politics, human behaviour, relationships, moral dilemmas)*

(Probe: if "yes") **How** does it try to help you? *(Probe for specific examples: e.g. in lessons – which?; in tutorial discussions?; in PSE?; in assemblies?; talking with teachers informally* How good is the school at doing this? How much does it help you?

(Probe: if "no") Do you think it should? *(If "yes")* What could the school do that would be helpful with this?

9l In general would you say that you liked coming to school?

9m Is there anything else about you and school that you would like to say but I haven't asked you?

10 That's the last question about school; but before we finish can I ask a little bit more about you? *(The aim is to have established sufficient rapport by this stage of the interview to gain accurate information about the interviewee's background and home life.)*

10a Would you please tell me a little about where you live? *(Probe for type of housing – council or private? house or flat?; size and space?; garden? location)*

10b And who lives with you? *(Probe for number and status of caring adults; resident brothers/sisters etc.; total number of people living together)*

10c Do any other people in your family live near? *(Probe for location of extended family – grandparents, aunts, uncles cousins; location of other members of divorced or separated families)*

10d What is it like living where you do? *(Probe for level of satisfaction – personal space at home, relationship to the external environment; restriction or facilitation of activity, sense of security/safety, attitude to neighbours, access to friends/facilities; distance from school)*

10e Have you lived there long? *(Probe for sense of transience/permanence)*

10f Can you tell me about the kind of work your mother/father (fill in as appropriate from answers to previous questions) does? *(Try to gain as accurate a description as possible of any paid employment – nature of work – inside/outside, manual/non-manual, permanent/casual/full-time/part-time/ self-employed, public/private sector; status and level of responsibility. Is there a full-time carer in the home? Is anyone unemployed?)*

10g Did your mother/father (fill in as appropriate from answers to previous questions) go to a school like this? *(Probe for educational level attained by BOTH – if present – parents. Try to establish exit point from formal education; any subsequent education or training e.g. craft training, study as a mature student. If possible gain corroborative detail about home attitudes to education.)*

10h When you are the same age as your parents what do you think your life will be like? What might you be doing? Where might you be living?

That really is the last question.
Thank you for talking to me and helping us with our research.

Appendix 3

ENCOMPASS
Group Interview Schedule

School: ....
Location: ....
Pupils: ....
....
....
....
....
....
Interviewers: ....
....
Date: ....

ENCOMPASS

Group Interviews, Jan, Feb, March 1999

Good pupils and peer groups

Themes: Gender, ethnicity, friendship, social background, success, 'coolness', conformity.

Good Pupil

1 *A good pupil is a little cute blonde girl with a brain which falls out of her mouth when she speaks.*
Prompt – Does it make a difference if the pupil is a girl or boy? Does what colour you are make a difference?

2 *A good pupil is a keener – a really clever person – posh – and they do everything proper*
Prompt – What does it mean to be a 'keener'? Does what kind of home you come from make a difference?

3 *A good pupil is someone who always does good work.*

Peer Groups

4 *A good pupil doesn't get into the wrong crowd.*
Prompt – What does 'getting into the wrong crowd' mean? What does being 'cool' mean?

5 *You can only be different if you're popular.*
Prompt – How important is it to fit in with your friends?

Teachers and assessment

Themes: Motivation, self esteem, identity as a learner, concept of 'interesting' lessons.

1 *Teachers judge pupils too much by their marks.*
Prompt – What effect does getting a bad mark/doing poor work have on you? What effect does getting a good mark/doing good work have on you? What does 'good work' mean?

2 *Teachers shouldn't make you feel like a loser.*

3 *I learn best when the teacher makes the lesson interesting and enjoyable.*
Prompt – What makes the lesson interesting? Enjoyable? Boring? Not enjoyable? Is that how **you** learn best? What sort of lessons do you learn best in?

Teacher and pupil relationships

Themes: Friendship between pupils and teachers, teachers knowing about pupils' home life, teachers knowing about how pupils think, pupils' fear of teachers, teachers' age, teachers' labelling of pupils.

1 *A teacher should be a kind of friend.*
Prompt – Can a teacher be a friend? Is it important for a teacher to be a friend?

2 *A teacher should know about your life outside school.*
Prompt – Does it matter for the teacher to know about your life outside school?

3 *A good teacher is someone who understands what is going on in your head.*
Prompt – What do you think is meant by 'what is going on in your head'? What do you think he or she wanted teachers to understand about?

4 *A teacher shouldn't be frightening to pupils.*

5 *Teachers should be able to understand the present and not be too old fashioned.*
Prompt – Does it matter how old a teacher is?

6 *Once a teacher gets an idea about you they don't change their minds easily.*
Prompt – What sort of ideas do teachers get about you? What sort of things don't teachers change their minds about?

Factors that make a good school

Themes: Physical environment, discipline, security, equality, ethos and belonging, respect, pupil influence, reputation and qualifications, 'having a laugh'.

1 *A modern school that doesn't look too sad.*
Prompt – How important to you are the surroundings in which you learn?

2 *A good school is one that has strict teachers and polite kids.*

3 *A good school is one which has good test results and a good name.*

4 *A good school is one where there is no violence and no differences are made.*
Prompt – If there are any differences what are they?

5 *Schools should make sure everyone is equal and has opportunities in life.*
Prompt – What does your school do to make sure that everyone is equal and has the same opportunities?

6 *A good school is one where there's a feeling of togetherness.*

7 *A good school is one where students and teachers respect each other.*

8 *A good school is one where pupils have a say in what goes on.*

Prompt – What sort of say do you think pupils should have? Over the curriculum? How you learn? School rules and school life?

9 *A good school is one where you can have a laugh.*

Bibliography

Abrahams, J. (1995) *Divide and School: Gender and Class Dynamics in Comprehensive Education*. London: Falmer Press.

Alexander, R. (1999) Culture in pedagogy, pedagogy across cultures, in R. Alexander, P. Broadfoot, D. Phillips (eds) *Learning from Comparing, Volume One: Contexts, Classrooms and Outcomes*. Oxford: Symposium Books.

Alexander, R. (2000) *Culture and Pedagogy: International Comparisons in Primary Education*. London: Blackwell Publishers.

Anderson, S. (1996) *Chronic Proximity and the Management of Difference: A study of the Danish School of Practice of Klasse*. Copenhagen: University of Copenhagen.

Andersson, B.E. (1995) Why am I in school? Paper presented at the European Conference on Educational Research, University of Bath, September 1995.

Archer, M. (1984) *Social Origins of Educational Systems*. London: Sage.

Audiger, F. and Motta, D. (1998) The strange concept of affective education: a French perspective, in P. Lang (ed.) *Affective Education: A Comparative View*. London: Cassell.

Bakhtin, M. (1986) *Speech Genres and Other Late Essays*. Austin, Tx: University of Texas Press.

Barber, M. (1996) *The Learning Game*. London: Victor Gollancz.

Bernstein, B. (1975) *Class Codes and Control Volume 3: Towards a Theory of Educational Transmission*. London: Routledge & Kegan Paul.

Best (1998) The development of affective education in England, in P. Lang (ed.) *Affective Education: A Comparative View*. London: Cassell.

Bloomer, M. and Hodkinson, P. (2000a) Continuity and change in young people's dispositions to learning, *British Education Research Journal*, 25(2).

Bloomer, M. and Hodkinson, P. (2000b) Stokingham Sixth Form College: institutional culture and dispositions to learning, *British Journal of Sociology of Education*, 21(2): 187–203.

Bourdieu, P. and Passeron, J-C. (1990) *Reproduction in Education, Society and Culture*, 2nd edn. London: Sage.

BRISTAIX (1988) *Final Report to ESRC*.

Broadfoot, P. (2000) Comparative education for the twenty-first Century: retrospect and prospect, *Comparative Education*, 36(3): 357–71.

Broadfoot, P. and Osborn, M. (1988) What professional responsibility means to teachers: national contexts and classroom constants, *British Journal of Sociology of Education*, 7(3): 265–82.

Broadfoot, P. and Osborn, M. (1992) French Lessons: comparative perspectives on what it means to be a teacher, *Oxford Studies in Comparative Education*, 1: 69–88.

Broadfoot, P., Osborn, M. and Planel, C. (1996) Teachers and change: a study of primary school teachers reactions to policy changes in England and France, in T. Winter-Jensen (ed.) *Challenges to European Education: Cultural Values, National Identities and Global Responsibilities*. Berne: Peter Lang.

Broadfoot, P., Osborn, M., Planel, C. and Sharpe, K. (2000) *Promoting Quality in Learning. Does England Have the Answer?* London: Cassell.

Bronfenbrenner, U. (1979) *The Ecology of Human Development: Experiments by Nature and Design*. Cambridge, MA: Harvard University Press.

Bruner, J.S. (1990) *Acts of Meaning*. Cambridge, MA: Harvard University Press.

Bruner, J. (1996) *The Culture of Education*. Cambridge, MA: Harvard University Press.

Castells, M. (1997) *The Power of Identity*. London: Routledge.

Callaghan, J. (1976) Towards a National Debate, (Ruskin College speech), *Education*, 148: 332–3.

Charlot, B., Bautier, E. and Rochex, J-Y. (1992) *École et savoir dans les banlieues . . . et ailleurs*. Paris: Armand Colin.

Coffield, F. (1999) Breaking the consensus: lifelong learning as social control, *British Educational Research Journal*, 25(4): 479–501.

Connelly, P. (1997) In search of authenticity: researching young children's perspectives, in A. Pollard, D. Thiessen and A. Filer (1997) *Children and Their Curriculum: The Perspectives of Primary and Elementary School Children*. London: Falmer Press.

Corbett, A. and Moon, R. (eds) (1996) *Education in France: Continuity and Change in the Mitterand Years, 1981–1995*. London: Routledge.

Cousin, O. (1998) *L'Efficacité des collèges: sociologie de l'effet établissement*. Paris: Presses Universitaires de France.

Cousin, O. and Felouzis, G. (1999) *Devenir collégien: de l'institution a l'établissement*. Bordeaux: Université Victor Segalen.

Cousin, O. and Felouzis, G. (2002) *Devenir collégien: l'entrée en classe de sixième*. Paris: ESF editeur.

Cox, T. and Sanders, S. (1994) *The impact of the National Curriculum on the Teaching of Five Year Olds*, London: Falmer Press.

Croll, P. (1996) Practitioners or policy-makers? Models of teachers and educational change, in P. Croll (ed.) *Teachers, Pupils and Primary Schooling*. London: Cassell Education.

Crossley, M. and Vulliamy, G. (1984) Case study research methods and comparative education, *Comparative Education*, 20: 193–207.

Crossley, M. and Vulliamy, G. (eds) (1997) *Qualitative Educational Research in Developing Countries*. New York: Garland.

Csikszentmihalyi, M., Rathunde, K. and Whalen, S. (1993) *Talented Teenagers: The Roots of Success and Failure*. Cambridge: Cambridge University Press.

Dale, R. (1999) Specifying globalization effects on national policy: a focus on the mechanisms, *Journal of Education Policy*, 14(1): 1–17.

Dale, R. (2000) Globalization and education: demonstrating a 'common world educational culture' or locating a 'globally structured educational agenda?', *Educational Theory*, 50(4): 427–48.

Denmark (1996) *1992 Act of the Folkeskole* (English language translation). Copenhagen: Undervisnings Ministeriet.

Department for Education and Employment (1997) *Excellence in Schools*. London: HMSO.

Deutscher, I. (1973) Asking questions cross-culturally: some problems of linguistic comparability, in D. Warwick and S. Osherton (eds) *Comparative Research Methods*. Englewood Cliffs, NJ: Prentice-Hall.

Dubet, F. and Martuccelli, D. (1996) *À l'école*. Paris: Editions du Seuil.

Dubet, F., Cousin, O. and Guillemet, J.P. (1996) A sociology of the lycée student, in A. Corbett and R. Moon (eds) *Education in France: Continuity and Change in the Mitterand Years, 1981–1995*. London: Routledge.

Dujykes, H.C.J. and Rokkan, S. (1954) Organisational aspects of cross-national social research, *Journal of Social Issues*, 10: 8–24.

Duru-Bellat, M. (1996) 'Social inequalities in French secondary schools: from figures to theories; *British Journal of Sociology of Education*, 17 (3): 341–50.

Duru-Bellat, M. and van Zanten, A. (1999) *Sociologie de l'école*. Paris: Armand Colin.

Duveen, G. and Lloyd, B. (1993) An ethnographic approach to social representations, in G.M. Breakwell and D.V. Canter (eds) *Empirical Approaches to Social Representations*. Oxford: OUP.

Dweck, C., Chiu, C. and Hong, Y. (1995) Implicit theories and their role in judgments and reactions: A world from two perspectives. *Psychological Inquiry*, 6: 267–285.

Eide, K. (1992) The future of European education as seen from the north, *Comparative Education*, 28(1): 9–17.

Elliott, J., Hufton, N., Hildreth, A. and Illushin, L. (1999) Factors influencing educational motivation: a study of attitudes, expectations and behaviour of children in Sunderland, Kentucky and St Petersburg, *British Educational Research Journal*, 25: 75–94.

Elliott, J., Hufton, N., Illushin, L. and Lauchlan, F. (2001) Motivation in the Junior Years: international perspectives on children's attitudes, expectations and behaviour and their relationship to educational achievement, *Oxford Review of Education*, 27(1).

Frønes, I. (1995) *Among Peers: On the Meaning of Peers in the Process of Socialization*. Copenhagen: Scandinavian University Press.

Galton, M., Simon, B. and Croll, C. (1980) *Inside the Primary Classroom*. London: Routledge & Kegan Paul.

Gewirtz, S., Ball, S.J. and Bowe, R. (1995) *Markets, Choice and Equity in Education*. Buckingham: Open University Press.

Giddens, A. (1993) *New Rules of Sociological Method*. Cambridge: Polity Press.

Glassman, M. (2001) 'Dewey & Vygotsky: Society, Experience and Inquiry in Educational Practice,' *Education Researcher*, 30 (4): 3–15.

Goffman, E. (1971) *The Presentation of Self in Everyday Life*. Harmondsworth: Penguin.

Goleman, D. (1996) *Emotional Intelligence: Why It Can Matter More Than IQ*. London: Bloomsbury.

Graudenz, I. and Randoll, D. (1997) So dänish wie möglich, so deutsch wie nötig?, *Studien und Dokumentationen zur vergleichenden Bildungsforschung*, 73, Deutsches Institut für Internationale Pädagogische Forschung, Böhlau-Verlag.

Green, A., Wolf, A. and Leney, T. (1999) *Convergence and Divergence in European Education and Training Systems*. Institute of Education: University of London.

Hall, S. (1990) Who Needs Identity?, in S. Hall and P. Du Gay (eds) *Questions of Culture and Identity*. London: Sage.

Halsey, A., Heath, A. and Ridge, J. (1980) *Origins and destinations: family, class and education in modern Britian*. Oxford: Clarendon Press.

Hans, N. (1949) *Comparative Education*. London: Routledge & Kegan Paul.

Hantrais, L. (1996) *Comparative Research Methods*, Social Research Update 13, University of Surrey.

Hargreaves, D. (1967) *Social Relations in a Secondary School*. London: RKP.

Harlen, W. and Deakin Crick, R. (2003) 'The impact of summative assessment on students' motivation for learning', Review of Research for Department of Education and Skills, Evidence for Policy & Practice Research reviews.

Hatcher, R. (2001) *Education Action Zones and Zones d'Education Prioritaires*. Paper presented at the University of the West of England, March.

Hodkinson, P. and Bloomer, M. (2000) 'Stokingham Sixth Form College: institutional culture & dispositions to learning' *British Journal of Sociology of Education* 21(2): 187–202.

Holmes, B. (ed.) (1985) Equality and Freedom in Education: A Comparative Study. London: George Allen & Unwin.

Hofstede, G. (1991) *Cultures and Organisation: Software of the Mind*. London: McGraw-Hill.

Hufton, N. and Elliott, J. (2000) Motivation to learn: the pedagogical values nexus in the Russian school: some implications for transnational research and policy borrowing, *Educational Studies*. 26(1): 115–36.

Ireson, J. (2001) Pedagogic culture and learning activity. Paper presented at the Conference on Cultures of Learning, University of Bristol, 19–22 April.

Jenkins, S. (2000) Why GCSEs Are Cheating Our Children, *The Times*, 25 August, p. 20.

Jensen, B., Nielsen, M. and Stenstrup, E. (1992) *The Danish Folkeskole: Visions and Consequences*. Copenhagen: The Danish Council for Educational Development in the Folkeskole.

Judge, H., Lemosse, M., Paine, L. and Sedlak, M. (1994) *The University and the Teachers: France, the United States, England*. Special Edition of Oxford Studies in Comparative Education, 4(1/2). Oxford: Triangle Books.

Kaplan, A., Gheen, M., Midgley, C. *et al.* (2002) 'British Journal of Educational Psychology' in *The Times*, 10 June, p. 4.

Kandel, I.L. (1933) *Studies in Comparative Education*. Boston MA: Houghton Mifflin.

Kenway, J. and Baller, E. (2000) 'Education in the age of uncertainty: an Eagle's edge view', *Compare*, 30(3): 265–275.

Keys, W. and Fernandes, C. (1993) *What Do Students Think About School?* Slough: National Foundation for Educational Research.

Kryger, A. and Reisby, K. (1998) The Danish class teacher: a mediator between the pastoral and the academic, in P. Lang (ed.) *Affective Education: A Comparative View*. London: Cassell.

Lacey, C. (1970) *Hightown Grammar: The School as a Social System*. Manchester: Manchester University Press.

Lang, P., Katz, Y. and Menezes, I. (eds) (1998) Affective education: a comparative view, *Cassell Studies in Pastoral Care and Personal and Social Education*. London: Cassell.

Lauder, H. (2000) The Dilemmas of Comparative Research and Policy Importation, *British Journal of Sociology of Education*, 21(3).

Lauglo, J. (1990) Factors behind decentralization in education systems: a comparative perspective and with special reference to Norway, *Compare*, 20(1): 21–39.

Lawton, D. and Gordon, P. (2002) *A History of Western Educational Ideas*. London: Woburn.

Laursen, F.P. (1999) *Didaktik og kognition, en grundbog*. Copenhagen: Gyldenhal.

Le Monde de l'Education (2003) It faut sauver les garçons, *Le Monde de l'Education*, January.

Lerner, D. (1956) Interviewing Frenchmen, *American Journal of Sociology*, 62: 193.

Letendre, G. and Akiba, M. (2001) Teacher beliefs about adolescent development: cultural and organisational impacts on Japanese and US middle school teachers' beliefs, *Compare*, 31(2).

Letendre, G., Baker, D., Akiba, M., Goesling, B. and Wiseman, A. (2001) Teachers' work: institutional isomorphism and cultural variation in the US, Germany, and Japan, *Educational Researcher*, 30(6).

Linn, M., Lewis, C., Tsuchida, I. and Butler-Songer, N. (2000) Beyond fourth-grade science: why do US and Japanese students diverge? *Educational Researcher*, 29(3).

MacLure, J.S. (1979) *Educational Documents: England and Wales 1816 to the present day*. London: Methuen.

MacLure, M. (1993) Arguing for Your Self: identity as an organising principle in teacher's jobs and lives. *British Education Research Journal*, 19(4): 311–322.

McNess, E., Broadfoot, P. and Osborn, M. (2003) Is the effective compromising the affective? *British Educational Research Journal*, 29(2).

Maden and Ruddock (1999) TES 6 August.

Masini, E. (1994) 'The futures of cultures: an overview', *The Futures of Cultures*. Paris: UNESCO Publishing.

Measor, L. and Woods, P. (1984) *Changing Schools: Pupil Perspectives on Transfer to a Comprehensive*. Buckingham: Open University Press.

Meyer, J., Boli, J., Thomas, G. and Ramirez, F. (1997) 'World Society and the Nation-State', *American Journal of Sociology*, 103(1): 144–181.

Miles, M. and Huberman, A. (1994) *Qualitative Data Analysis*. Second Edition. Sage Publications: London.

Moscovici, S. (1981) 'On Social Representation', in J. Forgas, (ed) *Social Cognition*. London: Academic Press.

Moscovici, S. (1984) 'The phenomenon of social representations', in R.M. Farr, and S. Moscovici (eds) *Social Representations*. Cambridge: CUP.

Moscovici, S. (1988) 'Notes towards a description of social representations', *European Journal of Social Psychology*, **18**, 211–250.

Ofsted (1998) *The Annual Report of Her Majesty's Chief Inspector of Schools in England: Standards and Quality in Education (1996–97)*. London: The Stationery Office.

Osborn, M. (2001) 'Constants and Contexts in Pupil Experience of Learning and Schooling: comparing learners in England, France and Denmark', *Comparative Education*, 37(3): 267–78.

Osborn, M. (2003) Life in school: pupil perspectives and pupil experience of schooling and learning in three European countries, *Doing Comparative Education Research: Issues and Problems*. Symposium Books.

Osborn, M. and Broadfoot, P. (1992) 'A Lesson in progress? Primary classrooms observed in England and France', *Oxford Review of Education*, 18(1): 3–15.

Osborn, M. and Planel, C. (1999) Comparing children's learning, attitude and performance in French and English primary schools, in R. Alexander, P. Broadfoot and D. Phillips (eds) *Learning from Comparing*, Vol. 1. Wallingford: Triangle Books.

Osborn, M., Broadfoot, P. and Planel, C. (1996) Social class, educational opportunity and equal entitlement: dilemmas of schooling in England and France, *Comparative Education*, 33(3).

Osborn, M., Broadfoot, P.M., Planel, C., Sharpe, K. and Ward, B. (1998) Being a pupil in England and France: findings from a comparative study, in A.M. Kazamias, with M.G. Spillane (eds) *Education and the Structuring of the European Space*. Athens: Seirios Editions.

Osborn, M., McNess, E. and Broadfoot, P. with Pollard, A. and Triggs, P. (2000) *What Teachers Do: Changing Policy and Practice in Primary Education*. London: Continuum Books.

Osborn, M., McNess, E., Planel, C. and Triggs, P. (2003) Culture, context and policy: comparing learners in three European countries, in R. Sutherland, G. Claxton and A. Pollard (eds) *Learning and Teaching where World Views Meet*, 35–57.

Organisation for Economic Co-operation and Development (OECD) (1996) *Reviews of National Policies for Education: France*. OECD: Paris.

Parsons, T. (1952) *The Social System*. London: Routledge & Kegan Paul.

Pepin, B. (1999) The influence of national cultural traditions in pedagogy: classroom practices in England, France and Germany, in J. Leach and B. Moon (eds) *Learners and Pedagogy*. London: Sage.

Pepin, B. and Haggarty, L. (2001) *Mathematics Textbooks and Their Use in English, French and German Classrooms*, Economic and Social Research Council, Ref. No. R000 22 3046. Milton Keynes: Centre for Research and Development in Teacher Education, Open University.

Planel, C. (1996) Children's experience of the learning process and the role of the teacher: A comparative study of English and French primary school classrooms, *European Educational Research Association Bulletin*, 2(1), March.

Pollard, A. (1985) *The Social World of the Primary School*. London: Cassell.

Pollard, A. and Filer, A. (1995) *The Social World of Children's Learning*. London: Cassell.

Pollard, A. and Filer, A. (1996) *The Social World of Pupil Career in Primary School*. London: Cassell.

Pollard, A. and Filer, A. (1999) *The Social World of Pupil Career Strategic Biographies through Primary School*. London: Cassell.

Pollard, A., Broadfoot, P., Croll, P., Osborn, M. and Abbott, D. (1994) *Changing English Primary Schools? The Impact of the Education Reform Act at Key Stage One*. London: Cassell.

Randoll, D. (1995) 'Schule im Urteil von Lehren', *Studien zur Pädagogischen Psychologie*, 32, Deutsches Institut für Internationale Pädagogische Forschung, Hofgrege-Verlag, pp. 1–117.

Raphael Reed, L. (1996) Working with boys: a new research agenda, *Redland Papers No. 3*. Bristol: University of the West of England.

Raveaud, M. (2003) Ethnic minorities and *enfants issus de l'immigration*. The social construction of difference through national educational policy in England and France. Paper given at RAPPE conference, Governance, Regulation and Equity in European Education Systems, London Institute of Education, 20–21 March.

Richards, M. and Light, P. (1986) *Children of Social Worlds*. Cambridge: Polity Press.

Rogoff, B. (1995) Observing sociocultural activity on three planes: participatory appropriation, guided participation and apprenticeship, in J.V. Wertsch, P. DelRio and A. Alvarez (eds) *Sociocultural Studies of Mind*. Cambridge: Cambridge University Press.

Rudduck, J. and Flutter, J. (2000) Pupil participation and pupil perspective: carving a new order of experience, *Cambridge Journal of Education*, 30: 75–89.

Rudduck, J., Chaplain, R. and Wallace, G. (1995) *School Improvement: What Pupils Can Tell Us*. London: Fulton.

Ryan, A. and Patrick, H. (2001) The classroom social enviroment and changes in adolescents' motivation and engagement during middle school, *American Educational Research Journal*, 38(2).

Schnapper, D. (1991) La France de l'intégration, *Sociologie de la nation*. Paris: Gallimard.

Schratz, M. (1992) *Qualitative Voices in Educational Research*. Basingstoke: Falmer Press.

Sharp, P. and Dunford, J. (1990) *The Education System in England and Wales*. London: Longman.

Sharpe, K. (1992) Educational homogeneity in French primary education: a double case study, *British Journal of Sociology of Education*, 13(3): 329–429.

Stenhouse, L. (1967) *Culture and Education*. London: Nelson.

Tajfel, H. (ed.) (1982) *Social Identity and Intergroup Relations*. Cambridge: Cambridge University Press.

Tajfel, H. and Forgas, J. (1981) Social categorization: cognitions, values and groups, in J. Forgas (ed.) *Social Cognition*. London: Academic Press.

Tobin, J. (1999) Method and meaning in comparative classroom ethnography, *Learning from Comparing*, Vol. 1. Oxford: Symposium.

van Zanten, A. (1997) Schooling immigrants in France in the 1990's: success or failure of the republican model of integration? *Anthropology and Education Quarterly*, 28(3): 351–74.

van Zanten, A. (2000) L'école de la périphérie. Scolarité et ségrégation en banlieue. Paris: PUF.

Vygotsky, L.S. (1978) *Mind in Society: The Development of Higher Psychological Processes*. Cambridge, MA: Harvard University Press.

Warwick, D. and Osherson, S. (eds) (1973) *Comparative Research Methods: An Overview*. Englewood Cliffs, NJ: Prentice-Hall.

Wertsch, J.V. (ed.) (1985) *Culture, Communication and Cognition: Vygotskian Perspectives*. Cambridge: Cambridge University Press.

Wertsch, J.V. (1991) *Voices of the Mind: A Socio-cultural Approach to Mediated Action*. Cambridge, MA: Harvard University Press.

Wertsch, J.V. and Smolka, A.L. (1993) Continuing the dialogue: Vygotsky, Bakhtin and Lotman, in H. Daniels (ed.) *Charting the Agenda: Educational Activity after Vygotsky*. London: Routledge.

Whiting, B.B. and Edwards, C.P. (1988) *Children of Different Worlds*. Cambridge, MA: Harvard University Press.

Winther-Jensen, T. (2000) Cultural changes and schools in Denmark, in D. Coulby, R. Cowen and C. Jones (eds) *World Yearbook of Education 2000: Education in Times of Transition*. London: Kogan Page.

Winther-Jenson, T. (2002) Tradition and Transition in Danish Education, in R. Griffin (ed.) *Education in Transition: International Perspectives on the Politics and Processes of Change*. London: Symposium Books.

Woods, P. (1990) *The Happiest Days? How Pupils Cope with School*. London: Falmer Press.

Woods, P., Jeffrey, B., Troman, G. and Boyle, M. (1997) *Restructuring Schools, Reconstructing Teachers*. Buckingham: Open University Press.

Index

Page numbers in *italics* refer to tables and boxes, *a* indicates appendix.

EDUCATION AND THE MIDDLE CLASS

Sally Power, Tony Edwards, Geoff Whitty and Valerie Wigfall

It is often assumed that for middle class and academically able children, schooling is a straightforward process that leads to academic success, higher education and entry into middle class occupations. However this fascinating book shows these relationships to be complex and often uncertain.

Based on the biographies of 350 young men and women who might have been considered 'destined for success' at the start of their secondary schooling, the book maps out the educational pathways they took. It analyses their subsequent achievements and entry into employment and compares them with their parents, with one another, and with their generation. Identifying patterns in the data, it also explores examples of extraordinary success and failure, and various forms of interrupted and disrupted careers.

As well as documenting a compelling human story, the findings have important implications for current policy debates about academic selection, access to elite universities, and the limits of meritocracy.

Contents

192pp 0 335 20555 0 (Paperback) 0 335 20556 9 (Hardback)

THE SCHOOL OF TOMORROW
VALUES AND VISION

Roger White

> I'd rather be in an environment where there's white people, black people, Asian people; all sorts. In my friendship groups it's all mixed.
>
> Jendayi

> You've got to have schools because otherwise you'd be thick.
>
> Alastair

> School is full of experiences: it's not just the learning.
>
> Donna

> Education is about picking up social skills, listening to authority, learning how to learn, working out what you really think about things, as well as learning actual subjects like maths and English.
>
> Nick

> Expectations and self esteem go hand in hand and both affect confidence. We've got to develop self esteem in all youngsters so that they have the confidence to build on those little nuggets that are inside every child.
>
> David Blunkett MP

> You will never see a list of grades put up in Denmark, not even for exams – never.
>
> Julia

> In Denmark we try to meet the child where it is.
>
> Margrethe Vestager, Minister for Education, Denmark

This is a book for anyone who cares about education and which brings to life the 'conversations between generations'. In the first part young people from secondary schools around Britain talk about what they enjoy and what they find difficult about school, what matters to them about teachers and classrooms, what it's like being at school in the UK and what changes they'd like to make. Their comments are interspersed with an analysis of the vision offered by contemporary writers as to how things might change as the 21st century gathers momentum. In the second part, David Blunkett, Tim Brighouse, Anita Higham, Richard Pring, Nick Tate and Ted Wragg respond to the young people's comments and offer their own ideas and beliefs as to what is important. Finally by drawing comparisons with Denmark and using the views of Danish young people and Margrethe Vestager, this book offers its own vision for education in the years ahead. It promises an exciting and thought provoking read.

Contents

200pp 0 335 20467 8 (Paperback) 0 335 20468 6 (Hardback)